CURRENT RESEARCH IN BIOCHEMISTRY AND MOLECULAR BIOLOGY

ENV BOOKS SERIES

CURRENT RESEARCH IN BIOCHEMISTRY AND MOLECULAR BIOLOGY

Editors

Dr. Prasann Kumar

Division of Research and Development
Lovely Professional University
Jalandhar - 144 411 (Punjab)
(India)

&

Dr. Pawan Kumar 'Bharti'

Society for Environment, Health Awareness of
Nutrition & Toxicology (SEHAT)
B-225/5D, Top Floor, Subhash Gali, Road No. 7, Block B
Ashok Nagar, Shahdara, Delhi - 110 093
(India)

DPH

DISCOVERY PUBLISHING HOUSE PVT. LTD.
INDIA

Published by:
Namit Wasan
DISCOVERY PUBLISHING HOUSE PVT. LTD.
4383/4B, Ansari Road, Darya Ganj
New Delhi-110 002 (India)
Phone : +91-11-23279245; 23253475; 43596065
E-mail : discoverybooksindia@gmail.com
discoverypublishinghouse@gmail.com
namitwasan9@gmail.com
web : www.discoverypublishinggroup.com

***First Edition:* 2020**

ISBN: 978-93-88854-33-7

Current Research in Biochemistry and Molecular Biology

Printed at:
Infinity Imaging Systems
Delhi

M.S. Swaminathan Research Foundation

M.S. Swaminathan
Founder Chairman
Ex-Member of Parliament (Rajya Sabha)

Foreword

I am very glad to know that a several books are being edited under the aegis of ENVBOOKS series, Delhi, India on various sub-themes of Agriculture and environment like:

'Cultivation Techniques for Agriculture Crops'
'Air Pollution and Control'
'Seed and Food Storage Technologies'
'Heavy Metals and Impacts on Plants'
'Climate Change and Agriculture Production'
'Scientific Writing and Research Methodology'
'Laboratory Management'
'Statistical Tools in Science'
'Advances in Chemistry and Chemical Sciences'
'Irrigation techniques in Crop management' 'Waste Management Practices'
'Vermitechnology, Farm and Fertilizers'
'Animal Science and Pest Control'
'Current Research in Biochemistry and Molecular Biology'
'Water Management and Sustainability'
'Soil Quality and Agriculture'

I am very happy to learn that a number of editors and authors from different institutions and university of different nations are involved in editing these books. The books are the compendium of screened-in manuscripts received from different countries like UK, Canada, Egypt, Nigeria, Ghana, Ethiopia, China, South Africa, Japan, Guyana, PNG, Nepal, South America, and various parts of India. I am feeling delighted in writing forward to these books and congratulate to Dr. Pawan Kumar Bharti, Editor-in-Chief and founder of ENVBOOKS series and of course his team for their tenacity and hard work in compiling these valuable compendiums.

I hope these books will be beneficial for academician, researchers, industrialist, policy makers and students as study material and will work as reference for further research work.

M.S. Swaminathan

Preface

Progress in science is achieved through observation and experiment. Biochemistry (and its close sister branch, molecular biology) is an experimental science that advances from well-thought out investigations in the laboratory. No serious scholar should neglect the opportunities which this branch provides to appreciate this fact. This stream includes experiments for researchers to gain some insight into how laboratory investigations are carried out and how data are processed and interpreted. To obtain useful results an experiment should be designed to answer a definite question and the detailed planning should be sufficiently rigorous to exclude adventitious errors.

Biochemistry, sometimes called biological chemistry, is the study of chemical processes within and relating to living organisms. Biochemical processes give rise to the complexity of life. A sub-discipline of both biology and chemistry, biochemistry can be divided in three fields; molecular genetics, protein science and metabolism. Over the last decades of the 20th century, biochemistry has through these three disciplines become successful at explaining living processes. Almost all areas of the life sciences are being uncovered and developed by biochemical methodology and research. Biochemistry and Molecular Biology focus on understanding how biological molecules give rise to the processes that occur within living cells and between cells, which in turn relates greatly to the study and understanding of tissues, organs, and organism structure and function.

Biochemistry is closely related to molecular biology, the study of the molecular mechanisms of biological phenomena. Molecular biology is a branch of biology that concerns the molecular basis of biological activity between bio-molecules in the various systems of a cell, including the interactions between DNA, RNA, proteins and their biosynthesis, as well as the regulation of these interactions.

Researchers in molecular biology use specific techniques native to molecular biology but increasingly combine these with techniques and ideas from genetics and biochemistry. There is not a defined line between these disciplines. This is shown in the following schematic that depicts one possible view of the relationships between the fields.

Biochemistry is the study of the chemical substances and vital processes occurring in live organisms. Biochemists focus heavily on the role, function, and structure of bio-molecules. The study of the chemistry behind biological processes and the synthesis of biologically active molecules are examples of biochemistry.

Genetics is the study of the effect of genetic differences in organisms. This can often be inferred by the absence of a normal component (e.g. one gene). The study of "mutants" – organisms which lack one or more functional components with respect to the so-called "wild type" or normal phenotype. Genetic interactions (epistasis) can often confound simple interpretations of such "knockout" studies.

Molecular biology is the study of molecular underpinnings of the processes of replication, transcription, translation, and cell function. The central dogma of molecular biology where genetic material is transcribed into RNA and then translated into protein, despite being oversimplified, still provides a good starting point for understanding the field. The picture has been revised in light of emerging novel roles for RNA.

Much of molecular biology is quantitative, and recently much work has been done at its interface with computer science in bioinformatics and computational biology.

The present book updates the subject content on Bacterial Genetics, Cloning Vectors in Molecular Biology, molecular tool to detect plant pathogen, Molecular Stress Response in Context with Abiotic and Biotic Factor, Plant Cells, Biochemistry of Methane Oxidation, Isolation of Secondary Metabolites, Silage, Polyamine and plant stress response, Photosynthesis, Transpiration, and Plant Hormones, Senescence and Abscission in Crops.

Thanks are due to publisher and contributors from various institutions and universities.

The book will be helpful for the researchers, academia working in the field of Genetics, Cloning Vectors, molecular tool to detect plant pathogen, Molecular Stress Response, Plant Cells, Biochemistry of Methane Oxidation, Secondary Metabolites, Polyamine and plant stress response, Photosynthesis, Transpiration, and Plant Hormones.

–Editors

(envbooks@gmail.com)

Contents

Pages: 1-11

Current Research in Biochemistry and Molecular Biology
Edited by: Dr. Prasann Kumar and Dr. Pawan Kumar 'Bharti'
ISBN: 978-93-88854-33-7
Edition: **2020**
Published by: **Discovery Publishing House Pvt. Ltd., New Delhi (India)**

CHAPTER
1

Bacterial Genetics and its Role in Research Innovation

Prasann Kumar[1,2*], Shipa Rani Dey[1]

GRAPHICAL ABSTRACT

Keywords: Bacteria, Crop, Energy, Genetics, Research, Innovation

INTRODUCTION

- The largest and most obvious division of living organisms is into prokaryotes vs. eukaryotes.

[1] Department of Agronomy, School of Agriculture, Lovely Professional University, Jalandhar - 144 411 (Punjab) (India)

[2] Divison of Research and Development, Lovely Professional University, Jalandhar - 144 411 (Punjab) (India)

- Eukaryotes are defined as having their genetic material enclosed in a membrane-bound nucleus, separate from the cytoplasm. In addition, eukaryotes have other membrane-bound organelles such as mitochondria, lysosomes, and endoplasmic reticulum. almost all multicellular organisms are eukaryotes.
- In contrast, the genome of prokaryotes is not in a separate compartment: it is located in the cytoplasm (although sometimes confined to a particular region called a "nucleoid"). Prokaryotes contain no membrane-bound organelles; their only membrane is the membrane that separates the cell form the outside world. Nearly all prokaryotes are unicellular.

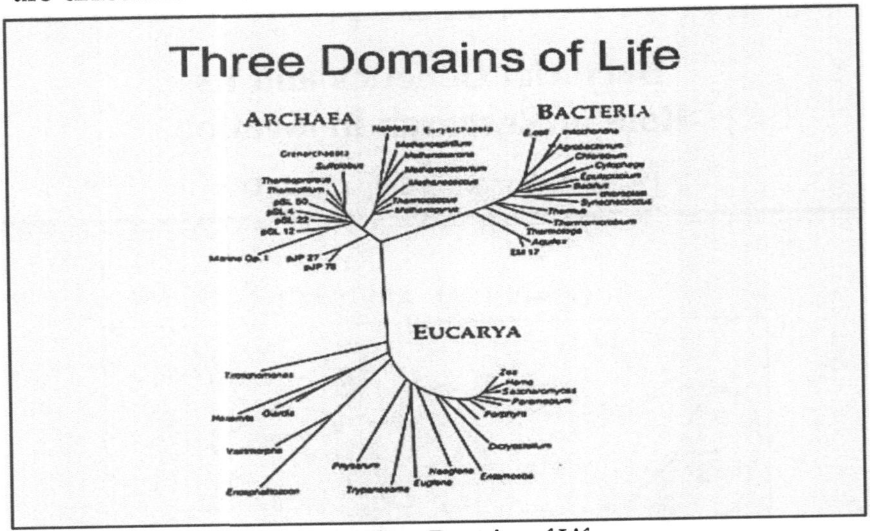

Fig. 1.1: Three Domains of Life
Source: based on review of literature

Prokaryote vs. Eukaryote Genetics

- Prokaryotes are haploid, and they contain a single circular chromosome. In addition, prokaryotes often contain small circular DNA molecules called "plasmids" that confer useful properties such as drug resistance. Only circular DNA molecules in prokaryotes can replicate.
- In contrast, eukaryotes are often diploid, and eukaryotes have linear chromosomes, usually more than 1.
- In eukaryotes, transcription of genes in RNA occurs in the nucleus, and translation of that RNA into protein occurs in the cytoplasm. The two processes are separated from each other.
- In prokaryotes, translation is coupled to transcription: translation of the new RNA molecule starts before transcription is finished.

Bacterial Culture

- Surprisingly, many, perhaps even most, of the bacteria on Earth cannot be grown in the laboratory today.
- Bacteria need a set of specific nutrients, the correct amount of oxygen, and a proper temperature to grow. The common gut bacterium *Escherichia coli* (E. coli) grows easily on partially digested extracts made from yeast and animal products, at 37 degrees in a normal atmosphere. These simple growth conditions have made E. coli a favorite lab organism, which is used as a model for other bacteria.

More Culture

- Bacteria are generally grown in either of 2 ways; on solid media as individual colonies , or in liquid culture.
- The nutrient broth for liquid culture allows rapid growth up to a maximum density. Liquid culture is easy and cheap.
- Solid media use the same nutrient broth as liquid culture, solidifying it with agar. Agar a polysaccharide derived from seaweed that most bacteria can't digest.
- The purpose of growth on solid media is to isolate individual bacterial cells, then grow each cell up into a colony. This is the standard way to create a pure culture of bacteria. All cells of a colony are closely related to the original cell that started the colony, with only a small amount of genetic variation possible.
- Solid media are also used to count the number of bacteria that were in a culture tube.

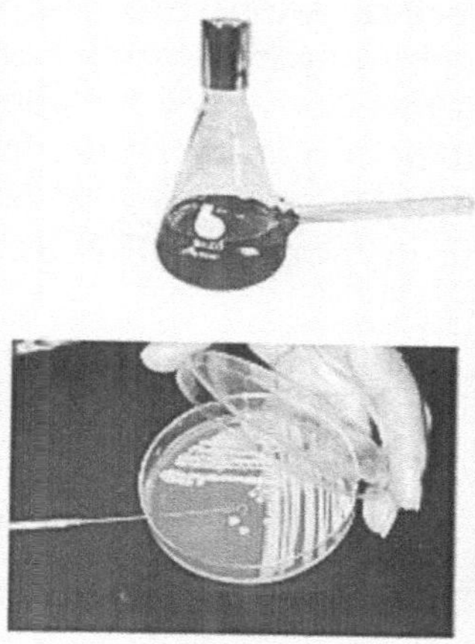

Fig. 1.2: More Culture

Source: based on review of literature

Bacterial Mutants

- Mutants in bacteria are mostly biochemical in nature, because we can't generally see the cells.
- The most important mutants are auxotrophs. An auxotroph needs some nutrient that the wild type strain (prototroph) can make for itself. For example, a trp- auxotroph can't make its own tryptophan (an amino acid). To grow trp- bacteria, you need to add tryptophan to the growth medium. Prototrophs are trp+; they don't need any tryptophan supplied since they make their own.
- Chemoauxotrophs are mutants that can't use some nutrient (usually a sugar) that prototrophs can use as food. For example, lac- mutants can't grow on lactose (milk sugar), but lac+ prototrophs can grow on lactose.

- Resistance mutants confer resistance to some environmental toxin: drugs, heavy metals, bacteriophages, etc. For instance, Amp^Rcauses bacteria to be resistant to ampicillin, a common antibiotic related to penicillin.
- Auxotrophs and chemoauxotrophs are usually recessive; drug resistance mutants are usually dominant.

Replica Plating

- A common way to find bacterial mutants is replica plating, which means making two identical copies of the colonies on a petri plate under different conditions.
- For instance, if you were looking for trp- auxotrophs, one plate would contain added tryptophan and the other plate would not have any tryptophan in it.
- Bacteria are first spread on the permissive plate, the plate that allows both mutants and wild type to grow, the plate containing tryptophan in this case. They are allowed to grow for a while, then a copy of the plate is made by pressing a piece of velvet onto the surface of the plate, then moving it to a fresh plate with the restrictive condition (no tryptophan). The velvet transfers some cells from each colony to an identical position on the restrictive plate.
- Colonies that grow on the permissive plate but not the restrictive plate are (probably) trp- auxotrophs, because they can only grow if tryptophan is supplied.

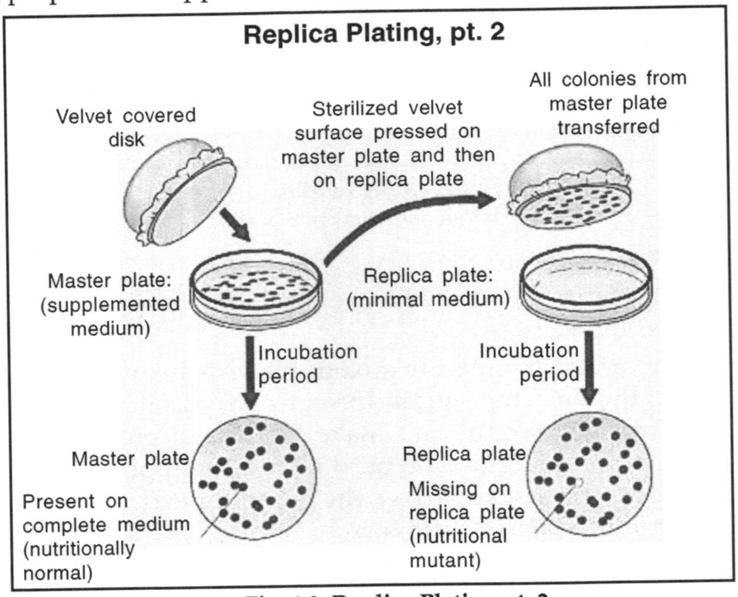

Fig. 1.3: Replica Plating pt. 2
Source: based on review of literature

Bacterial Sexual Processes

- Eukaryotes have the processes of meiosis to reduce diploids to haploidy, and fertilization to return the cells to the diploid state. Bacterial sexual processes are not so regular. However, they serve the same aim: to mix the genes from two different organisms together.
- The three bacterial sexual processes:
  1. conjugation: direct transfer of DNA from one bacterial cell to another.
  2. transduction: use of a bacteriophage (bacterial virus) to transfer DNA between cells.
  3. transformation: naked DNA is taken up from the environment by bacterial cells.

Transformation

- We aren't going to speak much of this process, except to note that it is very important for recombinant DNA work. The essence of recombinant DNA technology is to remove DNA from cells, manipulate it in the test tube, then put it back into living cells. In most cases this is done by transformation.
- In the case of E. coli, cells are made "competent" to be transformed by treatment with calcium ions and heat shock. E. coli cells in this condition readily pick up DNA from their surroundings and incorporate it into their genomes.

Conjugation

- Conjugation is the closest analogue in bacteria to eukaryotic sex.
- The ability to conjugate is conferred by the F plasmid. A plasmid is a small circle of DNA that replicates independently of the chromosome. Bacterial cells that contain an F plasmid are called "F+". Bacteria that don't have an F plasmid are called "F-".
- F+ cells grow special tubes called "sex pilli" from their bodies. When an F+ cell bumps into an F- cell, the sex pilli hold them together, and a copy of the F plasmid is transferred from the F+ to the F-. Now both cells are F+.
- Why aren't all E. coli F+, if it spreads like that? Because the F plasmid can be spontaneously lost.

Hfr Conjugation

- When it exists as a free plasmid, the F plasmid can only transfer itself. This isn't all that useful for genetics.
- However, sometimes the F plasmid can become incorporated into the bacterial chromosome, by a crossover between the F plasmid and the

chromosome. The resulting bacterial cell is called an "Hfr", which stands for "High frequency of recombination".

- Hfr bacteria conjugate just like F+ do, but they drag a copy of the entire chromosome into the F- cell.

Interrupted Mating

- Chromosome transfer from the Hfr into the F- is slow: it takes about 100 minutes to transfer the entire chromosome.
- The conjugation process can be interrupted using a kitchen blender.
- By interrupting the mating at various times you can determine the proportion of F-cells that have received a given marker.
- This technique can be used to make a map of the circular E. coli chromosome.

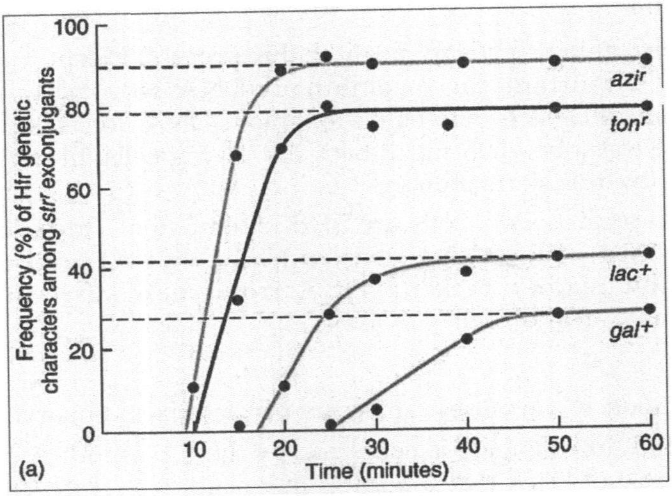

Fig. 1.4: Interrupted Mating

Source: based on review of literature

Different Hfr Strains

- The F plasmid can incorporate into the chromosome in almost any position, and in either orientation. Note that the genes stay in fixed positions, but the genes enter the F- in different orders and times, based on where the F was incorporated in the Hfr.
- Data are for initial time of entry of that gene into the F-.

gene	Hfr 1	Hfr 2	Hfr 3
azi	8	29	88
ton	10	27	90
lac	17	20	3
gal	25	12	11

Fig. 1.5: Different Hfr strains

Source: based on review of literature

Intracellular Events in Conjugation

- The piece of chromosome that enters the F- form the Hfr is linear. It is called the "exogenote".
- The F- cell's own chromosome is circular. It is called the "endogenote".
- Only circular DNA replicates in bacteria, so genes on the exogenote must be transferred to the endogenote for the F- to propagate them.
- This is done by recombination: 2 crossovers between homologous regions of the exogenote and the endogenote. In the absence of recombination, conjugation in ineffective: the exogenote enters the F, but all the genes on it are lost as the bacterial cell reproduces.

F-prime (F′)

- The process of making an Hfr from an F+ involves a crossover between the F plasmid and the chromosome. This process is reversible: an Hfr can revert to being F+ when the F plasmid DNA incorporated into the Hfr chromosome has a crossover and loops out of the chromosome forming an F plasmid once again.
- Sometimes the looping-out and crossing-over process doesn't happen at the proper place. When this happens, a piece of the bacterial chromosome can become incorporated into the F plasmid. This is called an F′ (F-prime) plasmid.
- F′ plasmids can be transferred by conjugation. Conjugation with an F′ (or a regular F plasmid) is much faster and more efficient than with an Hfr, because only a very small piece of DNA is transferred. Since the F′ carries a bacterial gene, this allele can be rapidly moved into a large number of other strains. This permits its function to be tested rapidly. Also, tests of dominance can be done.
- A cell containing an F′ is "merodiploid": part diploid and part haploid. It is diploid for the bacterial gene carried by the F′ (one copy on the F′ and the other on the chromosome), and haploid for all other genes.

Transduction

- Transduction is the process of moving bacterial DNA from one cell to another using a bacteriophage.
- Bacteriophage or just "phage" are bacterial viruses. They consist of a small piece of DNA inside a protein coat. The protein coat binds to the bacterial surface, then injects the phage DNA. The phage DNA then takes over the cell's machinery and replicates many virus particles.
- Two forms of transduction:
    1. generalized: any piece of the bacterial genome can be transferred
    2. specialized: only specific pieces of the chromosome can be transferred.

General Phage Life Cycle

- Phage attaches to the cell and injects its DNA.
- Phage DNA replicates, and is transcribed into RNA, then translated into new phage proteins.
- New phage particles are assembled.
- Cell is lysed, releasing about 200 new phage particles.
- Total time = about 15 minutes.

Generalized Transduction

- Some phages, such as phage P1, break up the bacterial chromosome into small pieces, and then package it into some phage particles instead of their own DNA.
- These chromosomal pieces are quite small: about 1 1/2 minutes of the E. coli chromosome, which has a total length of 100 minutes.
- A phage containing E. coli DNA can infect a fresh host, because the binding to the cell surface and injection of DNA is caused by the phage proteins.
- After infection by such a phage, the cell contains an exogenote (linear DNA injected by the phage) and an endogenote (circular DNA that is the host's chromosome).
- A double crossover event puts the exogenote's genes onto the chromosome, allowing them to be propagated.

Transduction Mapping

- Only a small amount of chromosome, a few genes, can be transferred by transduction. The closer 2 genes are to each other, the more likely they are to be transduced by the same phage. Thus, "co-transduction frequency" is the key parameter used in mapping genes by transduction.
- Transduction mapping is for fine-scale mapping only. Conjugation mapping is used for mapping the major features of the entire chromosome.

Mapping Experiment

- Important point: the closer 2 genes are to each other, the higher the co-transduction frequency.
- We are just trying to get the order of the genes here, not put actual distances on the map.
- Expt: donor strain is $azi^R leu^+ thr^+$. Phage P1 is grown on the donor strain, and then the resulting phage are mixed with the recipient strain: $azi^S leu^- thr^-$. The bacteria that survive are then tested for various markers.

- Of the leu$^+$ cells, 50% are azi^R, and 2% are thr$^+$. From this we can conclude that azi and leu are near each other, and that leu and thr are far apart.
- But: what is the order: leu—azi—thr, or azi—leu—thr ?

Mapping Experiment, pt. 2

- Do a second experiment to determine the order. Select the thr$^+$ cells, then determine how many of them have the other 2 markers. 3% are also leu$^+$ and 0% are also azi^R.
- By this we can see that thr is closer to leu than it is to azi, because thr and azi are so far apart that they are never co-transduced.
- Thus the order must be thr—leu—azi.
- Note that the co-transduction frequency for thr and leu are slightly different for the 2 experiments: 2% and 3%. This is attributable to experimental error.

Larger Experiment

- A few hints:
  1. There are 3 experiments shown. In each, 1 gene is selected, and the frequencies of co-transduction with the other genes is shown.
  2. start with 2 genes that are selected and that have a non-zero co-transduction frequency. Put them on the map.
  3. Then locate the other genes relative to the first 2

Selected	Co-transduced	Freq	Selected	Co-transduced	Freq	Selected	Co-transduced	Freq
e	a	0	f	a	90	c	a	74
e	b	85	f	b	2	c	b	32
e	c	29	f	c	41	c	d	0
e	d	62	f	d	0	c	e	21
e	f	0	f	e	0	c	f	39

Fig. 1.6: Larger Experiment

Source: based on review of literature

Intro to Specialized Transduction

- Some phages can transfer only particular genes to other bacteria.
- Phage lambda (λ) has this property. To understand specialized transduction, we need to examine the phage lambda life cycle.
- lambda has 2 distinct phases of its life cycle. The "lytic" phase is the same as we saw with the general phage life cycle: the phage infects the cell, makes more copies of itself, then lyses the cell to release the new phage.

Lysogenic Phase

- The "lysogenic" phase of the lambda life cycle starts the same way: the lambda phage binds to the bacterial cell and injects its DNA. Once inside the cell, the lambda DNA circularizes, then incorporates into the bacterial chromosome by a crossover, similar to the conversion of an F plasmid into an Hfr.
- Once incorporated into the chromosome, the lambda DNA becomes quiescent: its genes are not expressed and it remains a passive element on the chromosome, being replicated along with the rest of the chromosome. The lambda DNA in this condition is called the "prophage".
- After many generations of the cell, conditions might get harsh. For lambda, bad conditions are signaled when DNA damage occurs.
- When the lambda prophage receives the DNA damage signal, it loops out and has a crossover, removing itself from the chromosome. Then the lambda genes become active and it goes into the lytic phase, reproducing itself, then lysing the cell.

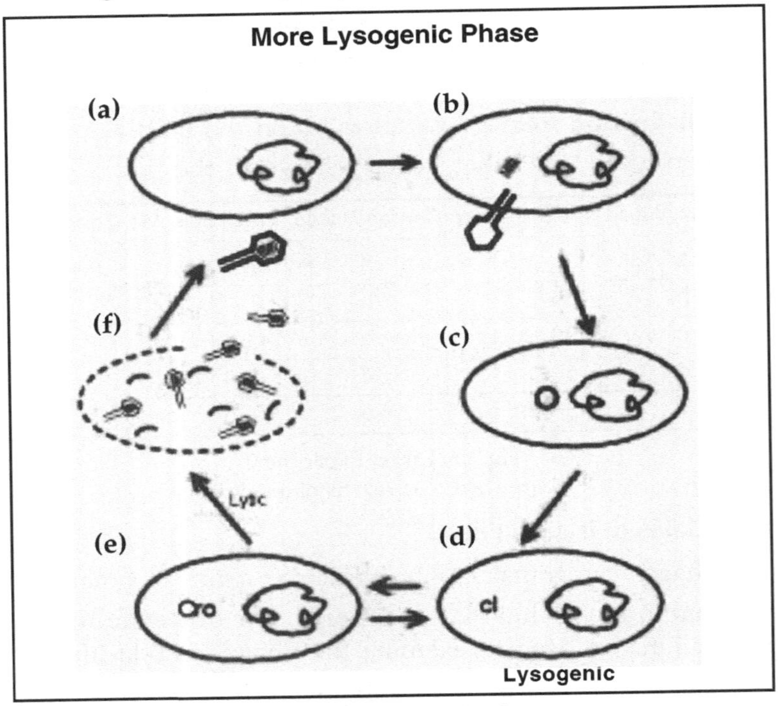

Fig. 1.7: More Lysogenic Phase
Source: based on review of literature

CONCLUSION

- Unlike the F plasmid that can incorporate anywhere in the E. coli genome, lambda can only incorporate into a specific site, called attë. The gal gene is on one side of attë and the bio gene (biotin synthesis) is on the other side.
- Sometimes when lambda come out of the chromosome at the end of the lysogenic phase, it crosses over at the wrong point. This is very similar to the production of an F′ from an Hfr.
- When this happens, a piece of the E. coli chromosome is incorporated into the lambda phage chromosome
- These phage that carry an E. coli gene in addition to the lambda genes are called "specialized transducing phages". They can carry either the gal gene or the bio gene to other E. coli.
- Thus it is possible to quickly develop merodiploids (partial diploids) for any allele you like of gal or bio. Note that this trick can't be used with other genes, but only for genes that flank the attachment site for lambda or another lysogenic phage.

REFERENCES

https://en.wikipedia.org/wiki/Bacterial_genetics

https://en.wikipedia.org/wiki/Bacterial_genetics

https://www.sciencedirect.com/topics/agricultural-and-biological.../bacterial-genetics

https://www.nature.com › subjects

https://www.slideshare.net/doctorrao/bacterial-genetics

https://www.microrao.com/micronotes/genetics.pdf

www.biologyreference.com › Ar-Bi

https://www.khanacademy.org › ... › Bacteria and archaea › Prokaryote structure

https://www.ncbi.nlm.nih.gov/books/NBK7908/

https://www.accessscience.com/content/bacterial-genetics/068700

Pages: 12-20

Current Research in Biochemistry and Molecular Biology
Edited by: **Dr. Prasann Kumar and Dr. Pawan Kumar 'Bharti'**
ISBN: 978-93-88854-33-7
Edition: **2020**
Published by: **Discovery Publishing House Pvt. Ltd., New Delhi (India)**

CHAPTER
2

Cloning Vectors in Molecular Biology

Prasann Kumar[1,2*], Johnson Yumnam[1]

GRAPHICAL ABSTRACT

Keywords: Biology, Cloning, Molecular, Vector

INTRODUCTION

- A cloning vector is a small DNA vehicle that carries a foreign DNA fragment. The insertion of the fragment into the cloning vector is

[1] Department of Agronomy, School of Agriculture, Lovely Professional University, Jalandhar - 144 411 (Punjab) (India)
[2] Divison of Research and Development, Lovely Professional University, Jalandhar - 144 411 (Punjab) (India)

carried out by treating the vehicle and the foreign DNA with the same restriction enzyme, then ligating the fragments together.

- A DNA molecule that carries foreign DNA into a host cell, replicates inside a bacterial (or yeast) cell and produces many copies of itself and the foreign DNA.
- There are many types of cloning vectors. Plasmids and bacteriophages (such as phage λ) are perhaps most commonly used for this purpose. Other types of cloning vectors include bacterial artificial chromosomes (BACs) and yeast artificial chromosomes (YACs).

Three features of all cloning vectors

- Sequences that permit the propagation of itself in bacteria (or in yeast for YACs)
- A cloning site to insert foreign DNA; the most versatile vectors contain A site that can be cut by many restriction enzymes
- A method of selecting for bacteria (or yeast for YACs) containing a vector with foreign DNA; usually accomplished by selectable markers for drug resistance

Types of Cloning Vectors

- **Plasmid** - an extrachromosomal circular DNA molecule that autonomously replicates inside the bacterial cell; cloning limit: 100 to 10,000 base pairs or 0.1-10 kilobases (kb)
- **Phage** - derivatives of bacteriophage lambda; linear DNA molecules, whose region can be replaced with foreign DNA without disrupting its life cycle; cloning limit: 8-20 kb
- **Cosmids** - an extrachromosomal circular DNA molecule that combines features of plasmids and phage; cloning limit - 35-50 kb
- **Bacterial Artificial Chromosomes (BAC)** - based on bacterial mini-F plasmids. cloning limit: 75-300 kb
- **Yeast Artificial Chromosomes (YAC)** - an artificial chromosome that contains telomeres, origin of replication, a yeast centromere, and a selectable marker for identification in yeast cells; cloning limit: 100-1000 kb

Plasmid cloning vectors (pUC19)

- Small size (2.69 kb)
- Origin of replication
- Selectable markers (lacZ and ampR genes)
- Unique cloning sites (polylinker/MCS)

- Plasmids are circular, double-stranded DNA molecules that exist in bacteria and in the nuclei of some eukaryotic cells. They can replicate independently of the host cell. The size of plasmids ranges from a few kb to near 100 kb.
- use a media that contains ampicillin and X-gal
- X-gal is a lactose analog that, when modified by β-galactosidase, turns the bacterial colony blue
- The polylinker is interior to the lacZ gene which separates the promoter from the coding region
- if a bacteria receives
- no plasmid: AmpS and lacZ-
- no growth
- intact plasmid: AmpR and lacZ+
- blue colony
- recombinant plasmid: AmpR and lacZ-
- white colony
- recombinant plasmids are restricted to about 7-8 kbp in size

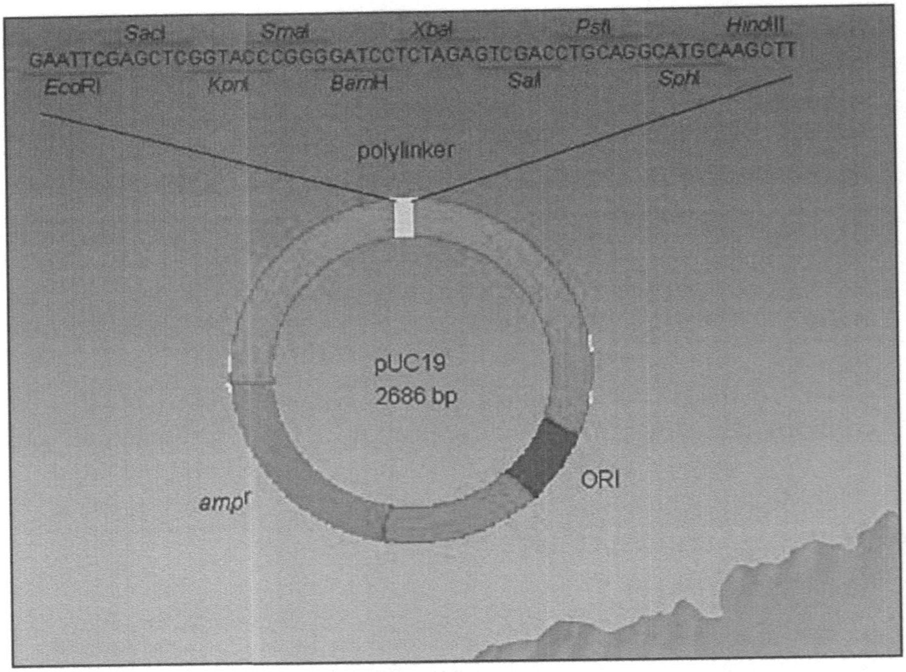

Fig. 2.1: pUC19

Source: based on review of literature

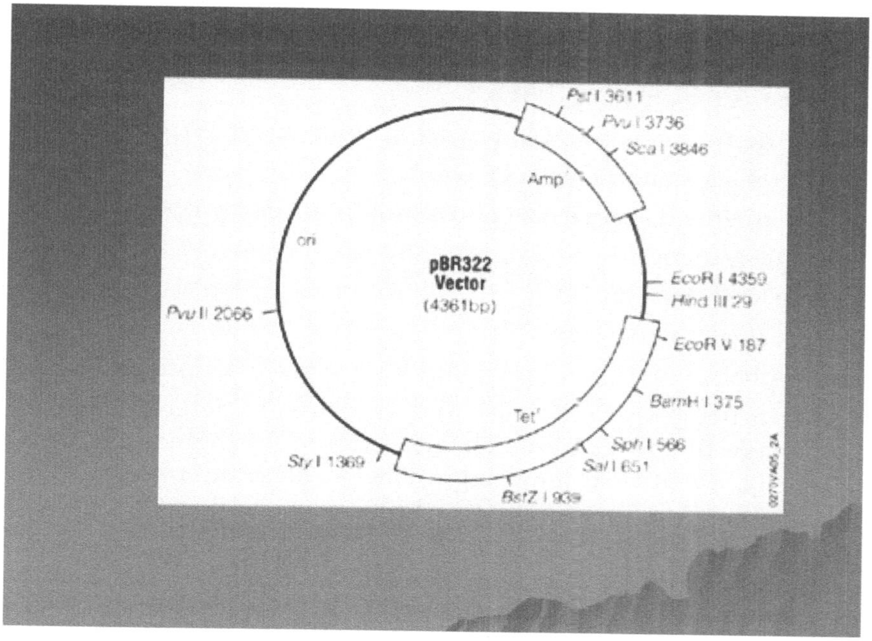

Fig. 2.2: pBR322 vector

Source: based on review of literature

- A plasmid vector is made from natural plasmids by removing unnecessary segments and adding essential sequences. To clone a DNA sample, the same restriction enzyme must be used to cut both the vector and the DNA sample. Therefore, a vector usually contains a sequence (polylinker) which can recognize several restriction enzymes so that the vector can be used for cloning a variety of DNA samples.
- A plasmid vector must also contain a drug-resistance gene for selective amplification. After the vector enters into a host cell, it may proliferate with the host cell. However, since the transformation efficiency of plasmids in *E. coli* is very low, most *E. coli* cells that proliferate in the medium would not contain the plasmids. Therefore, we must find a way to allow only the transformed *E. coli* to proliferate. Typically, antibiotics are used to kill *E. coli* cells which do not contain the vectors. The transformed *E. coli* cells are protected by the ampicillin-resistance gene (ampr) which can express the enzyme, b-lactamase, to inactivate the antibiotic ampicillin.

Bacteriophage

- lytic/lysogenic
- lambda, T4, M13
- 15 kb of the lambda-genome involved in lysogeny

- Not essential for cloning
- Packaging of lambda-DNA is size sensitive
- Must be between 45 and 51 kb
- Delete non-essential -DNA, replace it with insert DNA
- Charon 40, Lambda GT10, 11 etc.
- stuffer fragment, keeps size above minimum for propagation
- cut with enzyme
- swamp with foreign DNA
- 2 arms ligate, non-viable
- viable phages will be recombinant with a piece of foreign DNA
- Lambda phages are viruses that can infect bacteria. The major advantage of the Lambda phage vector is its high transformation efficiency, about 1000 times more efficient than the plasmid vector.
- The extreme ends of the Lambda DNA are known as COS sites, each is single stranded, 12 nucleotides long. Because their sequences are complementary to each other, one end of Lambda DNA may base-pair with the other end of a different Lambda DNA, forming concatemers. The two ends of a Lambda DNA may also bind together, forming a circular DNA. In the host cell, the Lambda DNA circularizes because ligase may seal the join of the COS sites.

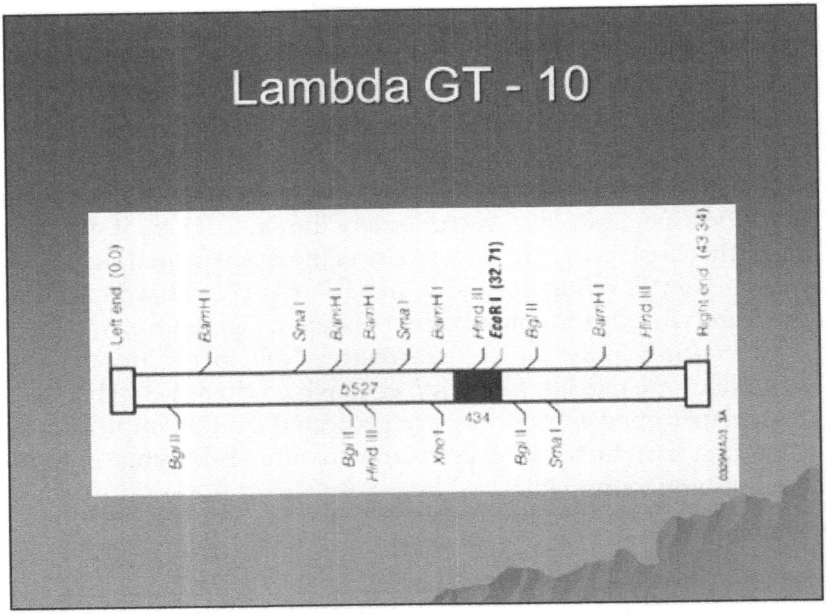

Fig. 2.3: Lambda GT-10

Source: based on review of literature

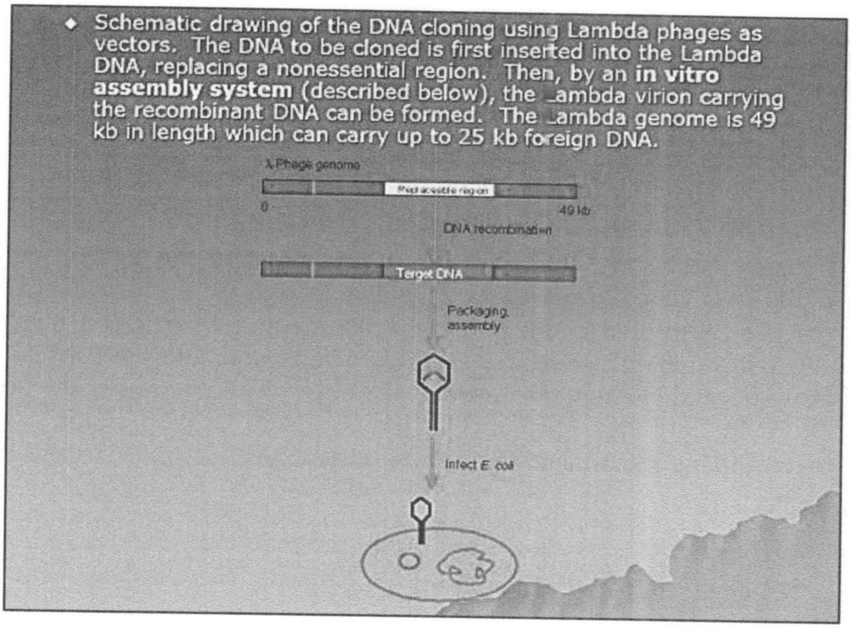

Fig. 2.4: DNA cloning

Source: based on review of literature

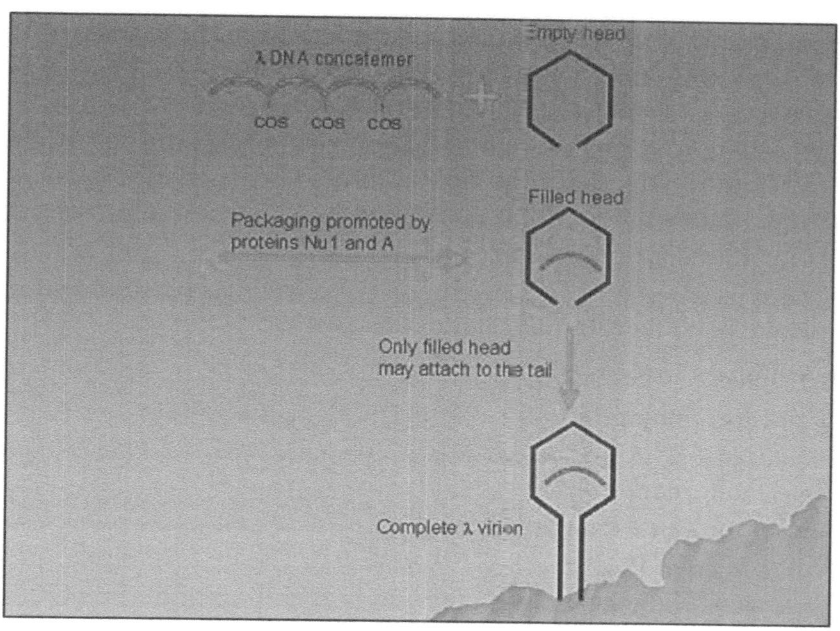

Fig. 2.5: Packaging promoted by protein

Source: based on review of literature

- In the assembly process of Lambda virions, two proteins Nu1 and A can recognize the COS site, directing the insertion of the Lambda DNA between them into an empty head. The filled head is then attached to the tail, forming a complete Lambda virion. The whole process normally takes place in the host cell. However, to prepare the Lambda virion carrying recombinant lambda DNA, the following in vitro assembly system is commonly used.
- Proteins Nu1 and A are encoded by the genes in the lambda genome. If the two genes are mutated, lambda DNA cannot be packaged into the pre-assembled head. Because tails attach only to filled heads, the cell will accumulate separate empty heads and tails, which can then be extracted. When the extract is mixed with recombinant lambda DNA and proteins Nu1 and A, the complete lambda virion carrying recombinant lambda DNA will be assembled.

COSMIDS

Lambda-DNA replicates via rolling circle replication

- "cos" sites are regularly spaced
- genome is snipped
- small plasmid with a cos site
- linearize and mix with foreign DNA
- ligate 2 cosmids on appropriately sized DNA (32-47 kb)
- will package into phage heads
- phage is infectious, injects into E. coli
- The cosmid vector is a combination of the plasmid vector and the COS site which allows the target DNA to be inserted into the lambda head. It has the following advantages:
- High transformation efficiency.
- The cosmid vector can carry up to 45 kb whereas plasmid and lambda phage vectors are limited to 25 kb.

Yeast Artificial Chromosome

- good for cloning large pieces of DNA (up to 500 kb)
- bacterial ori, Ampr, yeast ori, centromere, two telomere sequences, selectable markers
- grow YAC in bacteria, purify
- cut with two restriction enzymes
- creates two "arms"
- add foreign DNA, ligate
- two arms on either side of insert

- transform auxotrophic yeast - trp1- and ura3-
- properly ligated YAC will be Trp+ and Ura+
- will stably harbour the large piece of DNA
- Entire eukaryotic gene (introns and everything!)
- artificial chromosomes for bacteria (BAC) and mammalian (MAC) systems

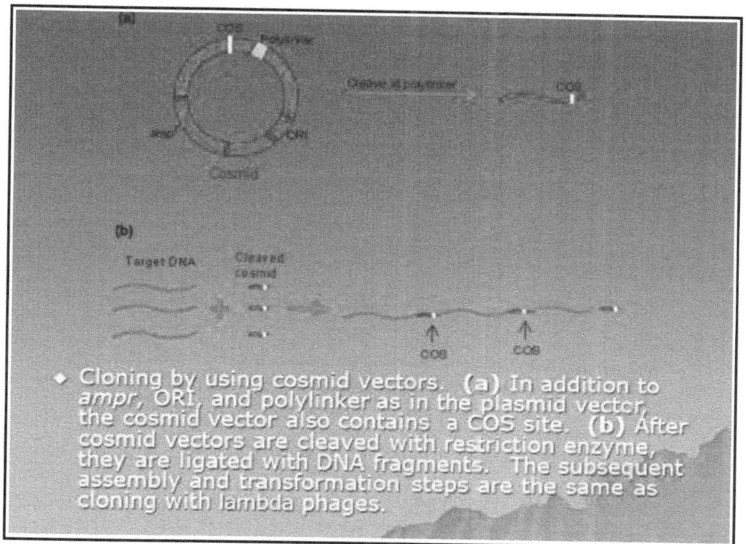

Fig. 2.6: Cosmid vectors

Source: based on review of literature

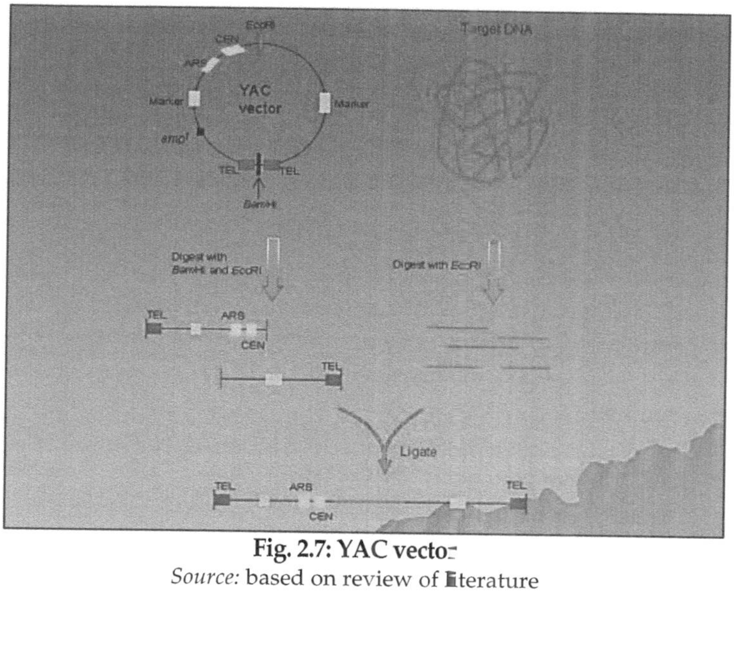

Fig. 2.7: YAC vector

Source: based on review of literature

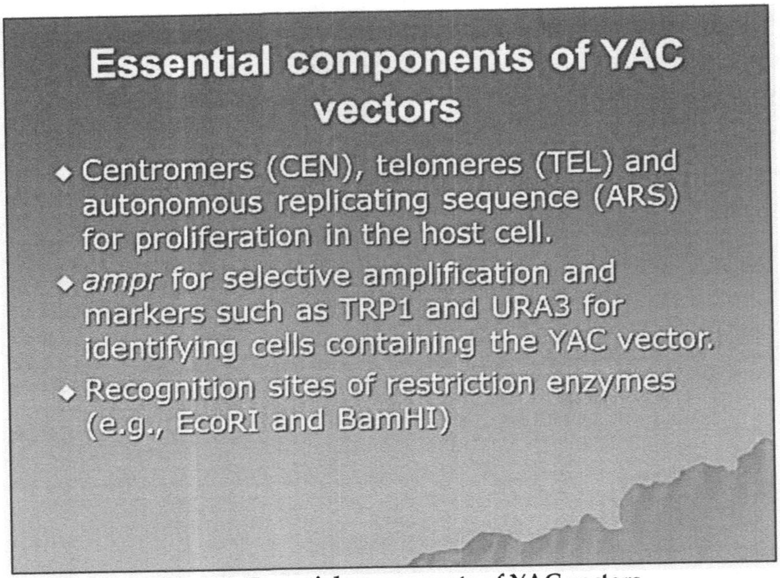

Fig. 2.8: Essential components of YAC vectors

Source: based on review of literature

Procedure

- The target DNA is partially digested by EcoRI and the YAC vector is cleaved by EcoRI and BamHI.
- Ligate the cleaved vector segments with a digested DNA fragment to form an artificial chromosome.
- Transform yeast cells to make a large number of copies.

CONCLUSION

A cloning vector is a small piece of DNA that can be stably maintained in an organism, and into which a foreign DNA fragment can be inserted for cloning purposes. Thecloning vector may be DNA taken from a virus, the cell of a higher organism, or it may be the plasmid of a bacterium.

REFERENCES

https://en.wikipedia.org/wiki/Cloning_vector

https://www.sciencedirect.com/topics/neuroscience/cloning-vector

https://nptel.ac.in/courses/102103013/module1/lec3/5.html

https://www.toppr.com/bytes/cloning-vectors/

www.genomecompiler.com › Blog

https://www.onlinebiologynotes.com/cloning-vector-characteristics-types/

https://www.ncbi.nlm.nih.gov/books/NBK21498/

https://www.thebalance.com › ... › Biotech Industry › Biotech Glossary

https://www.promega.com/products/cloning-and.../cloning-vectors-and-kits...

https://www.longdom.org/.../cloning-vector-journals-articles-ppts-list-31.ht...

Pages: 21-49

Current Research in Biochemistry and Molecular Biology
Edited by: Dr. Prasann Kumar and Dr. Pawan Kumar 'Bharti'
ISBN: 978-93-88854-33-7
Edition: **2020**
Published by: **Discovery Publishing House Pvt. Ltd., New Delhi (India)**

CHAPTER

3

Advance Molecular tool to Detect Plant Pathogen *A Review*

R. Kannan[a], A. Solaimalai[b] and M. Jayakumar[*]

ABSTRACT

Plant pathogenic bacteria, phytoplasmas, viruses and viroids are difficult to control, and preventive measures are essential to minimize the losses they cause each year in different crops. In this context, rapid and accurate methods for detection and diagnosis of these plant pathogens are required to apply treatments, undertake agronomic measures or proceed with eradication practices, particularly for quarantine pathogens. In recent years, there has been an exponential increase in the number of protocols based on nucleic-acid tools being those based on PCR or RT-PCR now routinely applied worldwide. Nucleic acid extraction is still necessary in many cases and in practice inhibition problems are decreasing the theoretical sensitivity of molecular detection. For these reasons, integrated protocols that include the use of molecular techniques as screening methods, followed by confirmation by other techniques supported by different biological principles are advisable.

Overall, molecular techniques based on different types of PCR amplification and very especially on real-time PCR are leading to high throughput, faster and more accurate detection methods for the most severe plant pathogens, with important

[a] Assistant Professor (Plant Pathology), Department of Plant Pathology, Faculty of Agriculture, Annamalai University, AnnamalaiNagar - 608 002 (Tamil Nadu) (India)

[b] Associate Professor (Agronomy), Agricultural Research Station, Tamil Nadu Agricultural University, Kovilpatti - 628 501, (Tamil Nadu) (India)

[*] Subject Matter Specialist (Agronomy), Regional Coffee Research Station, Thandigudi - 624 216, Dindigul (Dt), (Tamil Nadu) (India)

benefits for agriculture. Other technologies, such as isothermal amplification, microarrays, etc. have great potential, but their practical development in plant pathology is still underway. Despite these advances, there are some unsolved problems concerning the detection of many plant pathogens due to their low titre in the plants, their uneven distribution, the existence of latent infections and the lack of validated sampling protocols. Research based on genomic advances and innovative detection methods as well as better knowledge of the pathogens' lifecycle will facilitate their early and accurate detection, thus improving the sanitary status of cultivated plants in the near future.

Keywords: Advance molecular tools, plant pathogen, PCR and ELISA

INTRODUCTION

Plant diseases cause major production and economic losses in agriculture and forestry. For example, soybean rust (a fungal disease in soybeans) has caused a significant economic loss and just by removing 20% of the infection, the farmers may benefit with an approximately 11 million-dollar profit (Roberts *et al.,* 2006). It is estimated that the crop losses due to plant pathogens in United Stated result in about 33 *billion* dollars every year. Of this, about 65% (21 billion dollars) could be attributed to non-native plant pathogens (Pimentel *et al.,*2005). Some of the diseases caused by introduced pathogenic species are chestnut blight fungus, Dutch elm disease, and huanglongbing citrus disease (Pimentel *et al.,* 2005; Li *et al.,* 2006). The bacterial, fungal, and viral infections, along with infestations by insects result in plant diseases and damage. There are about 50,000 parasitic and non-parasitic plant diseases of plants in United States (Pimentel *et al.,* 2005). Upon infection, a plant develops symptoms that appear on different parts of the plants causing a significant agronomic impact (López *et al.,* 2003). Many such microbial diseases with time spread over a larger area in groves and plantations through accidental introduction of vectors or through infected plant materials.

Presently, the plant disease detection techniques available are enzyme-linked immunosorbent assay (ELISA), based on proteins produced by the pathogen, and polymerase chain reaction (PCR), based on specific deoxyribose nucleic acid (DNA) sequences of the pathogen (Prithiviraj *et al.,* 2004; Das, 2004; Li *et al.,* 2006; Saponari *et al.,* 2008; Ruiz-Ruiz *et al.,* 2009; Yvon *et al.,* 2009). In spite of availability of these techniques, there is a demand for a fast, sensitive, and selective method for the rapid detection of plant diseases. Disease detection techniques can be broadly classified into direct and indirect methods. Summarizes some of these methods of disease detection. An advanced plant disease detection technique can provide rapid, accurate, and reliable detection of plant diseases in early stages for economic, production, and agricultural benefits. In the present paper, advanced techniques of ground-based disease detection that could be possibly integrated with an automated agricultural vehicle are reviewed. In ground-based disease detection studies, both field-based and laboratory-based experiments are discussed in this paper. The field-based studies refer to studies that involve spectral data collection under field conditions, whereas laboratory-based studies refer to data collection under laboratory conditions. The laboratory-based experiments provide strong background knowledge (such as the experimental protocol and statistical algorithm for classification) for the field-based applications.

MOLECULAR TECHNIQUES OF PLANT DISEASE DETECTION

In recent years, molecular techniques of plant disease detection have been well established. The sensitivity of the molecular techniques refers to the minimum amount of microorganism that can be detected in the sample. López *et al.*, (2003) reported that the sensitivity of the molecular techniques for detecting bacteria ranged from 10 to 106 colony forming units/ml. The commonly used molecular techniques for disease detection are ELISA and PCR (PCR and real-time PCR). Other molecular techniques include immune fluorescence (IF), flow cytometry, fluorescence in situ hybridization (FISH), and DNA microarrays. In the ELISA-based disease detection, the microbial protein (antigen) associated with a plant disease is injected into an animal that produces antibodies against the antigen. These antibodies are extracted from the animal's body and used for antigen detection with a fluorescence dye and enzymes. In presence of the disease causing microorganism (antigen), the sample would fluoresce, thus confirming the presence of a particular plant disease. In PCR-based disease detection, the genetic material (DNA) of the disease-causing microorganism is extracted, purified, and amplified before performing the gel electrophoresis. The presence of a specific band in gel electrophoresis confirms the presence of the plant-disease causing organism.

Different types of immunological and PCR techniques are described by López *et al.*, (2003). There are number of studies on disease detection using the molecular techniques. Efforts are ongoing to improve the efficiency of these techniques. Table 3.1 summarizes few studies on plant disease detection using molecular techniques. López*et al.*, (2003) reviewed the various molecular techniques used for detecting pathogenic viruses and bacteria in plants. Their review paper elaborates the molecular methods of plant disease detection, including different types of PCR and ELISAbased techniques. Schaad and Frederick (2002), and Henson and French (1993) described the applications of PCR technique for the diagnosis of plant diseases. Alvarez (2004) reported that there are about 97 commercially available immuno diagnostic test kits for the detection of bacterial pathogens in plants.

Table 3.1

Comparison of the current methods for detecting plant diseases resulting from bacterial pathogens

Techniques	Limit of Detection (CFU/mL)	Advantages	Limitations
PCR	10^3-io^4	Mature and common technology, portable, easy to operate.	Effectiveness is subjected to DNA extraction, inhibitors, polymerase activity, concentration of PCR buffer and deoxynucleoside triphosphate.
FISH	10^3	High sensitivity	Autofluorescence, photobleaching.
ELISA	10^5-10^6	Low cost, visual color change can be used for detection.	Low sensitivity for bacteria.
IF	10^3	High sensitivity, target distribution can be visualized.	Photobleaching.
FCM$^{S''}$	10^4	Simultaneous measurement of Several parameters, rapid detection.	High cost, overwhelming Unnecessary information.

PCR: polymerase chain reaction; FISH: fluorescence in-situ hybridization; ELISA: enzyme-linked immunosorbent assay; IF: immunofluorescence; FCM: flow cytometry; CFU: colony forming unit.

Some of the limitations of the molecular techniques are that they are time-consuming and labour-intensive, and require an elaborate procedure, especially during sample preparation (collection and extraction) to obtain reliable and accurate results on plant disease detection. In addition, these techniques require consumable reagents that must be tailored to detect each specific pathogen (e.g. sequence-specific primers for PCR). The molecular techniques could be used as robust tool to ensure the presence of plant diseases, but cannot be used as a preliminary screening tool for processing large number of plant samples due to the time involved in the process.

SPECTROSCOPIC AND IMAGING TECHNIQUES

Recent developments in agricultural technology have led to a demand for a new era of automated non-destructive methods of plant disease detection. It is desirable that the plant disease detection tool should be rapid, specific to a particular disease, and sensitive for detection at the early onset of the symptoms (López *et al.,* 2003). The spectroscopic and imaging techniques are unique disease monitoring methods that have been used to detect diseases and stress due to various factors, in plants and trees. Current research activities are towards the development of such technologies to create a practical tool for a large-scale real-time disease monitoring under field conditions. Various spectroscopic and imaging techniques have been studied for the detection of symptomatic and asymptomatic plant diseases.

Some the methods are: fluorescence imaging (Bravo *et al.,*2004; Moshou *et al.,* 2005; Chaerle *et al.,* 2007), multispectral or hyperspectral imaging (Moshou *et al.,* 2004; Shafri and Hamdan, 2009; Qin *et al.,* 2009), infrared spectroscopy (Spinelli *et al.,* 2006; Purcell *et al.,*2009), fluorescence spectroscopy (Marcassa *et al.,* 2006; Belasque *et al.,*2008; Lins *et al.,* 2009), visible/multiband spectroscopy (Yang *et al.,* 2007; Delalieux *et al.,* 2007; Chen *et al.,* 2008), and nuclear magnetic resonance (NMR) spectroscopy (Choi *et al.,* 2004). Hahn (2009) reviewed multiple methods (sensors and algorithms) for pathogen detection, with special emphasis on postharvest diseases. The spectroscopic and imaging techniques could be integrated with an autonomous agricultural vehicle that can provide information on disease detection at early stages to control the spread of plant diseases. This technology can also be applied to identify stress levels and nutrient deficiencies in plants. In regard to plant disease detection, significant research is ongoing on the prospective of this technology from last few decades. Spectroscopic technology has been successfully applied for plant stress detection such as water-stress detection and nutrient-stress detection. In addition, there have also been significant applications for monitoring the quality of postharvest fruits and vegetables. Some of the commonly used spectroscopic and imaging techniques are described in the following sections.

FLUORESCENCE SPECTROSCOPY

Fluorescence spectroscopy refers to a type of spectroscopic method, where the fluorescence from the object of interest is measured after excitation with a beam of light (usually ultraviolet spectra). For the last twenty years, the laser-induced fluorescence has been used for vegetative studies, such as to monitor stress levels and physiological states in plants (Belasque *et al.*, 2008). Two types of fluorescence: (i) blue-green fluorescence in about 400-600 nm range, and (ii) chlorophyll fluorescence in about 650-800 nm range, are produced by green leaves. The fluorescence spectroscopy can be utilized to monitor nutrient deficiencies, environmental conditions based stress levels, and diseases in plants (Cerovic *et al.*, 1999; Belasque *et al.*, 2008). Belasque *et al.*, (2008) employed fluorescence spectroscopy to detect stress caused by citrus canker (bacterial disease caused by Xanthomonascitri–X. axonopodispv. citri) and mechanical injury.

A portable fluorescence spectroscopy system was taken to the greenhouse and the measurement probe was placed 2 mm above the leaf (attached to greenhouse plants) for collecting data from different samples during the period of study (60 days). The spectral data were further processed and analyzed in the laboratory. A 532 nm 10 mW excitation laser was used for excitation and ratios between fluorescence at different wavelengths were employed to monitor the stress caused by bacterial infection. The samples of leaves collected from the field (detached leaves) as well as leaves from greenhouse plants (attached leaves) were analyzed using the system. The three ratios used were: (i) ratio between fluorescence intensity at 452 and 685 nm, (ii) ratio between fluorescence intensity at 452 nm and 735 nm, and (iii) ratio between fluorescence intensity at 685 nm and 735 nm. Fluorescence of citrus leaves was monitored for 60 days under four different conditions: leaves with no stress, leaves with mechanical stress, leaves with disease, and leaves with disease and mechanical stress.

The studies reported the potential of fluorescence spectroscopy for disease detection and discrimination between the mechanical and diseased stress. A similar approach was taken to detect water stress and differentiate citrus canker leaves from variegated chlorosis leaves (Marcassa *et al.*, 2006). The above studies could classify healthy from citrus canker-affected leaves, but were unable to identify water stress and distinguish between variegated chlorosis and citrus canker-infected leaves. The authors did not yet present any statistical analysis to evaluate theability of the technique to discriminate or classify different plant conditions. Lins *et al.*, (2009) conducted field experiments to discriminate citrus canker-stressed leaves from chlorosis-infected (caused by *Xylellafastidiosa* bacteria) and healthy leaves. Methods such as principal component analysis (PCA), discriminant analysis, and neural network-based classification algorithms can be applied to analyze the results obtained from fluorescence spectroscopy. Methods such as PCA, parallel factor analysis, cluster analysis, partial least square (PLS) regression, and Fischer's linear discriminant analysis (LDA) can be applied for classifying fluorescent spectrometric data having two or more classes (Guimet, 2005).

VISIBLE AND INFRARED SPECTROSCOPY

Similar to fluorescence spectroscopy, visible and infrared spectroscopy have been used as a rapid, non-destructive, and cost-effective method for the detection of plant diseases. It is a fastdeveloping technology used for varied applications (Ramon *et al.*, 2002; Delwiche and Graybosch, 2002; Pontius *et al.*, 2005; Gomez *et al.*, 2006; Zhang *et al.*, 2008a,b; Guo *et al.*, 2009; Sundaram *et al.*, 2009). Studies have also been conducted on the detection of stress, injury, and diseases in plants using this technology (Polischuk *et al.*, 1997; Spinelli *et al.*, 2006; Naidu *et al.*,2009). The visible and infrared regions of the electromagnetic spectra are known to provide the maximum information on the physiological stress levels in the plants (Muhammed, 2002, 2005; Xu *et al.*, 2007) and thus, some of these wavebands specific to a disease can be used to detect plant diseases (West *et al.*, 2003), even before the symptoms are visible. In general, visible spectroscopy is used for disease detection in plants in combination with infrared spectroscopy (Malthus and Madeira, 1993; Bravo *et al.*, 2003; Huang *et al.*, 2004; Larsolle and Muhammed, 2007).

Spinelli *et al.*, (2006) assessed the near infrared (NIR)-based technique for detecting fire blight disease in the asymptomatic pear plants under greenhouse conditions. The NIR technique did not exhibit potential for classifying infected plants from that of healthy ones, while electronic nose system showed a better potential to classify diseased plants. The authors reported that the possible reason for the inability of the NIR based technique to distinguish diseased from healthy plants could be due to a very small leaf scan area (2 mm^2 in this study). Purcell *et al.*, (2009) investigated the application of NIR spectroscopy for the determination and rating of sugarcane resistance against Australian sugarcane disease, Fiji leaf gall. The leaf samples from the cane stalks were analyzed with a Fourier transform (FT)-NIR instrument in 2-4 days after the sugarcane stalks were removed. The signal in the spectral range of 11,000 - 4000 cm^{-1} was procured.

Principal component analysis and PLS-based statistical methods were used to analyze the data. The second derivative of the signal in the spectral range was also determined to verify if the signal is better represented the disease for analysis. The authors reported that the PLS-based method was effective in predicting the disease rating in sugarcane. The data analysis procedure used for the classification of postharvest food products can be applicable for plant disease detection. Thus, the knowledge from one application (on statistical algorithm, data processing, experimental protocol, etc.) can be transferred to other possible applications. For example, Sirisomboon *et al.*, (2009) used visible spectra along with NIR spectra (600-1100 nm) to identify defective pods during soybean processing.

In addition to PCA, soft independent modelling of class analogy (SIMCA) and PLS-discriminant analysis were used to classify the groups. The authors reported that the SIMCA-based model was able to discriminate different groups of soybean better than the PLS-based model. Naidu *et al.*, (2009) used leaf spectral reflectance to identify viral infection (under field conditions) in grapevines (*Vitisvinifera* L.) that cause grapevine leafroll disease. A portable spectrometer was used to collect reflectance data from each leaf of the plant using a plant-probe attachment device having a leaf clip. In addition to the green, near infrared, and mid infrared region of the spectra, vegetative indices were used to assess the applicability of spectral reflectance in identifying the disease.

Discriminant analysis was performed to classify the infected leaves with and without symptoms with that of non-infected leaves. The different categories of leaves could be clearly differentiated with improved accuracies when both the vegetative indices and individual reflectance bands were used. A maximum of 75% accuracy was achieved in the study. Huang and Apan (2006) collected hyperspectral data using portable spectrometer under field conditions to detect Sclerotinia rot disease in celery. PLS regression analysis was performed to analyze the spectral reflectance data. The first and second derivatives were estimated to test their effectiveness in reducing the root mean square error during the validation of the developed model.

The raw data-based model produced lower root mean square errors than the first and second derivatives. The authors also stated that the reflectance in the visible and infrared range from 400 to 1300 nm were sufficient in acquiring similar results as that of entire spectra (400-2500 nm). The cross-validation results using raw, first derivative, and second derivative data provided a prediction error of 11-13%. Chen *et al.*, (2008) investigated the application of hyper spectral reflectance to identify cotton canopy infected with Verticillium wilt. The data were collected using a portable spectroradiometer under field conditions and it was analyzed in the laboratory.

The authors reported that among the visible and infrared spectra, the first derivative of the infrared spectra in the wavelength range between 731 and 1317 nm were most effective in predicting the Verticillium wilt in cotton canopy accurately based on the developed models. Other sensitive regions for prediction of infection severity levels were found to be from 780 to 1300 nm and the first derivative of the spectra from 680 to 760 nm. Yang *et al.*, (2007) studied brown planthoppers and leaf-folder infestations in rice plants. The infested conditions of the plants were ranked and efforts were made to identify the extent of infestations using spectroscopic reflectance (350-2400 nm) data collected under field conditions. The results indicated that the spectral range from 426 to 1450 nm showed the maximum correlation intensity.

The changes in spectral properties were low in visible and ultraviolet (UV) range, whereas the infrared region (740-2400 nm) yielded the maximum change in spectral signature. Delalieux *et al.,* (2007) used hyper spectral reflectance data (350-2500 nm) to detect apple scab caused by *Venturiainaequalis*. The study involved the identification of infected trees and selection of wavelengths best suited for classifying the infected leaves from those of the healthy leaves. The spectral data were analyzed using methods as LDA, logistic regression analysis (for each wavelength), partial least squares logistic discriminant analysis (PLS-LDA), and tree-based modelling for classifying the infected and healthy leaves. The paper reported that the spectral features from 1350 to 1750 nm and 2200 to 2500 nm were effective for the classification of the infected leaves from healthy leaves at early stages, whereas 580-660 nm and 688-715 nm were effective in identifying infected leaves at their developed stages of infection. Among the statistical methods, logistic regression analysis, PLS-LDA, and tree-based modelling were preferred for classification.

The authors recommended PLS-LDA and tree-based modelling methods as they are simpler, and less computationally and time-intensive. Kobayashi *et al.,* (2001) utilized multispectral radiometer and airborne multispectral scanner for the identification of panicle blast in rice. The spectral range for airborne multispectral scan was selected based on ground experiments. The four spectral bands of 400-460 nm, 490-530 nm or 530-570 nm, 650-700 nm, and 950-1100 nm were utilized for scanning (instantaneous field of view = 2.5 mrad, ground resolution = 0.94 m at 300 m height). The magnitude of reflectance ratios (R470/R570, R520/R675, and R570/R675) decreased with an increase in frequency of panicle blast occurrence.

Wang *et al.,* (2002) used PLS and artificial neural network (ANN) models on the visible-IR reflectance data for classifying damaged soybean seeds. The authors reported that the ANN yielded higher overall as well as individual-class classification accuracies than PLS models. Various studies have used different methods/models for the classification of diseases/conditions of plants based on spectral data. For an instance, Roggo *et al.,* (2003) utilized eight classification models (linear discriminant analysis, k-nearest neighbours, soft independent modelling of class analogy, discriminant partial least squares (DPLS), procrustes discriminant analysis (PDA), classification and regression tree, probabilistic neural network, and learning vector quantization-based neural network) for qualitative determination of sugarbeet. They found that SIMCA, DPLS, and PDA yielded the highest classification accuracies that those of other models.

Wu *et al.,* (2008) used PCA-based back-propagation neural network (BPNN) model and PLS wave length-based BPNN for detection of *Botrytis cinerea* affected eggplant leaves prior to the visibility of symptoms under laboratory conditions. The BPNN model yielded a maximum of 85% classification accuracy for predicting fungal infections. In addition to the statistical models for classification, many spectroscopy-based studies use different vegetative indices for evaluating the change in spectral reflectance at different plant conditions (diseased or healthy plant).

FLUORESCENCE IMAGING

The change in blue-green fluorescence and chlorophyll florescence of the plants upon ultraviolet excitation could provide the status of physiological condition of the plant (Belasque *et al.,* 2008). Fluorescence imaging is an advancement of fluorescence spectroscopy, where fluorescence images (rather than single spectra) are obtained using a camera. A xenon or halogen lamp is used as a UV light source for fluorescence excitation, and the fluorescence at specific wavelengths are recorded using the charge coupled device (CCD)-based camera system (Bravo *et al.,* 2004; Lenk and Buschmann, 2006; Chaerle *et al.,* 2007; Lenk *et al.,* 2007). The regions of electromagnetic spectra that are commonly used for fluorescence imaging are blue (440 nm), green (520-550 nm), red (690 nm), far red (740 nm), and near infrared (800 nm) (Lenk and Buschmann, 2006; Chaerle *et al.,* 2007).

Lenk *et al.,*(2007) described the multispectral fluorescence and its possible application in monitoring fruit quality, photosynthetic activities, tissue structures, and disease symptoms in plants; and the basic instrumentation required. The chlorophyll fluorescence imaging can be an effective tool in monitoring leaf diseases (Chaerle *et al.,* 2004; Scharte *et al.,* 2005; Lenk *et al.,* 2007). Chaerle *et al.,* (2007) used blue-green fluorescence to evaluate the effectiveness of this technique in observing the development of tobacco mosaic virus (TMV) infection in tobacco plants. A temporal effect of TMV infection on the fluorescence (blue-green and chlorophyll fluorescence) of infected plants was observed. The reflectance image at 550 and 800 nm were acquired and considered as the reference images. The authors reported an increase in blue, green, and chlorophyll fluorescence after about 40-55 h upon inoculation of TMV.

The fluorescence imaging demonstrated a visible difference between the infected and non-infected leaves in short period of time (50 h) in comparison to the reference images (14 days for visible symptoms of infection). Bravo *et al.,* (2004) used fluorescence imaging for detecting yellow rust in winter wheat. They acquired two fluorescence images: a background image without the xenon lamp source and a fluorescence image with the xenon lamp source during the experiments. The fluorescence image utilized for the analysis was obtained by subtracting fluorescence image from the background image. The fluorescence was measured at 450, 550, 690, and 740 nm. The authors stated that the difference between the fluorescence at 550 and 690 nm were higher in the diseased portion of the leaves, while it was very low for healthy regions of the leaves.

Moshou *et al.,* (2005) investigated the applicability of hyper spectral reflectance imaging in combination with multispectral fluorescence imaging through sensor fusion to detect yellow rust (*Pucciniastriiformis*) disease of winter wheat. The hyper spectral imaging was performed under ambient condition in winter wheat plots, whereas fluorescence images were procured upon UVexcitation. The authors reported that when the sensor information from the fluorescence and multispectral imaging were combined, QDA-based classification accuracy of the healthy plants improved from 71to 97%. The classification accuracy of the diseased plants and healthy plants further improved to 98.7% and 99.4%, respectively, when the self-organizing map (SOM) based neural network was used for the plant classification. The above studies indicate the possibility for using imaging techniques for disease identification.

HYPER SPECTRAL IMAGING

In recent years, hyper spectral imaging is gaining considerable interest for its application in precision agriculture (Okamoto *et al.,* 2009). In the hyper spectral imaging, the spectral reflectance of each pixel is acquired for a range of wavelengths in the electromagnetic spectra. The wavelengths may include the visible and infrared regions of the electromagnetic spectra. The hyper spectral imaging is similar to multispectral imaging, the difference being a broader range of wavelengths (more number of spectral bands) being scanned for each pixel in the hyper spectral imaging. The resulting information is a set of pixel values (intensity of the reflectance) at each wavelength of the spectra in the form of an image.

Hyper spectral imaging is often used for monitoring the quality of food products (Kim *et al.,* 2001, 2002; Mehl *et al.,* 2004; Yao *et al.,* 2005; Lee *et al.,* 2005; Tallada *et al.,* 2006; Gowen *et al.,* 2007; Mahesh *et al.,,* 2008; Sighicelli *et al.,* 2009). Aleixos *et al.,* (2002) used multispectral imaging of citrus fruits to assess the quality of the fruits for developing a machine vision system. Gowen *et al.,* (2007) revealed that the application of hyper spectral imaging for food quality control and food safety applications. The authors discussed the components of hyper spectral imaging system, different image processing techniques, and various applications in food quality and safety.

Some of the major challenges in hyper spectral imaging-based plant disease detection are the selection of disease-specific spectral band and selection of statistical classification algorithm for a particular application, which depends on the data acquisition setup under field conditions. For an example, Lu (2003), Xing and Baerdemaeker (2005), Xing *et al.*, (2005), Nicolaï *et al.*, (2006) and ElMasry *et al.*, (2008) reported that used hyper spectral imaging for the detection of bruises in apples and acquired different results. Lu (2003) reported that 1000 nm to 1340 nm were best for bruise detection, whereas Xing *et al.*, (2005) and ElMasry *et al.*, (2008) reported bands within range 558-960 nm were suitable for the identification of bruises in apple. Blasco *et al.*,(2007) indicated that applied multi-spectral computer vision using non-visible (ultraviolet, IR, and fluorescence) and visible multiple spectra for citrus sorting. The anthracnose was classified better with NIR images (86%), whereas green mold was more accurately classified with fluorescence imaging (94%).

The stem-end injury was classified up to 100% using the ultraviolet spectra in this study. This study showed the utilization of hyper spectral bands for detecting different aspects of a single problem. Similarly, the hyper spectral imaging could be used for detecting different features within a plant to identify diseases. Each spectral region provides unique information about the plant. For instance, the reflectance at visible wavelength provides the information on the leaf pigmentations while, reflectance at infrared wavelength provides the physiological condition of the plant (Huang *et al.*, 2007). Much attention has been drawn towards utilizing this technology for the plant disease detection for precision agriculture-based applications.

Bravo *et al.*, (2003) investigated that the application of visible-NIR hyper spectral imaging for the early detection of yellow rust disease (*Pucciniastriiformis*) in winter wheat. A discrimination model was developed using quadratic discriminant analysis for the classification of diseases from the healthy plants. The classification model yielded about 92-98% classification accuracy while classifying diseased plants. Similarly, Moshou *et al.*, (2004) utilized a spectrograph to acquire spectral images from 460 to 900 nm to detect yellow rust in wheat. Shafri and Hamdan (2009) reported that used air-borne hyper spectral imaging for the detection of ganoderma basal stem rot disease in oil palm plantations. The authors used various vegetative indices and red edge techniques to classify the diseased from healthy plantations. The classification reported accuracies using different methods ranged from 73 to 84%. The results indicated that an aerial hyper spectral imaging could be used for disease detection and management of plantations in large scale.

Qin *et al.*, (2009) obtained that hyper spectral image in the wavelength range 450-930 nm to detect citrus canker and other damages to Ruby red grape fruit. A spectral information divergence (SID)-based classification method yielded about 96% classification accuracy for discriminating the diseased, damaged, and healthy fruits. Similarly, Lee *et al.*, (2008) investigated the applicability of aerial hyper spectral imaging for the detection of greening in citrus plantation.

OTHER IMAGING TECHNIQUES

The other imaging techniques that can used for detecting plant diseases are infrared thermography, terahetz spectroscopy, NMR spectroscopy, and X-ray imaging. As these techniques are not cost effective, the present paper provides an overview of these methods and does not discuss them in detail. Infrared thermography refers to an imaging technique that utilizes the thermal energy of the infrared band and transforms the procured information into a visible image. Infrared thermography similar to other imaging techniques can be used for non-destructive monitoring of physiological status of plants (Chaerle *et al.*, 1999, 2001). Lenthe *et al.*, (2007) used infrared thermography to examine the possible relationship between the leaf microclimate and fungal diseases in wheat fields. Although microclimate can be determined from infrared thermography, direct diseased leaf area identification could not be established. Chaerle *et al.*, (2003) and Chaerle and Van Der Straeten (2000) reviewed the application of imaging techniques in agronomy and stress detection. They reported that the stomatal changes in the leaves of the plants upon pathogen infection could be monitored by thermography (e.g. hydrogen peroxide produced by Pseudomonas syringae induces stomata in the leaves to close).

Similarly, local temperature changes due to plant defence mechanisms against diseases can also help in monitoring plant diseases. Tobacco leaves produces salicylic acid (promoting thermal and stomatal change) that can be monitored using thermography. Other studies include presymptomatic detection of cucumber downy mildew - Pseudoperonospora cubensis (Lindenthal *et al.*, 2005; Oerke *et al.*, 2005, 2006), fungal infection by *Cercosporabeticola* in sugarbeet (Chaerle *et al.*, 2004), and *Brassica napus* infection with Phoma lingam (Lamkadmi *et al.*, 1996) among others. In recent years, terahertz (THz) frequencies (0.1-10 THz) are being utilized for measuring the water content in leaves.

The water stress can be observed by utilizing this frequency, as terahertz frequency is absorbed greatly by water molecules (Hadjiloucas *et al.*, 2009). Nuclear magnetic resonance and X-ray-based imaging techniques can also be used for detecting infections, different types of stress, and other health conditions in trees/fruits (Goodman *et al.*, 1992; Williamson *et al.*, 1992; Karunakaran *et al.*, 2004; Pearson and Wicklow, 2006). Goodman *et al.*, (1992) used NMR microscopic imaging for identification of the fungal pathogen Botrytis cinerea in red raspberry. Narvankar *et al.*, (2009) applied X-ray imaging to identify fungal infections in wheat. The authors employed statistical discriminant models and ANN to classify the images of the wheat kernels. Statistical classifiers, especially the Mahalanobis discriminant classifier performed better (92-99% accuracy) than the ANNbased classification.

PROFILING OF PLANT VOLATILE ORGANIC COMPOUNDS

The volatile organic compounds (VOC) released by plants and trees contribute about two-thirds of the total VOC emissions present in the atmosphere (Guenther, 1997). There are number of factors that affect the volatile metabolic profile of a plant or tree. The VOCs released by the plants depend on various physico-chemical factors such as humidity, temperature, light, soil condition, and fertilization, as well as biological factors such as growth and developmental stage of the plant, insects, and presence of other herbs (Vallat *et al.,* 2005; Vuorinen *et al.,* 2007).

These plant volatiles in turn influence their relationship between the plants and other organisms including pathogens (Vuorinen *et al.,* 2007). For example, acetaldehyde is released by the leaves of young poplar trees are controlled by the transfer of ethanol to leaves through transpiration. Dudareva *et al.,* (2006) reviewed a range of plant volatiles released by the plants due to biotic and abiotic interactions. Some of the commonly found secondary plant volatiles are terpeniods, volatile fatty acids (such as trans-2-hexenal, cis-3-hexenol and methyl jasmonate), phenylpropanoids and benzenoids, and amino acid volatiles (such as aldehydes, alcohols, esters, acids, and nitrogen- and sulfur-containing volatiles derived from amino acids).

Cevallos-Cevallos *et al.,* (2009) reported that the compounds (extracted from leaves) such as hesperidin, naringenin, and quercetin present in the leaves could be used as a biomarker to identify huanglongbing diseases in citrus trees. The volatiles of these compounds could be tested in the atmosphere near the citrus plantations to detect the presence of huanglongbing disease. Tholl *et al.,* (2006) reviewed practical methods to study the plant volatiles suitable for various applications. The authors described the methods for VOC sampling and analysis for in-situ experiments as well as some for field experiments. The focus of the present paper is towards the application of plant VOC profile monitoring for detecting diseases in plants. The VOCs released by the plants change when the plant is infected with a disease due to change in its physiology. These emissions are expected to vary from the VOCs released under normal plant health conditions.

ELECTRONIC NOSE SYSTEM

An electronic nose system consists of a series of gas sensors that are sensitive to a range of organic compounds. As each sensor has specific sensitivities, the sensitivities of a series of sensors could be used to discriminate different compounds present in the atmosphere. Electronic nose systems have been used for multiple applications. They have been used to determine food quality (Evans *et al.,* 2000; Di Natale *et al.,* 2001; Zhang *et al.,* 2008a&b), identify diseases in humans (Gardner *et al.,* 2000; Lin *et al.,* 2001; Dragonieri *et al.,* 2007), and detect microorganisms in food products (Falasconi *et al.*, 2005; Rajamäki *et al.*, 2006; Balasubramanian *et al.*, 2008; Concina *et al.*, 2009) among others. The application of electronic nose systems for identifying plant diseases is relatively new domain for its application. Li *et al.*, (2009b) used a Cyranose @ 320 (an array of 32 conducting polymer-based sensors) to detect postharvest fungal disease in blueberries in a controlled environment.

Blueberries were disinfected with ethanol to eliminate any naturally present fungal spores and bacteria. Once the blueberries were rinsed with distilled water to remove residual ethanol, they were inoculated with spore suspensions of three fungal species: *Botrytis cinerea, Colletotrichum gloeosporioides,* and *Alternaria spp.* that cause graymold, anthracnose, and Alternaria fruit rot in postharvest blueberries, respectively. The berries were placed in a 500 mL bottle and headspace gases were tested using Cyranose @ 320. GC–MS (Gas chromatography–mass spectroscopy) analysis was also performed to identify specific compounds that could be related to fungal diseases. Principal component analysis plots indicated a clear delineation between the control (fresh berries) and berries with fungal infections. The berries with *C. gloeosporioides* could be distinctively differentiated from the other groups, though there was some overlap in the VOC profiles of the berries infected with *B. cinerea* and *Alternaria spp.*

Laothawornkitkul *et al.*, (2008) evaluated the potential of plant volatile signature for pest and disease monitoring in cucumber, pepper, and tomato plants. Similar to Li *et al.*, (2009b), an electronic nose system and GC–MS were used to identify and distinguish the volatiles released by the plants under different conditions. The authors used Bloodhound @ ST214 electronic nose (an array of 14 conducting polymer-based sensors with one sensor as a reference) for determining sensors' responses to VOCs released by the plant leaves in experiments conducted in a greenhouse. Markom *et al.*, (2009) used an electronic nose system to detect basal stem rot disease in oil palm plantation during field experiments. The authors reported that two principal components based on PCA were able to account for 99.32% variability in the data, and MLP-based artificial neural network could classify infected from healthy trees with high accuracy.

GC–MS

The GC–MS is commonly used technique for a qualitative as well as quantitative analysis of volatile metabolites released by plants/trees in different environmental and physiological conditions. The GC–MS studies have been performed to evaluate the change in volatiles caused by bacterial or fungal infection in various food products. Prithiviraj *et al.*, (2004) assessed the variability in the volatiles released from onion bulbs infected with bacterial (*Erwiniacarotovora* causing soft rot) and fungal species (*Fusarium oxysporum* and *Botrytis allii* causing basal and neck rots) using HAPSITE, commercial portable GC–MS instrument. The study indicated that 25 volatile compounds (among the 59 consistently detected compounds) released from onion can be used to identify the disease based on VOC profiling. Although no statistical analyses were performed to determine the discriminatory ability of an algorithm in classifying the VOC profiles for disease detection, model development and software development were recommended for the purpose.

Similar studies on potato tubers inoculated with *Erwiniacarotovora* subsp. carotovora, *E. carotovora* subsp. *atroseptica, Pythium ultimum, Phytophthora infestans, or Fusarium sambucinum* using solid phase microextraction (SPME) fiber along with GC-flame ionization detector (FID) indicated the potential of the VOC profiling for disease detection (Kushalappa *et al.*, 2002). The amount of volatiles increased with an increase in disease severity. A BPNN model was applied to classify the volatile metabolite profiles with respect to the diseases. The gas retention time of the volatile compounds (GC feature) was used as the input data and two hidden layers were used for cross-validation. The cross-validation probabilities (using BPNN) were >67% (67-75%) for all groups except potato tubers infected with *Phytophtho rainfestans.* Unlike other studies, this study did not determine the specific compounds that resulted in VOC peaks in the FID. Lui *et al.*, (2005) inoculated potato tubers with *Phytophthora infestans, Pythium ultimum,* or *Botrytis cinerea* and analyzed the VOC profile using GC–MS. The compounds in the headspace of the potatoes were identified and their abundance in terms of peak area was determined. Stepwise discriminant analysis was performed using the 32 compounds that were consistently present in the headspace and mass ions from the MS data as the input. The developed discriminant analysis models categorized the diseases with a classification accuracy of 13-100%. Comparing studies conducted by Lui *et al.*, (2005) and Kushalappa *et al.*, (2002), BPNN-based classification provided higher classification accuracy than discriminant analysis basedmodels.

Vuorinen *et al.*, (2007) utilized VOC emission pattern of silver birch to determine whether the plants were damaged by larvae (herbivore arthropod Epirritaautumnata), infected with pathogenic leaf spot (Marssoninabetulae) or if they were healthy. The VOCs were collected from pathogen-inoculated leaves, herbivore damaged leaves, and undamaged leaves from the top of the branches as well as undamaged detached twigs. Different plant conditions produced specific patterns of VOCs. The herbivore damaged leaves released VOCs such as methyl salicylate, linalool etc., especially after 72 h of feeding.

Staudt and Lhoutellier (2007) evaluated the VOC release profile of the damaged and undamaged leaves of holm oak tree infested by gypsy moth larvae. The researchers stated that the leaves released linalool, homoterpene (E)-4, 8-dimethyl1,3,7-nonatriene, germacrene D, caryophyllene, and several other sesquiterpenes upon days of caterpillar growth on the leaves. These gases were not present in the VOCs released by the control plants. Moalemiyan *et al.*, (2006, 2007) employed VOC profiling to detect fungal diseases (Lasiodiplodia theobromae causing stemend rot and *Colletotrichum gloeosporioides* causing anthracnose) in mangoes. Discriminant analysis models were used to classify the groups using the gaseous metabolite profile and mass ions. Though the methods showed potential for detecting fungal diseases. the classification accuracy of the models needs to be further increased to make it a feasible method for postharvest disease detection.

FLUORESCENCE *IN-SITU* HYBRIDIZATION

Another type of molecular detection technique is fluorescence *in-situ* hybridization (FISH), which is applied for bacterial detection in combination with microscopy and hybridization of DNA probes and target gene from plant samples. Due to the presence of pathogen-specific ribosomal RNA (rRNA) sequences in plants, recognizing this specific information by FISH can help detect the pathogen infections in plants. In addition to bacterial pathogens, FISH could also be used to detect fungi and viruses and other endosymbiotic bacteria that infect the plant. The high affinity and specificity of DNA probes provide high single-cell sensitivity in FISH, because the probe will bind to each of the ribosomes in the sample. However, the practical limit of detection lies in the range of around 10^3 CFU/mL. In addition to the detection of culturable microorganisms that cause the plant diseases, FISH could also be used to detect yet-to-be cultured (so called unculturable) organisms in order to investigate complex microbial communities.

HYPER SPECTRAL TECHNIQUES

Hyper spectral imaging can be used to obtain useful information about the plant health over a wide range of spectrum between 350 and 2500 nm. Hyper spectral imaging is increasingly being used for plant phenotyping and crop disease identification in large scale agriculture. The technique is highly robust and it provides a rapid analysis of the imaging data. Furthermore, hyper spectral imaging cameras facilitate the data collection in three dimension, with X- and Y- axes for spatial and Z- for spectral, which contributes to more detailed and accurate information about plant health across a large geographic area. Hyper spectral techniques have been widely used for plant disease detection by measuring the changes in reflectance resulting from the biophysical and biochemical characteristic changes upon infection. *Magnaporthe grisea* infection of rice, *Phytophthora infestans* infection of tomato and *Venturia inaequalis* infection of apple trees have been identified and reported using hyperspectral imaging techniques.

BIOSENSOR PLATFORMS BASED ON NONMATERIALS

For biosensing application, the limit of detection and the overall performance of a biosensor can be greatly improved by using nonmaterials for their construction. The popularity of nonmaterial's for sensor development could be attributed to the friendly platform it provides for the assembly of bio-recognition element, the high surface area, high electronic conductivity and plasmonic properties of nonmaterial's that enhance the limit of detection. Various types of nanostructures have been evaluated as platforms for the immobilization of a bio-recognition element to construct a biosensor. The immobilization of the biorecognition element, such as DNA, antibody and enzyme, can be achieved using various approaches including biomolecule adsorption, covalent attachment, encapsulation or a sophisticated combination of these methods. The nanomaterials used for biosensor construction include metal and metal oxide nanoparticles, quantum dots, carbon nanomaterials such as carbon nanotubes and graphene as well as polymeric nanomatenals. Nanoparticles have been utilized with other biological materials such as antibody for detecting *Xanthomonas axonopodis* that causesbacterial spot disease. Fluorescent silica nanoparticles (FSNPs) combined with antibody as a biomarker has been studied as the probe, which successfully detected plant pathogens such as *Xanthomonas axonopodis*pv. *Vesicatoria* that cause bacterial spot disease in Solanaceae plant.

AFFINITY BIOSENSORS

Compared to the non-specific nanoparticle-based biosensors, inclusion of a bio-recognition element can greatly increase the specificity of the sensor. Consequently, other types of biosensors have been developed and among them affinity biosensors are popular. In affinity biosensors, the sensing is achieved based on the reaction of the bio-recognition element and the target analyte. Affinity biosensors can be developed using antibody and DNA as recognition elements.

ANTIBODY-BASED BIOSENSORS

Antibodies are versatile and are suitable for diverse immune sensing applications. Antibody-based iosensor allows rapid and sensitive detection of a range of pathogens especially for food borne diseases and this technique has already been developed for food safety monitoring. The antibody-based biosensors provide several advantages such as fast detection, improved sensitivity, real-time analysis and potential for quantification. Antibody-based biosensors hold great value for agricultural plant pathogen detection. The biosensors enable the pathogen detection in air, water and seeds with different platforms for greenhouses, on-field and postharvest storages of processors and distributors of crops and fruits.

DNA/RNA-BASED AFFINITY BIOSENSOR

A recently developed new type of affinity biosensor uses nucleic acid fragments as elements for pathogen detection. The detection of specific DNA sequence is of significance in a variety of applications such as clinical human disease detection, environmental, horticulture and food analysis. Due to the possibility of detection at a molecular level, the DNA-based biosensor enables early detection of diseases before any visual symptoms appear. The application of specific DNA sequences has been widely used for detection of bacteria, fungi and genetically modified organisms. Based on the specific nucleic acid hybridization of the immobilized DNA probe on the sensor and the analyte DNA sequence, DNA-based biosensor allows rapid, simple and economical testing of genetic and infectious diseases. The most commonly adopted DNA probe is single stranded DNA (ssDNA) on electrodes with electroactive indicators to measure hybridization between probe DNA and the complementary DNA analyte. There are four major types of DNA-based biosensors depending on their mode of transduction: optical, piezoelectric, strip type and electrochemical DNA biosensors. Optical DNA biosensors transduce the emission signal of a fluorescent label. The detection of DNA analyte is realized through a variation in physio-chemical properties such as mass, temperature, optical property and electrical property as a result of double-stranded DNA (dsDNA) hybridization occurs during the analyte recognition.

ENZYMATIC ELECTROCHEMICAL BIOSENSORS

The use of enzyme as bio-recognition element can provide highly selective detection of the target analyte due to the high specificity of enzymes towards the analyte. An enzyme specific for the analyte of interest is immobilized on the nanomaterial modified-electrode. The amperometric detection is based on the bio-electro catalytic reaction between the target analyte and electrode, which results in an electrical signal (current) that can be used for quantitative detection of the analyte. The amperometric signal can be obtained through either direct or mediated electron transfer based electrochemical reactions. Unlike other types of biosensors, which are not widely commercialized, the enzymatic electrochemical biosensors have been successfully commercialized, thanks to the invention of glucose biosensors, which are widely used in personal diabetes monitors;a similar biosensing methodology can be adopted for plant pathogen detection, food quality detection and environmental monitoring (Table 3.2). For plant pathogen detection, enzymatic biosensors could be used if the target VOC could be collected in the form of a liquid sample.

Table 3.2

VOCs emitted from whole, intact tomato plants or detached leaves, and biotic stress causing agents responsible for increases in VOC emissions

Volatiles	Biotic Stress Causing Agents that Increase VOC Emissions
Cis-3-hexen-1-ol	*Botrytis cinerea, Spodopteralittoralis, Lirimyzahuidobrensis, Spodopteraexigua, manducasexta, Macrosiphumeurhorbiae, Helicoverpaarmigera*
Trans-2-hexanal	*Botrytis cinerea, Spodopteralittoralis, Lirimyzahuidobrensis, Spodopteraexigua, Manducasexta, Helicoverpaarmigera*
Methyl salicylate	*Botrytis cinera, Spodopteralittoralis, Tetranychusurticae, Manducasexta, Macrosiphum euphoria,* Tobacco mosaic virus.

BACTERIOPHAGE BASED BIOSENSORS

Bacteriophage is a virus, composed of protein capsid that encapsulates a DNA or RNA genome. It infects the bacteria and replicates within the bacteria and finally lyses the bacterial host to propagate. Being able to lyse the bacteria, bacteriophage has been widely studied and used in phage therapy to cure bacterial infections. Phage therapy has been used for not only human diseases, but also plant disease control. In addition to phage therapy, bacteriophage is also emerging as a promising alternative for pathogen detection due to its high sensitivity, selectivity, low cost and higher thermo stability. Upon the interaction between the bacteriophage and the target analyte, the impedance of charge transfer reactions at the interface changes which are used as a signal for detection.

AFFINITY-BASED BIOSENSORS

Receptor proteins can provide some of the same properties as enzymes, and well-selected antibodies provide highly selective and high affinity recognition for almost any soluble analyte. Receptors are not always suitable, often due to lability or requirement for a membrane. Antibodies on the other hand are robust and versatile and have been adapted into diverse immune sensor systems. Affinity recognition need not be based on biomolecules as the recognition element and some robust sensor systems make use of molecular imprinted materials and volume-sensitive hologram-based biosensor surfaces. The most recent addition to the family of affinity-based sensor technologies is the development of nucleic acid fragments as recognition species, especially the use of selected or designed aptamers (eg short 20-40 nucleotide, single stranded DNA) which bind the analyte.

GENETICALLY-ENCODED BIOSENSORS

The optical biosensor field has been led and enlightened, in particular, by calcium sensitive reporters such as aequorin and its successors the cameleons. The cameleons utilise the large conformational rearrangement induced by calcium binding to calmodulin to change the proximity of paired FPs fused at either end, frequently CFP and YFP or their variants, and the sensor is interrogated using FRET microscopy. Second generation versions were improved for selectivity by using engineered versions of calmodulin and a calmodulin-binding peptide in the bridge between FPs so that on binding calcium the sensor folds up on itself to promote FRET.

SPECTROSCOPIC AND IMAGING TECHNIQUES

Recent developments in agricultural technology have led to a demand for a new era of automated non-destructive methods of plant disease detection. It is desirable that the plant disease detection tool should be rapid, specific to a particular disease, and sensitive for detection at the early onset of the symptoms (Lopez *et al.,* 2003). The spectroscopic and imaging techniques are unique disease monitoring methods that have been used to detect diseases and stress due to various factors, in plants and trees. Current research activities are towards the development of such technologies to create a practical tool for a large-scale real-time disease monitoring under field conditions.

FLUORESCENCE SPECTROSCOPY

Fluorescence spectroscopy refers to a type of spectroscopic method, where the fluorescence from the object of interest is mea-sured after excitation with a beam of light (usually ultraviolet spectra). For the last twenty years, the laser-induced fluorescence has been used for vegetative studies, such as to monitor stress levels and physiological states in plants (Belasque *et al.,* 2008). Two types of fluorescence: (i) blue-green fluorescence in about 400-600 nm range and (ii) chlorophyll fluorescence in about 650-800 nm range, are produced by green leaves. The fluorescence spectroscopy can be utilized to monitor nutrient deficiencies, environmental conditions based stress levels and diseases in plants (Cerovic *et al.,* 1999; Belasque *et al.,* 2008).

VISIBLE AND INFRARED SPECTROSCOPY

Similar to fluorescence spectroscopy, visible and infrared Spectroscopy have been used as a rapid, non-destructive, and cost-effective method for the detection of plant diseases. It is a fast-developing technology used for varied applications (Ramon *et al.,* 2002: Delwiche and Graybosch, 2002: Pontius *et al.,* 2005; Gomez *et al.,* 2006; Zhang *et al.,* 2008a, b; Guo *et al.,* 2009; Sundaram *et al.,* 2009). Studies have also been conducted on the detection of stress, injury, and diseases in plants using this technology (Polischuk *et al.,* 1997; Spinelli *et al.,* 2006; Naidu *et al.,* 2009). The visible and infrared regions of the electromagnetic spectra are known to pro-vide the maximum information on the physiological stress levels in the plants (Muhammed, 2002, 2005; Xu *et al.,* 2007) and thus, some of these wavebands specific to a disease can be used to detect plant diseases (West *et al.*, 2003), even before the symptoms are visible. In general, visible spectroscopy is used for disease detection in plants in combination with infrared spectroscopy (Malthus and Madeira, 1993; Bravo *et al.*, 2003; Huang *et al.*, 2004; Larsolle and Muhammed. 2007).

CONCLUSION

Developing detection methods is both an art and an ever-ending story, and the concept of accurate detection of plant pathogenic bacteria and viruses, is moving from conventional methods to molecular techniques, included in integrated approaches. PCR and especially real-time PCR are the methods of choice for rapid and accurate diagnosis of plant pathogenic bacteria but conventional serological methods, such as immune fluorescence, are still widely used and ELISA is the most frequently applied method for virus detection. Consequently, trying to answer the question: "Are nucleic-acid tools solving the challenges posed by specific and sensitive detection of plant pathogenic bacteria and viruses?" we could answer yes, when a rapid analysis of a reduced number of samples is performed and the protocols have been suitably optimised and also when the presence of false positives is not crucial because the main goal is the quality of the negatives. However, for quarantine pathogens or in critical cases of export-import, experience advises the use of more than one technique.

REFERENCES

Aleixos, N., Blasco, J., Navarron, F., Molto, E. (2002): Multispectral Inspection of Citrus in Real-time using Machine Vision and Digital Signal Processors. *Computers and Electronics in Agriculture*, 33 (2): 121-137.

Alvarez, A.M. (2004): Integrated Approaches for Detection of Plant Pathogenic Bacteria and Diagnosis of Bacterial Diseases. *Annual Review of Plant Pathology*, 42: 339-366.

Balasubramanian, S., Panigrahi, S., Logue, C.M., Doetkott, C., Marchello, M., Sherwood, J.S. (2008): Independent Component Analysis-processed Electronic Nose Data for Predicting Salmonella Typhimurium Populations in Contaminated Beef. *Food Control*, 19 (3): 236-246.

Belasque, L., Gasparoto, M.C.G., Marcassa, L.G. (2008): Detection of Mechanical and Disease Stresses in Citrus Plants by Fluorescence Spectroscopy. *Applied Optics*, 47 (11): 1922-1926.

Blasco, J., Alexios, N., Gomez, J., Molto, E. (2007): Citrus Sorting by Identification of the most Common Defects using Multispectral Computer Vision. *Journal of Food Engineering*, 83 (3): 384-393.

Bravo, C., Moshou, D., West, J., McCartney, A., Ramon, H. (2003): Early Disease Detection in Wheat Fields using Spectral Reflectance. *Biosystems engineering*, 84 (2): 137-145.

Bravo, C., Moshou, D., Oberti, R., West, J., McCartney, A., Bodria, L., Ramon, H. (2004): Foliar Disease Detection in the Field using Optical Sensor Fusion. Agricultural Engineering International: *The CIGR Journal of Scientific Research and Development*, Manuscript FP 04 008, Vol. VI. December 2004.

Cerovic, Z.G., Samson, G., Morales, F., Tremblay, N., Moya, I. (1999): Ultraviolet Induced Fluorescence for Plant Monitoring: Present State and Prospects. *Agronomie,*19: 543-578.

Cevallos-Cevallos, J.M., Rouseff, R., Reyes-De-Corcuera, J.I. (2009): Untargeted Metabolite Analysis of Healthy and Huanglongbing-infected Orange Leaves by *CE-DAD. Electrophoresis,* 30: 1-8.

Chaerle, L., Caeneghem, W.V., Messens, E., Lamber, H., Van Montagu, M., Van Der Straeten, D. (1999): Presymptomatic Visualization of Plant-virus Interactions by Thermography. *Nature Biotechnology,* 17: 813-816.

Chaerle, L., Van Der Straeten, D. (2000): Imaging Techniques and the Early Detection of Plant Stress. *Trends in Plant Science,* 5 (11): 495-501.

Chaerle, L., De Boever, F., Van Montagu, M., Van Der Straeten, D. (2001): Thermographic Visualization of Cell Death in Tobacco and Arabidopsis. *Plant, Cell and Environment,* 24 (1): 15-25.

Chaerle, L., Hulsen, K., Hermans, C., Strasser, R.J., Valcke, R., Hofte, M., Van Der Straeten, D. (2003): Robotized Time-lapse Imaging to Assess in-plant uptake of Phenylurea Herbicides and their Microbial Degradation.*Physiologia Plantarium,* 118: 613-619.

Chaerle, L., Hagenbeek, D., De Bruyne, E., Valcke, R., Van Der Straeten, D. (2004): Thermal and Chlorophyll-fluorescence Imaging Distinguish Plant-pathogen Interactions at an Early Stage. *Plant and Cell Physiology,* 45: 887-896.

Chaerle, L., Lenk, S., Hagenbeek, D., Buschmann, C., Van Der Straeten, D. (2007): Multicolor Fluorescence Imaging for Early Detection of the Hypersensitive Reaction to Tobacco Mosaic Virus. *Journal of Plant Physiology,* 164 (3): 253-262.

Chen, B., Wang, K., Li, S., Wang, J., Bai, J., Xiao, C., Lai, J. (2008): Spectrum Characteristics of Cotton Canopy Infected with Verticillium Wilt and Inversion of Severity Level. *In IFIP International Federation for Information Processing,* Volume 259; Computer and Computing Technologies in Agriculture, Vol. 2, Daoliang Li, Springer, Boston, pp. 1169-1180.

Choi, Y.H., Tapias, E.C., Kim, H.K., Lefeber, A.W.M , Erkelens, C., Verhoeven, J.T.J., Brzin, J., Zel, J., Verpoorte, R. (2004): Metabolic Discrimination of Catharanthusroseus Leaves Infected by Phytoplasma using 1H-NMR Spectroscopy and Multivariate Data Analysis. *Plant Physiology,* 135: 2398-2410.

Concina, I., Falasconi, M., Gobbi, E., Bianchi, F., Musci, M. Mattarozzi, M., Pardo, M., Mangia, A., Careri, M., Sberveglieri, G. (2009): Early Detection of Microbial Contamination in Processed Tomatoes by Electronic Nose. *Food Control,* 20 (10): 873-880.

Das, A.K. (2004): Rapid Detection of Candidatus Liberibacter asiaticus, the Bacterium Associated with Citrus Huanglongbing (Greening) Disease using PCR. *Current Science,* 87 (9): 1183-1185.

Delalieux, S., van Aardt, J., Keulemans, W., Schrevens, E., Coppin, P. (2007): Detection of Biotic Stress (Venturiainaequalis) in Apple Trees using Hyperspectral Data: Non-parametric Statistical Approaches and Physiological Implications. *European Journal of Agronomy,* 27 (1): 130-143.

Delwiche, S.R., Graybosch, R.A. (2002): Identification of Waxy Wheat by near-infrared Reflectance Spectroscopy. *Journal of Cereal Science,* 35 (1): 29-38.

Di Natale, C., Macagnano, A., Martinelli, E., Paolesse, R., Proietti, E., D'Amico, A. (2001): The Evaluation of Quality of Post-harvest Oranges and Apples by means of an Electronic Nose. Sensors and Actuators B: *Chemical,* 78 (1-3): 26-31.

Dragonieri, S., Schot, R., Mertens, B.J.A., Le Cessie, S., Gauw, S.A., Spanevello, A., Resta, O.,Willard, N.P., Vink, T.J., Rabe, K.F., Bel, E.H., Sterk, P.J. (2007): An Electronic Nose in the Discrimination of Patients with Asthma and Controls. *Journal of Allergy and Clinical Immunology*, 120 (4): 856-862.

Dudareva, N., Negre, F., Nagegowda, D.A., Orlova, I. (2006): Plant Volatiles: Recent Advances and Future Perspectives. *Critical Reviews in Plant Sciences*, 25: 417-440.

ElMasry, G., Wang, N., Vigneault, C., Qiao, J., ElSayed, A. (2008): Early Detection of Apple Bruises on Different Background Colors using hyper Spectral Imaging. *LWT Food Science and Technology*,41 (2): 337-345.

Evans, P., Persaud, K.C., McNeish, A.S., Sneath, R.W., Hobson, N., Magan, N. (2000): Evaluation of a Radial basis Function Neural Network for the Determination of Wheat Quality from Electronic Nose Data. Sensors and Actuators B: *Chemical*, 69 (3): 348-358.

Falasconi, M., Gobbi, E., Pardo, M., Della Torre, M., Bresciani, A., Sberveglieri, G. (2005): Detection of Toxigenic Strains of Fusarium verticillioides in Corn by Electronic Olfactory System. Sensors and Actuators B: *Chemical*,108 (1-2): 250-257.

Gardner, J.W., Shin, H.W., Hines, E.L. (2000): An Electronic Nose System to Diagnose Illness. Sensors and Actuators B: *Chemical*, 70 (1-3): 19-24.

Gomez, A.H., He, Y., Garcia Pereira, A. (2006): Non-destructive Measurement of Acidity, Soluble Solids and Firmness of Satsuma Mandarin using Vis/NIR Spectroscopy Techniques. *Journal of Food Engineering*, 77 (3): 313-319.

Goodman, B.A., Williamson, B., Chudek, A. (1992): Non-invasive Observation of the Development of Fungal Infection in Fruit. *Protoplasma*, 166: 107-109.

Gowen, A.A., O'Donnell, C.P., Cullen, P.J., Downey, G., Frias, J.M. (2007): Hyper spectral Imaging—an Emerging Process Analytical Tool for Food Quality and Safety Control. *Trends in Food Science & Technology*, 18 (12): 590-598.

Guenther, A. (1997): Seasonal and Spatial Variations in Natural Volatile Organic Compound Emissions. *Ecological Applications*, 7 (1): 34-45.

Guimet, F. (2005): Olive Oil Characterization using Excitation-emission Fluorescence Spectroscopy and Three-way methods of Analysis. Ph.D. Thesis, Rovirai Virgili University, Spain.

Guo, T.T., Guo, L., Wang, X.H., Li, M. (2009): Application of NIR Spectroscopy in Classification of Plant Species. *In: International Workshop on Education Technology and Computer Science*, Wuhan, Hubei, China, vol. 3, pp: 879-883.

Hadjiloucas, S., Walker, G.C., Bowen, J.W., Zafiropoulos, A. (2009): Propagation of Errors from a Null Balance Terahertz Reflect Meter to a Sample's Relative Water Content. *Journal of Physics: Conference Series, Sensors & their Applications* XV 178, 012012, 1-5.

Hahn, F. (2009): Actual Pathogen Detection: Sensors and Algorithms—A Review. *Algorithms*, 2: 301-338.

Henson, J.M., French, R. (1993): The Polymerase Chain Reaction and Plant Disease Diagnosis. *Annual Review of Plant Pathology*, 31: 81-109.

Huang, J.F., Apan, A. (2006): Detection of Sclerotiniarot Disease on Celery using Hyper Spectral Data and Partial Least Squares Regression. *Journal of Spatial Science*, 51 (2): 129-142.

Huang, M.Y., Huang, W.H., Liu, L.Y., Huang, Y.D., Wang, J.H., Zhao, C.H., Wan, A.M. (2004): Spectral Reflectance Feature of Winter Wheat Single Leaf Infested with Stripe Rust and Severity Level Inversion. *Transactions of the CSAE*, 20 (1): 176-180.

Huang, W., Lamb, D.W., Niu, Z., Zhang, Y., Liu, L., Wang, J. (2007): Identification of Yellow Rust in Wheat using *in-situ* Spectral Reflectance Measurements and Airborne Hyper Spectral Imaging. *Precision Agriculture*, 8: 187-197.

Karunakaran, C., Jayas, D.S., White, N.D.G. (2004): Identification of Wheat Kernels Damaged by the Red Flour Beetle using X-ray Images. *Biosystems Engineering*, 87 (3): 267-274.

Kim, M.S., Chen, Y.R., Mehl, P.M. (2001): Hyper Spectral Reflectance and Fluorescence Imaging System for Food Quality and Safety. *Transactions of the ASAE*, 44 (3): 721-729.

Kim, M.S., Lefcourt, A.M., Chao, K., Chen, Y.R., Kim, I., Chan, D.E. (2002): Multispectral Detection of Fecal Contamination on Apples based on Hyper Spectral Imagery: Part I. Application of Visible and Near-infrared Reflectance Imaging. *Transactions of the ASAE*, 45 (6): 2027-2037.

Kobayashi, T., Kanda, E., Kitada, K., Ishiguro, K., Torigoe, Y. (2001): Detection of Rice Panicle Blast with Multispectral Radiometer and the Potential of using Airborne Multispectral Scanners. *Phytopathology*, 91 (3): 316-323.

Kushalappa, A.C., Lui, L.H., Chen, C.R., Lee, B. (2002): Volatile Fingerprinting (SPMEGCFID) to Detect and Discriminate Diseases of Potato Tubers. *Plant Disease*, 86: 131-137.

Lamkadmi, Z., Esnault, M.A., Le Normand, M. (1996): Characterization of a 23 kDa Polypeptide induced by Phoma lingam in *Brassica napus* Leaves. *Plant Physiology and Biochemistry*, 34 (4): 589-598.

Laothawornkitkul, J., Moore, J.P., Taylor, J.E., Possell, M , Gibson, T.D., Hewitt, C.N., Paul, N.D. (2008): Discrimination of Plant Volatile Signatures by an Electronic Nose: A Potential Technology for Plant Pest and Disease Monitoring. *Environmental Science and Technology*, 42: 8433-8439.

Larsolle, A., Muhammed, H.H. (2007): Measuring Crop Status using Multivariate Analysis of Hyper Spectral Field Reflectance with Application to Disease Severity and Plant Density. *Precision Agriculture*, 8 (1-2): 37-47.

Lee, K.J., Kang, S., Kim, M.S., Noh, S.H. (2005): Hyper Spectral Imaging for Detecting Defect on Apples. ASABE Paper No. 053075, 2005 *ASAE Annual International Meeting*, Tampa, FL, 17-20 July, 2005.

Lee, W.S., Ehsani, R., Albrigo, L.G. (2008): Citrus Greening Disease (Huanglongbing) Detection using Aerial Hyper Spectral Imaging. In: *The Proceedings of the 9th International Conference on Precision Agriculture*, July 20-23, 2008, Denver, CO.

Lenk, S., Buschmann, C. (2006): Distribution of UV-shielding of the Epidermis of Sun and Shade Leaves of the Beech (*Fagus sylvatica* L.) as monitored by Multi-colour Fluorescence Imaging. *Journal of Plant Physiology*, 163 (12): 1273-1283.

Lenk, S., Chaerle, L., Pfundel, E.E., Langsdorf, G., Hagenbeek, D., Lichtenthaler, H.K., Van Der Straeten, D., Buschmann, C.(2007): Multispectral Fluorescence and Reflectance Imaging at the Leaf Level and its Possible Applications. *Journal of Experimental Botany*, 58 (4): 807-814.

Lenthe, J.H., Oerke, E.C., Dehne, H.W. (2007): Digital Infrared Thermography for Monitoring Canopy Health of Wheat. *Precision Agriculture*, 8 (1-2): 15-26.

Li, W., Hartung, J.S., Levy, L. (2006): Quantitative Real-time PCR for Detection and Identification of Candidatus Liberibacter Species associated with Citrus Huanglongbing. *Journal of Microbiological Methods*, 66 (1): 104-115.

Li, C., Krewer, G., Kays, S. J. (2009b): Blueberry Postharvest Disease Detection using an Electronic Nose. *ASABE Paper No. 096783, ASABE Annual International Meeting,* Reno, NV, June 21-June 24, 2009.

Lin, Y.J., Guo, H.R., Chang, Y.H., Kao, M.T., Wang, H.H., Hong, R.I. (2001): Application of the Electronic Nose for Uremia Diagnosis. Sensors and Actuators B: *Chemical,* 76 (1-3), 177-180.

Lindenthal, M., Steiner, U., Dehne, H.W., Oerke, E. C. (2005): Effect of Downy Mildew Development on Transpiration of Cucumber Leaves Visualized by Digital Infrared Thermography. *Phytopathology,* 95 (3): 233-240.

Lins, E.C., Belasque Junior, J., Marcassa, L.G. (2009): Detection of Citrus Canker in Citrus Plants using Laser Induced Fluorescence Spectroscopy. *Precision Agriculture,* 10: 319-330.

Lopez, M.M., Bertolini, E., Olmos, A., Caruso, P., Gorris, M.T., Llop, P., Penyalver, R., Cambra, M. (2003): Innovative Tools for Detection of Plant Pathogenic Viruses and Bacteria. *International Microbiology,* 6: 233-243.

Lu, R. (2003): Detection of Bruises on Apples using Near-infrared Hyper Spectral Imaging. *Transactions of the ASAE,* 46 (2): 523-530.

Lui, L., Vikram, A., Hamzehzarghani, H., Kushalappa, A.C. (2005): Discrimination of Three Fungal Diseases of Potato Tubers based on Volatile Metabolic Profiles Developed using GC/MS. *Potato Research,* 48: 85-96.

Mahesh, S., Manickavasagan, A., Jayas, D.S., Paliwal, J., White, N.D.G. (2008): Feasibility of near-infrared Hyper Spectral Imaging to Differentiate Canadian Wheat Classes. *Biosystems Engineering,* 101 (1): 50-57.

Malthus, T.J., Madeira, A.C. (1993): High Resolution Spectroradiometry: Spectral Reflectance of Field Bean Leaves Infected by Botrytis Fabae. *Remote Sensing of Environment,* 45: 107-116.

Marcassa, L.G., Gasparoto, M.C.G., Belasque Junior, J., Lins, E.C., Dias Nunes, F., Bagnato, V.S. (2006): Fluorescence Spectroscopy Applied to Orange Trees. *Laser Physics,* 16 (5): 884-888.

Markom, M.A., MdShakaff, A.Y., Adom, A.H., Ahmad, M.N., WahyuHidayat, Abdullah, A.H., AhmadFikri, N. (2009): Intelligent Electronic Nose System for Basal Stem Rot Disease Detection. *Computers and Electronics in Agriculture,* 66 (2): 140-146.

Mehl, P.M., Chen, Y.R., Kim, M.S., Chan, D.E. (2004): Development of Hyper Spectral Imaging Technique for the Detection of Apple Surface Defects and Contaminations. *Journal of Food Engineering,* 61 (1): 67-81.

Moshou, D., Bravo, C., West, J., Wahlen, S., McCartney, A., Ramon, H. (2004): Automatic Detection of 'Yellow Rust' in Wheat using Reflectance Measurements and Neural Networks. *Computers and Electronics in Agriculture,* 44 (3): 173-188.

Moshou, D., Bravo, C., Oberti, R., West, J., Bodria, L., McCartney, A., Ramon, H. (2005): Plant Disease Detection based on Data Fusion of Hyper-spectral and Multi-spectral Fluorescence Imaging using Kohonen Maps. *Real-Time Imaging,* 11 (2): 75-83.

Muhammed, H.H. (2002): Using Hyper Spectral Reflectance Data for Discrimination between Healthy and Diseased Plants, and Determination of Damage-level in Diseased Plants. *In: IEEE: Proceedings of the 31st Applied Imagery Pattern Recognition Workshop,* pp: 49-54.

Muhammed, H.H. (2005): Hyper Spectral Crop Reflectance Data for Characterizing and Estimating Fungal Disease Severity in Wheat. *Biosystems Engineering,* 91 (1): 9-20.

Naidu, R.A., Perry, E.M., Pierce, F.J., Mekuria, T. (2009): The Potential of Spectral Reflectance Technique for the Detection of Grapevine Leaf Roll-associated Virus-3 in Two Red-berried Wine Grape Cultivars. *Computers and Electronics in Agriculture*, 66: 38-45.

Narvankar, D.S., Singh, C.B., Jayas, D.S., White, N.D.G. (2009): Assessment of Soft X-ray Imaging for Detection of Fungal Infection in Wheat. *Biosystems Engineering*, 103 (1): 49-56.

Nicolai, B.M., Lotze, E., Peirs, A., Scheerlinck, N., Theron, K.I. (2006): Non-destructive Measurement of Bitter Pit in Apple Fruit using NIR Hyper Spectral Imaging. *Postharvest Biology and Technology*,40 (1): 1-6.

Oerke, E.C., Lindenthal, M., Frohling, P., Steiner, U. (2005): Digital Infrared Thermography for the Assessment of Leaf Pathogens. In: Stafford, J.V. (Ed.), *Precision Agriculture '05*.Wageningen University Press, Wageningen, The Netherlands, pp: 91-98.

Oerke, E.C., Steiner, U., Dehne, H.W., Lindenthal, M. (2006): Thermal Imaging of Cucumber Leaves Affected by Downy Mildew and Environmental Conditions. *Journal of Experimental Botany*, 57 (9): 2121-2132.

Okamoto, H., Suzuki, Y., Kataoka, T., Sakai, K. (2009): Unified Hyperspectral Imaging Methodology for Agricultural Sensing using Software Framework. *ActaHorticulturae*, 824: 49-56.

Pearson, T.C., Wicklow, D.T. (2006): Detection of Kernels Infected by Fungi. *Transactions of the ASABE*, 49 (4): 1235-1245.

Pimentel, D., Zuniga, R., Morrison, D. (2005): Update on the Environmental and Economic Costs associated with Alien-invasive Species in the United States. *Ecological Economics*, 52 (3): 273-288.

Polischuk, V.P., Shadchina, T.M., Kompanetz, T.I., Budzanivskaya, I.G., Sozinov, A. (1997): Changes in Reflectance Spectrum Characteristic of Nicotianadebneyi Plant under the Influence of Viral Infection. *Archives of Phytopathology and Plant Protection*, 31 (1): 115-119.

Pontius, J., Hallett, R., Martin, M. (2005): Assessing Hemlock Decline using Visible and near-infrared Spectroscopy: Indices Comparison and Algorithm Development. *Applied Spectroscopy*, 59 (6): 836-843.

Prithiviraj, B., Vikram, A., Kushalappa, A.C., Yaylayan, V. (2004): Volatile Metabolite Profiling for the Discrimination of Onion Bulbs Infected by *Erwinia carotovora* ssp. *carotovora, Fusarium oxysporum* and *Botrytis allii*. *European Journal of Plant Physiology*, 110: 371-377.

Purcell, D.E., O'Shea, M.G., Johnson, R.A., Kokot, S. (2009): Near-infrared Spectroscopy for the Prediction of Disease Rating for Fiji Leaf Gall in Sugarcane Clones. *Applied Spectroscopy*, 63 (4): 450-457.

Qin, J., Burks, T.F., Ritenour, M.A., Bonn, W.G. (2009): Detection of Citrus Canker using Hyperspectral Reflectance Imaging with Spectral Information Divergence. *Journal of Food Engineering*, 93 (2): 183-191.

Rajamaki, T., Alakomi, H.L., Ritvanen, T., Skytta, E., Smolander, M., Ahvenainen, R. (2006): Application of an Electronic Nose for Quality Assessment of Modified Atmosphere Packaged Poultry Meat. *Food Control*, 17 (1): 5-13.

Ramon, H., Anthonis, J., Vrindts, E., Delen, R., Reumers, J., Moshou, D., Deprez, K., De Baerdemaeker, J., Feyaerts, F., Van Gool, L., De Winne, R., Van den Bulcke, R. (2002): Development of a Weed Activated Spraying Machine for Targeted Application of Herbicides. *Aspects of Applied Biology*, 66: 147-164.

Roberts, M.J., Schimmelpfennig, D., Ashley, E., Livingston, M., Ash, M., Vasavada, U. (2006): The Value of Plant Disease Early-warning Systems. *Economic Research Service*, No. 18, United States Department of Agriculture.

Roggo, Y., Duponchel, L., Huvenne, J.P. (2003): Comparison of Supervised Pattern Recognition methods with McNemar's Statistical Test: Application to Qualitative Analysis of Sugar Beet by Near-infrared Spectroscopy. *Analytica Chimica Acta*, 477 (2): 187-200.

Ruiz-Ruiz, S., Ambros, S., Carmen Vives, M., Navarro, L., Moreno, P., Guerri, J. (2009): Detection and Quantification of Citrus Leaf Blotch Virus by TaqMan Real-time RTPCR. *Journal of Virological Methods*, 160 (1-2): 57-62.

Saponari, M., Manjunath, K., Yokomi, R.K. (2008): Quantitative Detection of Citrus tristeza Virus in Citrus and Aphids by Real-time Reverse Transcription-PCR (TaqMan). *Journal of Virological Methods*, 147 (1): 43-53.

Schaad, N.W., Frederick, R.D. (2002): Real-time PCR and its Application for Rapid Plant Disease Diagnostics. *Canadian Journal of Plant Pathology*, 24 (3): 250-258.

Scharte, J., Schon, H., Weis, E. (2005): Photosynthesis and Carbohydrate Metabolism in Tobacco Leaves during an Incompatible Interaction with Phytophthoranicotianae. *Plant, Cell and Environment*, 28: 1421-1435.

Shafri, H.Z.M., Hamdan, N. (2009): Hyper Spectral Imagery for Mapping Disease Infection in Oil Palm Plantation using Vegetation Indices and Red Edge Techniques. *American Journal of Applied Sciences*, 6 (6): 1031-1035.

Sighicelli, M., Colao, F., Lai, A., Patsaeva, S. (2009): Monitoring Post-harvest Orange Fruit Disease by Fluorescence and Reflectance Hyper Spectral Imaging. ISHS *Acta Horticulturae*,817: 277-284.

Sirisomboon, P., Hashimoto, Y., Tanaka, M. (2009): Study on Non-destructive Evaluation methods for Defect Pods for Green Soybean Processing by near-infrared Spectroscopy. *Journal of Food Engineering*, 93: 502-512.

Spinelli, F., Noferini, M., Costa, G. (2006): Near Infrared Spectroscopy (NIRs): Perspective of Fire Blight Detection in Asymptomatic Plant Material. Proceeding of 10th International Workshop on Fire Blight. *ActaHorticulturae*, 704: 87-90.

Staudt, M., Lhoutellier, L. (2007): Volatile Organic Compound Emission from Holm Oak Infested by Gypsy Moth Larvae: Evidence for Distinct Responses in Damaged and Undamaged Leaves. *Tree Physiology*, 27: 1433-1440.

Sundaram, J., Kandala, C.V., Butts, C.L. (2009): Application of Near Infrared (NIR) Spectroscopy to Peanut Grading and Quality Analysis: Overview. *Sensing and Instrumentation for Food Quality and Safety*, 3 (3): 156-164.

Tallada, J.G., Nagata, M., Kobayashi, T. (2006): Detection of Bruises in Strawberries by Hyperspectral Imaging. ASABE Paper No. 063014, 2006 *ASABE, Annual International Meeting*, Portland, Oregon, 9-12 July 2006.

Tholl, D., Boland, W., Hansel, A., Loreto, F., Rose, U.S.R., Schnitzler, J.P. (2006): Practical Approaches to Plant Volatile Analysis. *The Plant Journal*, 45: 540-560.

Vallat, A., Gu, H., Dorn, S. (2005): How Rainfall, Relative Humidity and Temperature Influence Volatile Emissions from Apple Trees *in situ*. *Phytochemistry*, 66: 1540-1550.

Vikram, A., Lui, L.H., Hossain, A., Kushalappa, A.C. (2006): Metabolic Fingerprinting to Discriminate Diseases of Stored Carrots. *Annals of Applied Biology*, 148: 17-26.

Vuorinen, T., Nerg, A.M., Syrjala, L.,Peltonen, P., Holopainen, J.K. (2007): Epirritaautumnata Induced VOC Emission of Silver Birch Differ from Emission Induced by Leaf Fungal Pathogen. *Arthropod-Plant Interactions,* 1: 159-165.

Wang, D., Ram, M.S., Dowell, F.E. (2002): Classification of Damaged Soybean Seeds using Near-infrared Spectroscopy. *Transactions of the ASAE,* 45 (6): 1943-1948.

West, J.S., Bravo, C., Oberti, R., Lemaire, D., Moshou, D., McCartney, H.A. (2003): The Potential of Optical Canopy Measurement for Targeted Control of Field Crop Disease. *Annual Review of Phytopathology,* 41: 593-614.

Williamson, B., Goodman, B.A., Chudek, J.A. (1992): Nuclear Magnetic Resonance (NMR) Micro-imaging of Ripening Red Raspberry Fruits. *New Phytologist,* 120: 21-28.

Wu, D., Feng, L., Zhang, C., He, Y. (2008): Early Detection of *Botrytis cinerea* on Eggplant Leaves based on Visible and near-infrared Spectroscopy. *Transactions of the ASABE,*51 (3): 1133-1139.

Xing, J., Baerdemaeker, J.D. (2005): Bruise detection on 'Jonagold' Apples using Hyper Spectral Imaging. *Postharvest Biology and Technology,* 37 (2): 152-162.

Xing, J., Bravo, C., Jancsok, P.T.,Ramon,H., Baerdemaeker, J.D.(2005): Detecting Bruises on 'Golden Delicious' Apples using Hyper Spectral Imaging with Multiple Wavebands. *Biosystems Engineering,* 90 (1): 27-36.

Xu, H.R., Ying, Y.B., Fu, X.P., Zhu, S.P. (2007): Near-infrared Spectroscopy in Detecting Leaf Minor Damage on Tomato Leaf. *Biosystems Engineering,* 96 (4): 447-454.

Yang, C.M., Cheng, C.H. (2001): Spectral Characteristics of Rice Plants Infested by brown Planthoppers. Proceedings of the National Science Council, Republic of China. Part B, *Life Sciences,* 25 (3): 180-186.

Yang, C.M., Cheng, C.H., Chen, R.K. (2007): Changes in Spectral Characteristics of Rice Canopy Infested with Brown Planthopper and Leaf Folder. *Crop Science,* 47: 329-335.

Yao, H., Hruska, Z., DiCrispino, K., Brabham, K., Lewis, D., Beach, J., Brown, R.L., Cleveland, T.E. (2005): Differentiation of Fungi using Hyper Spectral Imagery for Food Inspection.ASAE Paper No. 053127, 2005 *ASAE Annual International Meeting,* Tampa, FL, 17-20 July 2005.

Yvon, M., Thebaud, G., Alary, R., Labonne, G. (2009): Specific Detection and Quantification of the Phytopathogenic Agent *'Candidatus Phytoplasmaprunorum'. Molecular and Cellular Probes,* 23 (5): 227-234.

Zhang, C., Shen, Y., Chen, J., Xiao, P., Bao, J. (2008a): Non-destructive Prediction of Total Phenolics, Flavonoid Contents and Antioxidant Capacity of Rice Grain using Near-infrared Spectroscopy. *Journal of Agricultural and Food Chemistry,* 56 (18): 8268-8272.

Zhang, H., Chang, M., Wang, J., Ye, S. (2008b): Evaluation of Peach Quality Indices using an Electronic Nose by MLR, QPST and BP Network. Sensors and Actuators B: *Chemical,* 134 (1): 332-338.

Pages: 50-65

Current Research in Biochemistry and Molecular Biology
Edited by: **Dr. Prasann Kumar and Dr. Pawan Kumar 'Bharti'**
ISBN: 978-93-88854-33-7
Edition: **2020**
Published by: **Discovery Publishing House Pvt. Ltd., New Delhi (India)**

CHAPTER

4

Molecular Stress Response in Context with Abiotic and Biotic Factor

Prasann Kumar[1,2*], Shipa Rani Dey[1]

GRAPHICAL ABSTRACT

Keywords: Abiotic, Biotic, Context, Factor, Stress

INTRODUCTION

The various processes involved in cellular stress responses serve the adaptive purpose of protecting a cell against unfavourable environmental

[1] Department of Agronomy, School of Agriculture, Lovely Professional University, Jalandhar - 144 411 (Punjab) (India)
[2] Divison of Research and Development,, Lovely Professional University, Jalandhar - 144 411 (Punjab) (India)

conditions, both through short term mechanisms that minimize acute damage to the cell's overall integrity, and through longer term mechanisms which provide the cell a measure of resiliency against similar adverse conditions.Cellular stress response is the wide range of molecular changes that cells undergo in response to environmental stressors, including extremes of temperature, exposure to toxins, and mechanical damage.

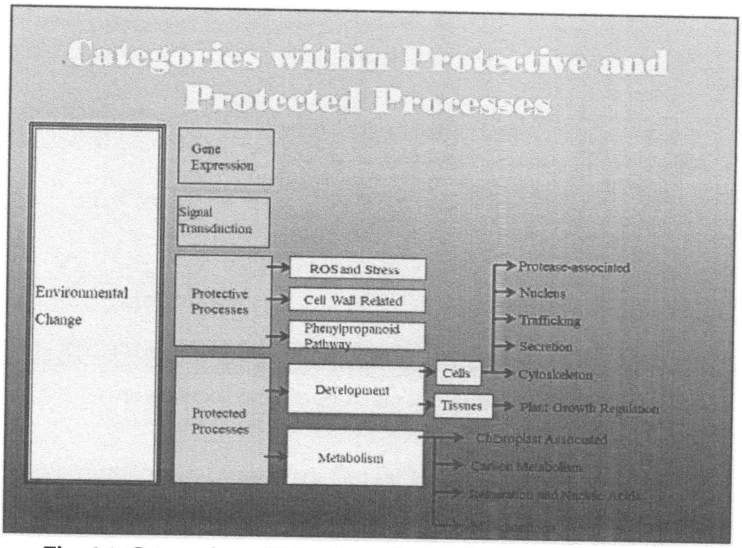

Fig. 4.1: Categories within protective and protected processes

Source: Based on review of literature

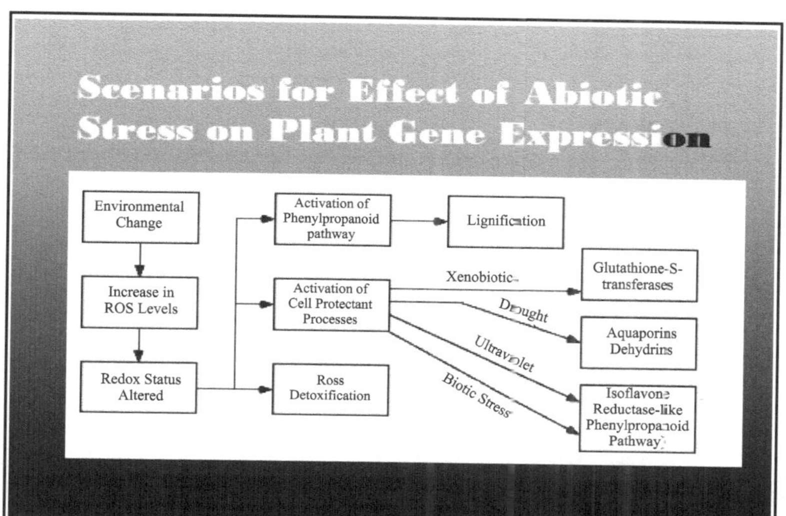

Fig. 4.2: Scenarios for Effect of Abiotic and stress on plant

Source: Based on review of literature

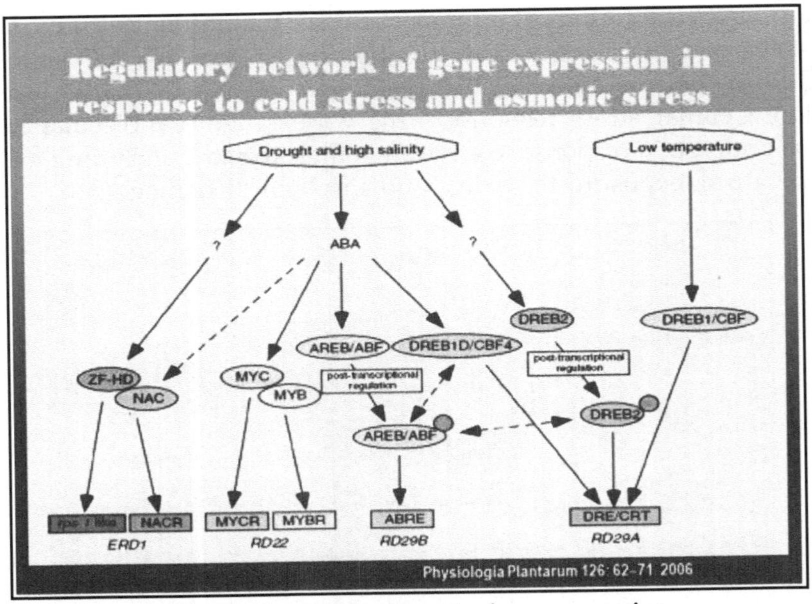

Fig. 4.3: Regulatory network of gene expression

Source: Based on review of literature

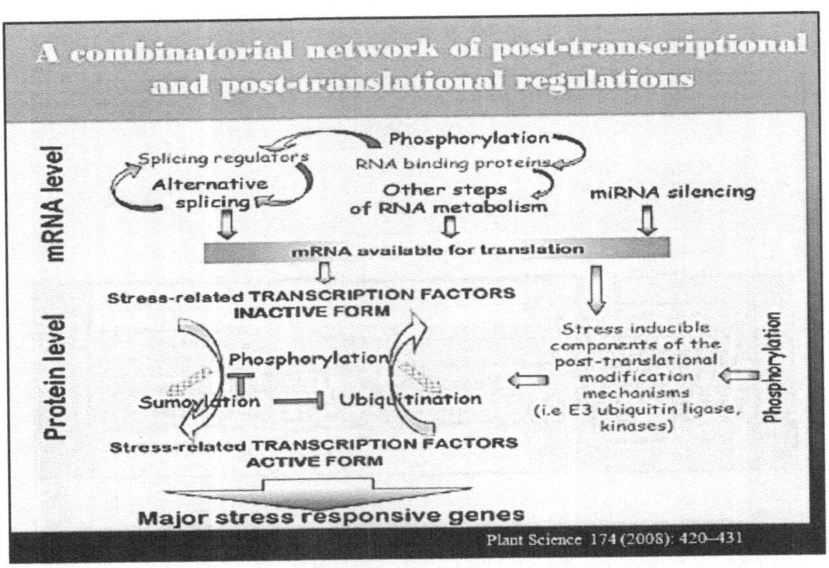

Fig. 4.4: Post-transcriptional regulations

Source: Based on review of literature

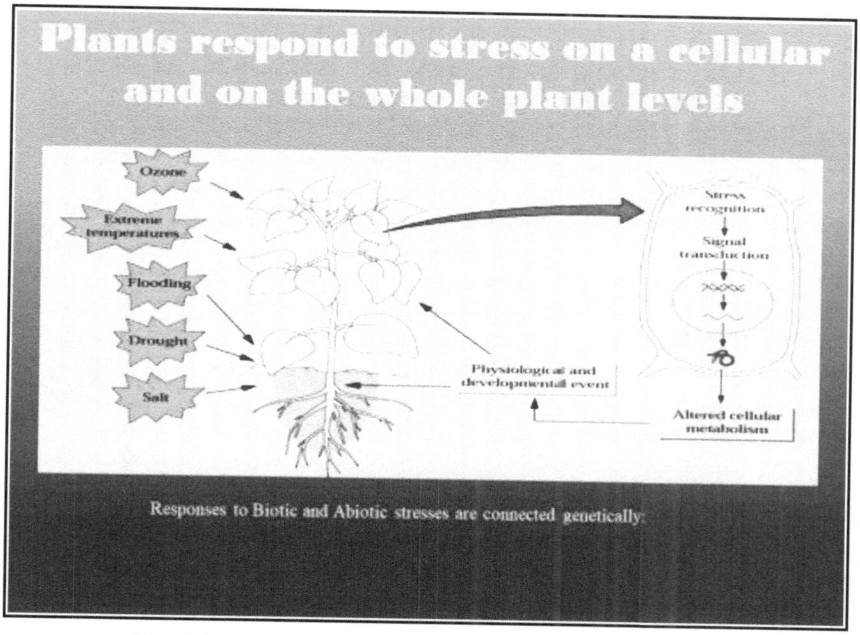

Fig. 4.5: Response on a cellular and whole plant levels
Source: Based on review of literature

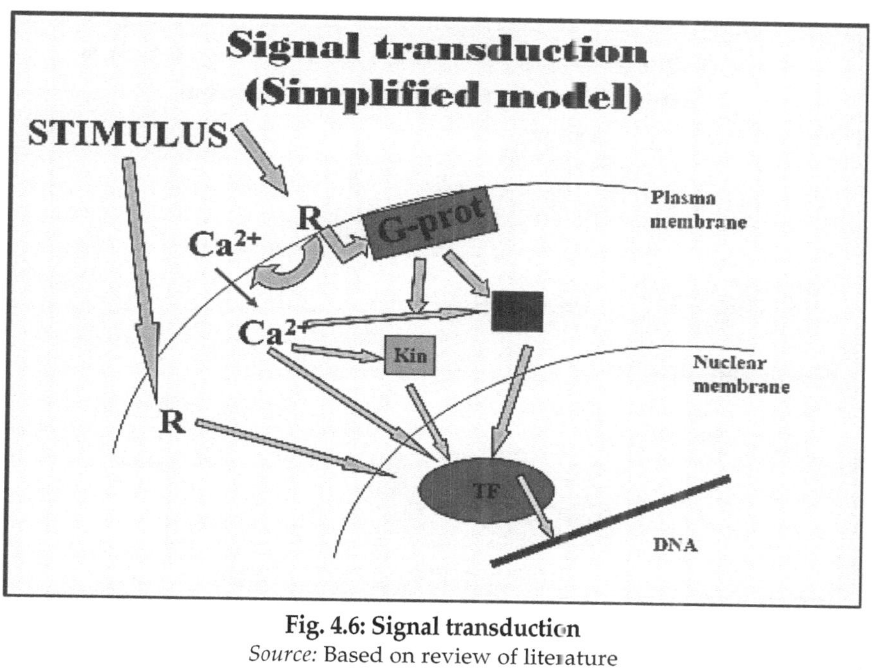

Fig. 4.6: Signal transduction
Source: Based on review of literature

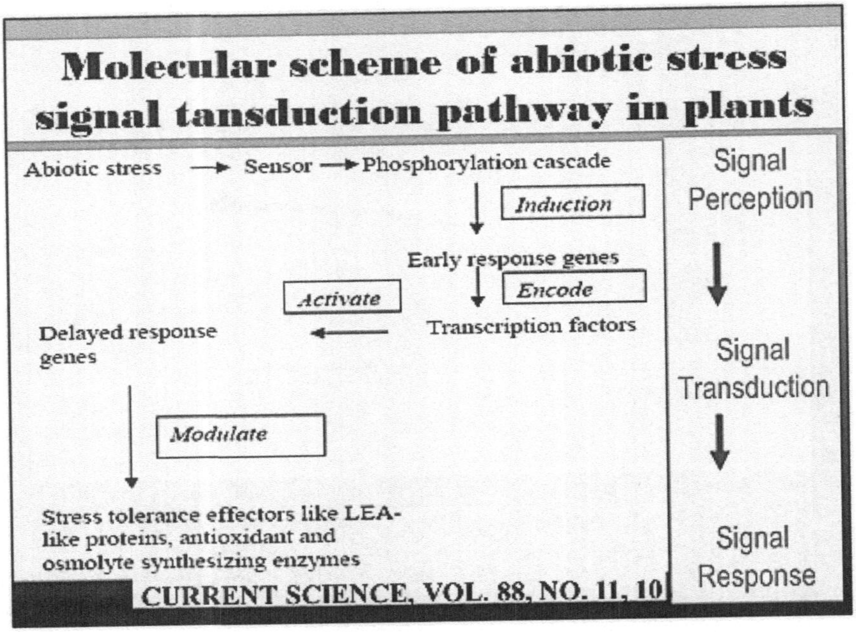

Fig. 4.7: Molecular pathway of abiotic stress

Source: Based on review of literature

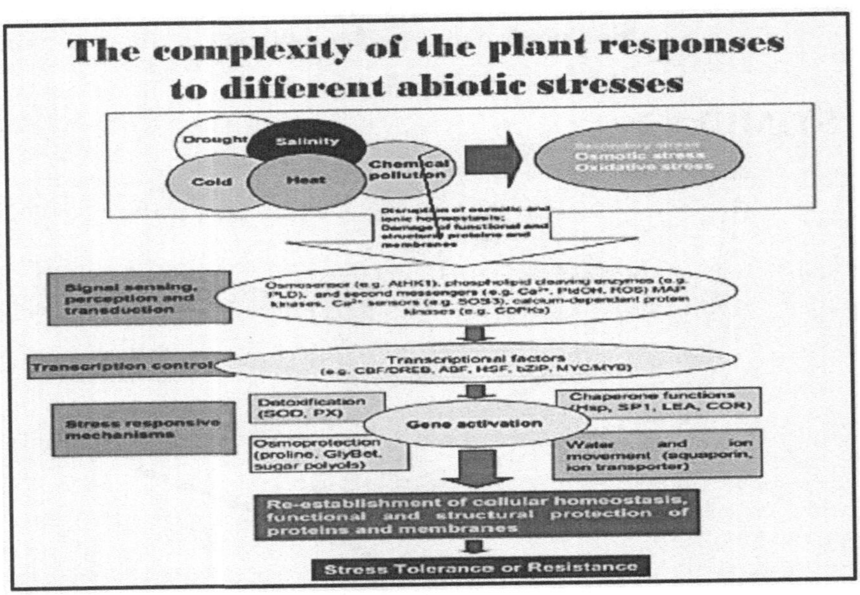

Fig. 4.8: Cross talk of plant responses

Source: Based on review of literature

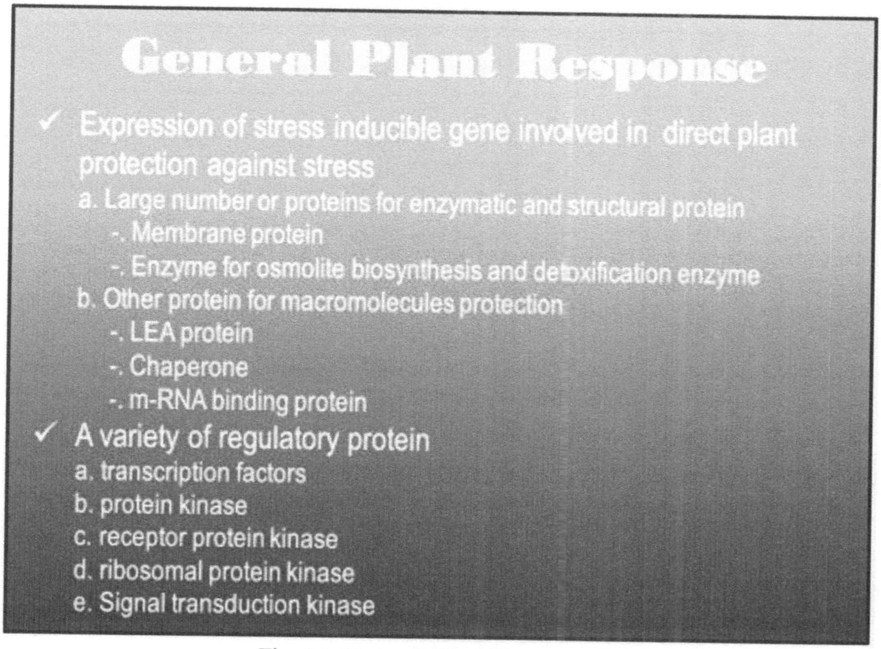

Fig. 4.9: General Plant Response
Source: Based on review of literature

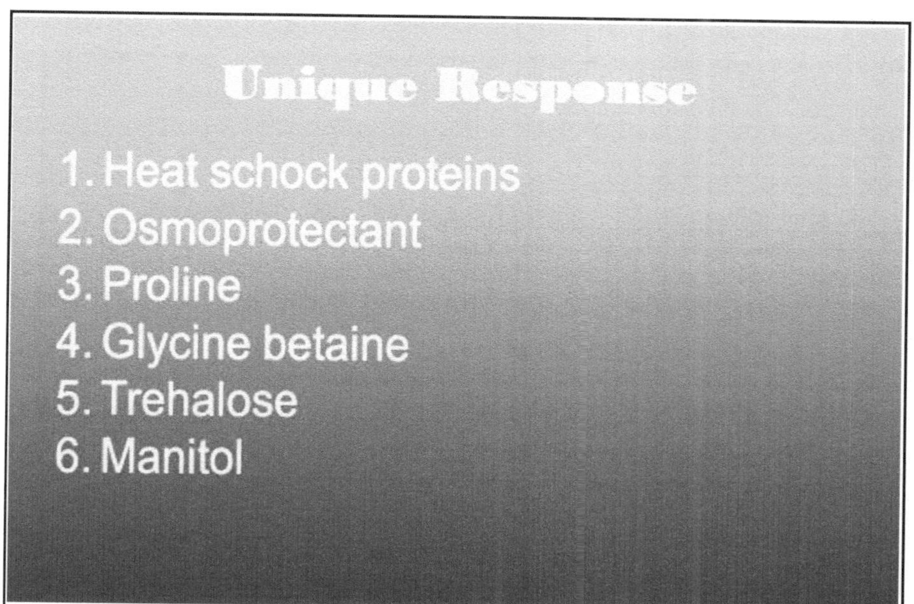

Fig. 4.10: Unique response
Source: Based on review of literature

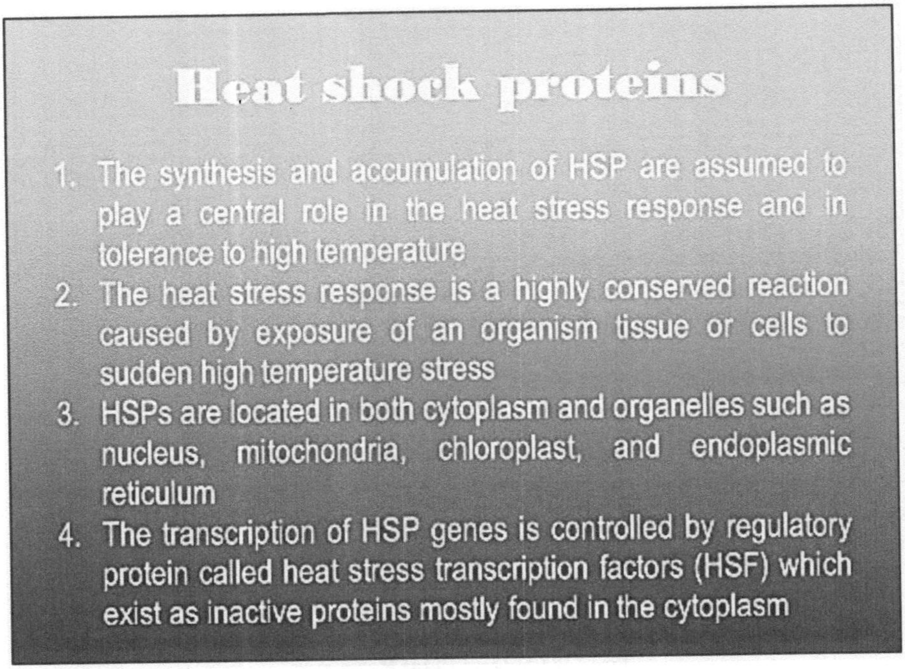

Fig. 4.11: Heat shock proteins
Source: Based on review of literature

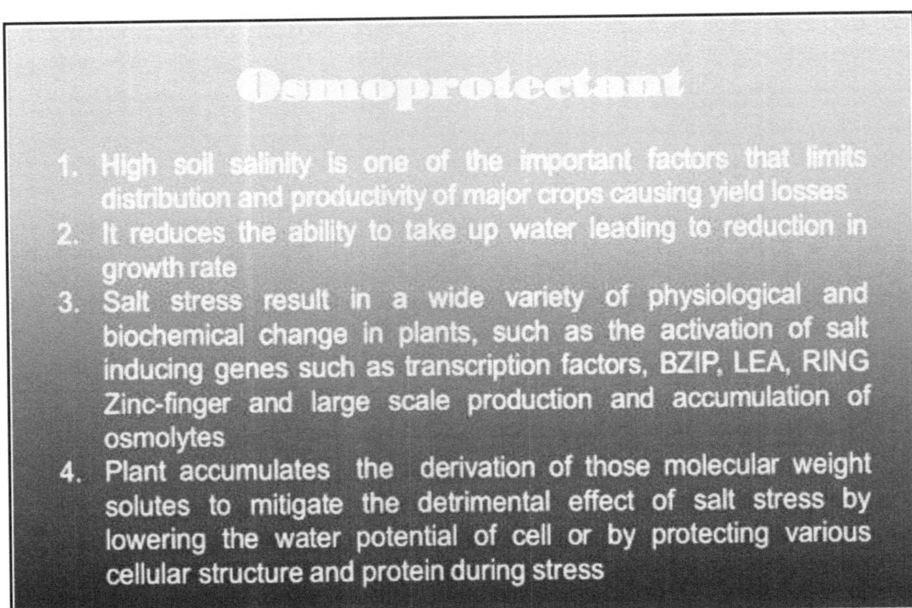

Fig. 4.12: Osmoprotectant
Source: Based on review of literature

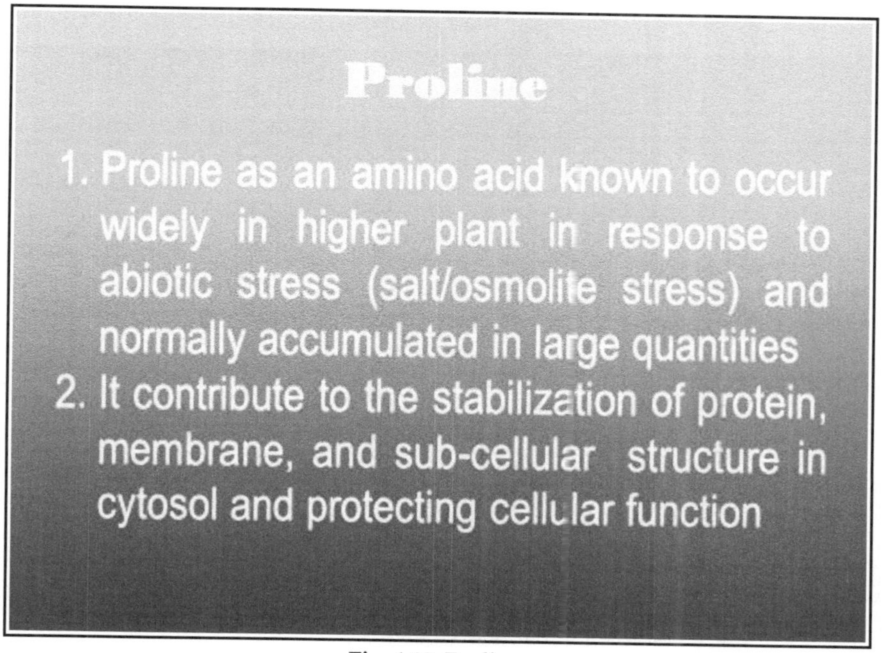

Fig. 4.13: Proline

Source: Based on review of literature

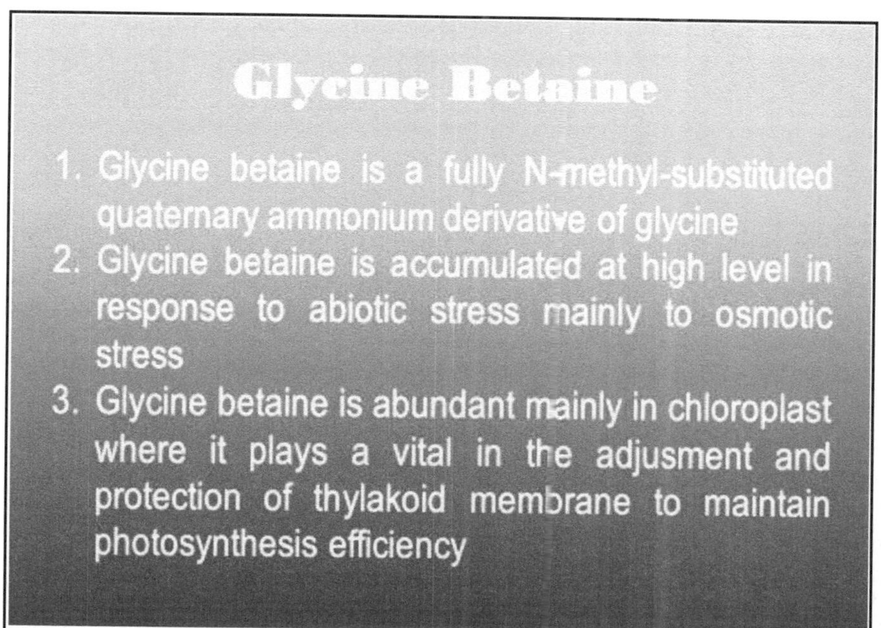

Fig. 4.14: Glycine Betaine

Source: Based on review of literature

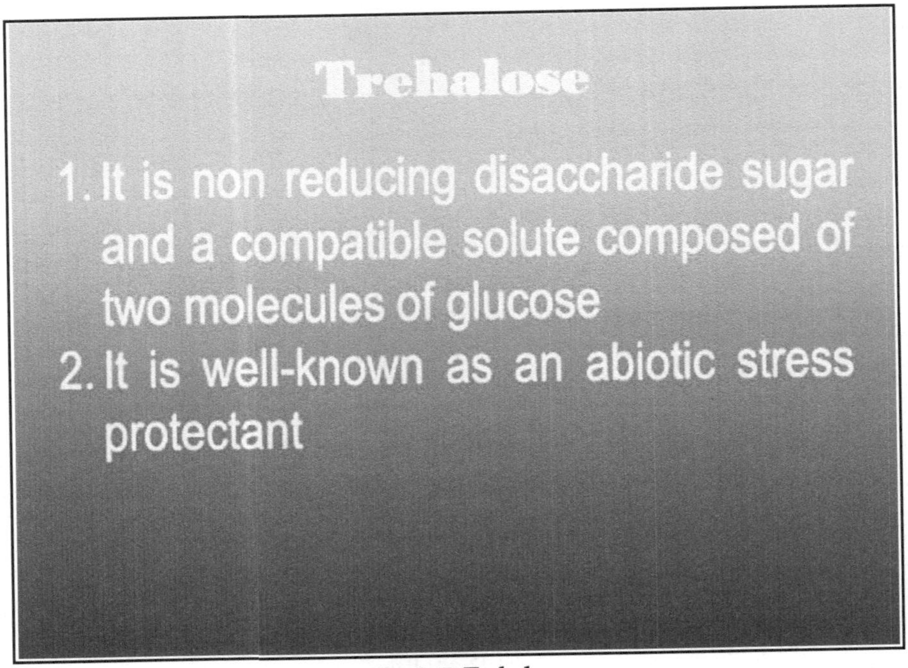

Fig. 4.15: Trehalose
Source: Based on review of literature

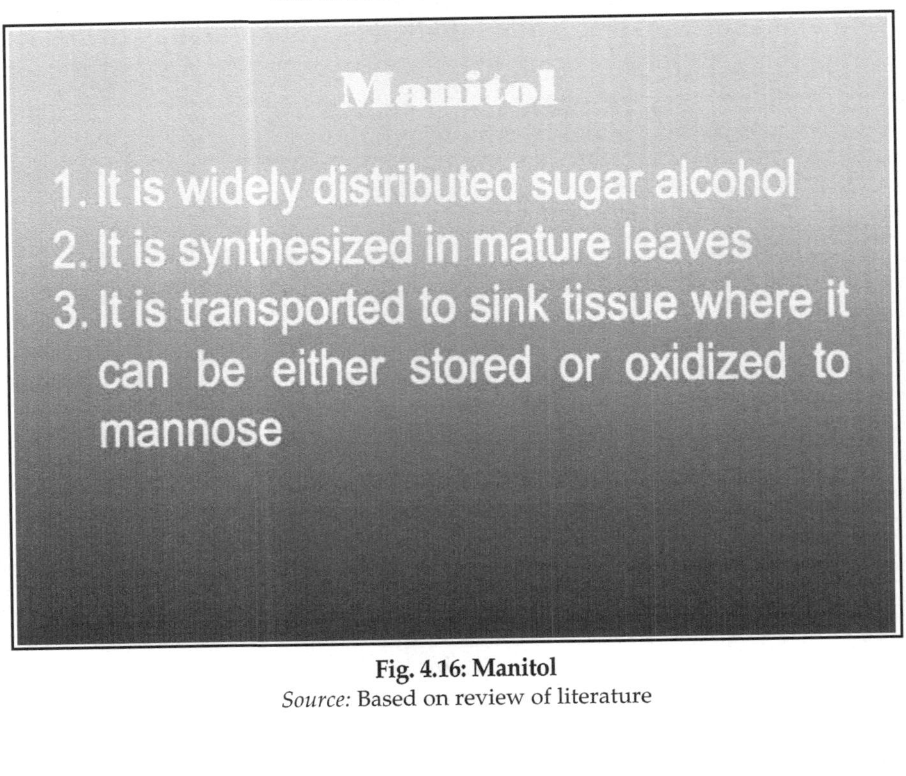

Fig. 4.16: Manitol
Source: Based on review of literature

Fig. 4.17: Physiological stress responses
Source: Based on review of literature

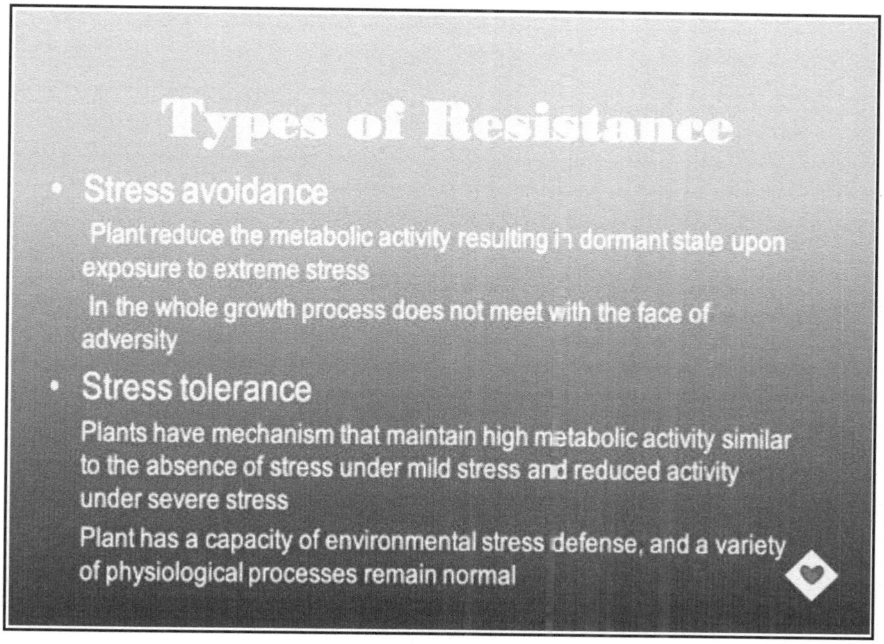

Fig. 4.18: Types of Resistance
Source: Based on review of literature

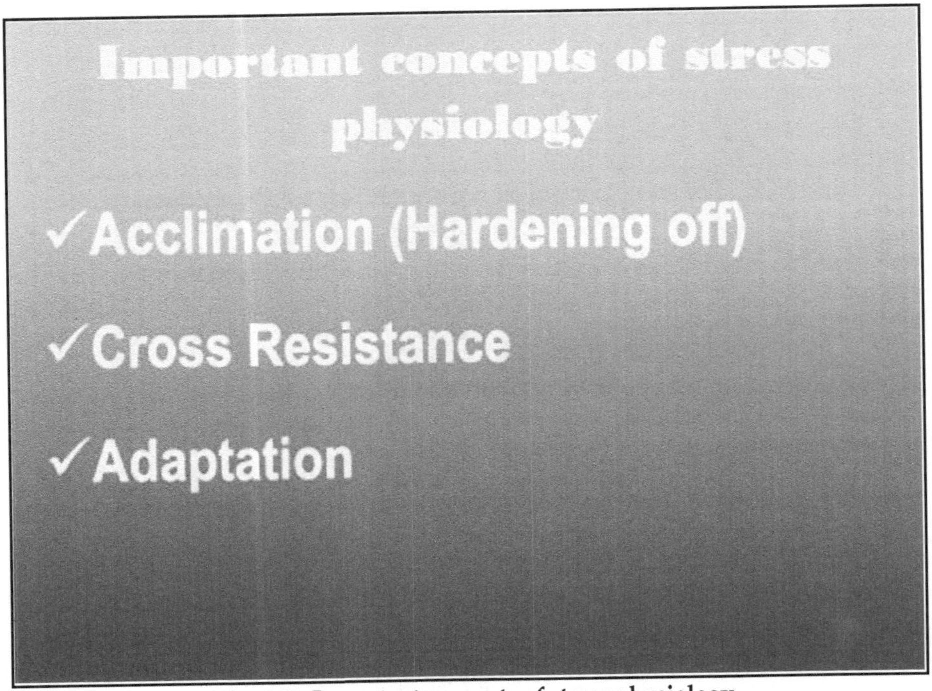

Fig. 4.19: Important concepts of stress physiology

Source: Based on review of literature

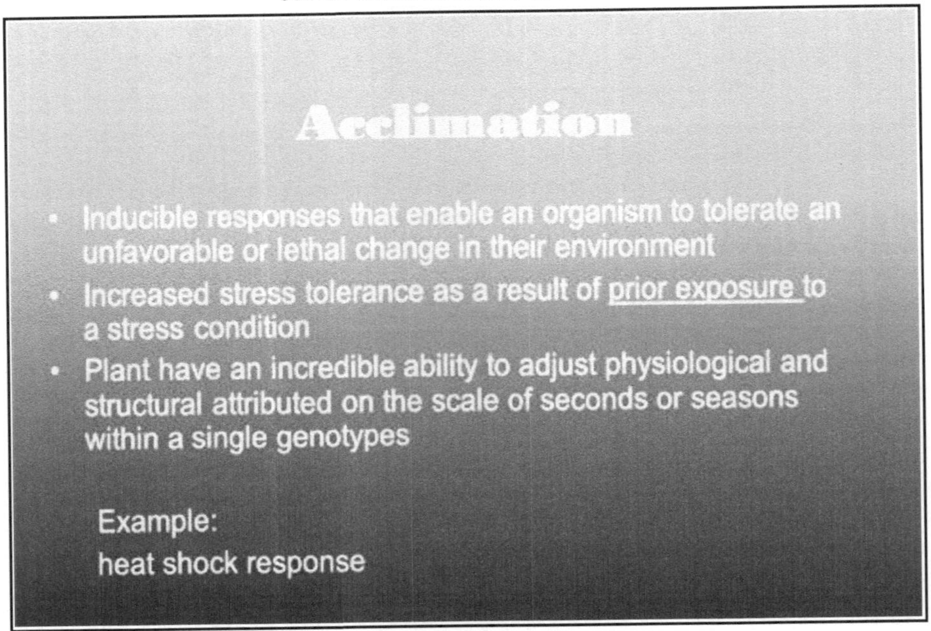

Fig. 4.20: Acclimation

Source: Based on review of literature

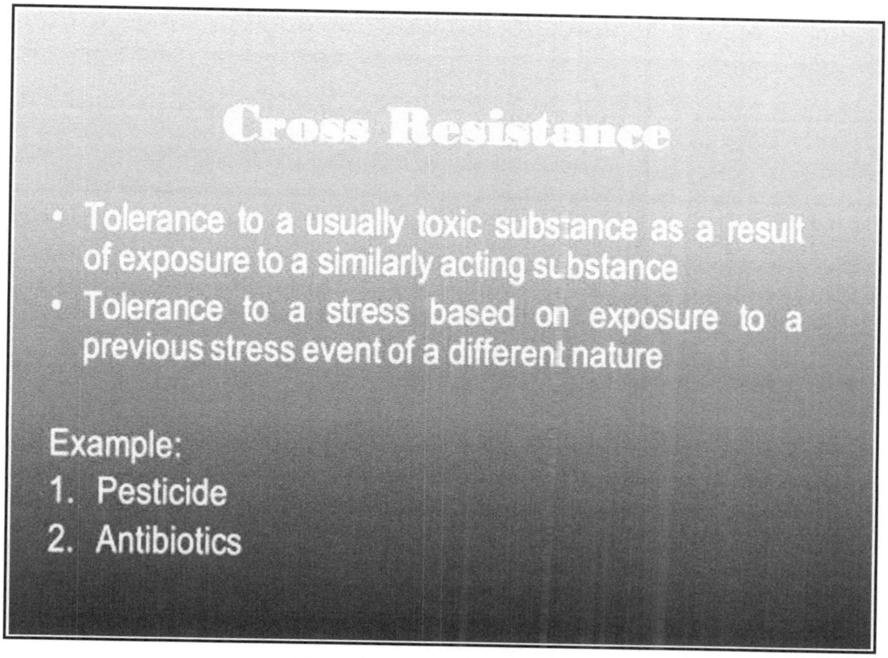

Fig. 4.21: Cross resistance

Source: Based on review of literature

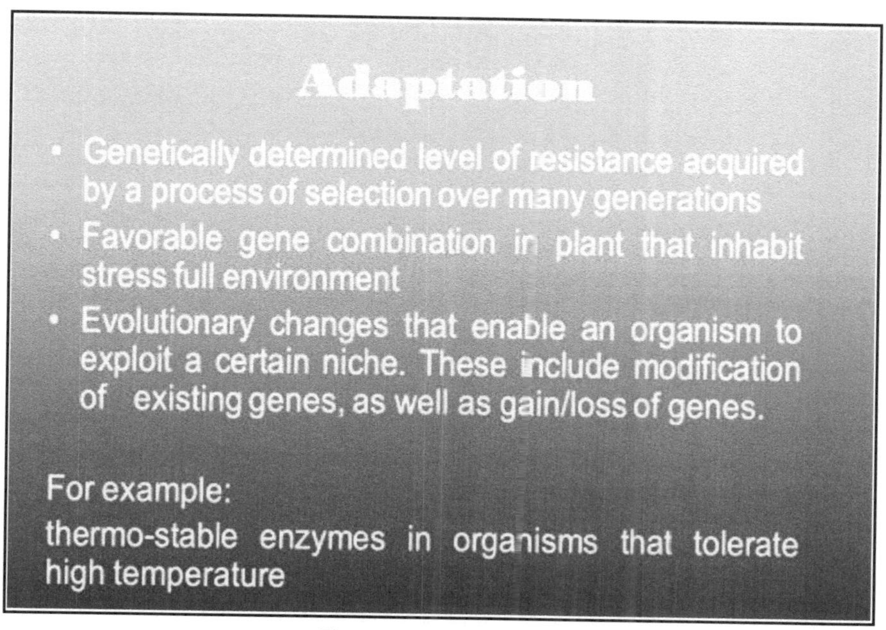

Fig. 4.22: Adaptation

Source: Based on review of literature

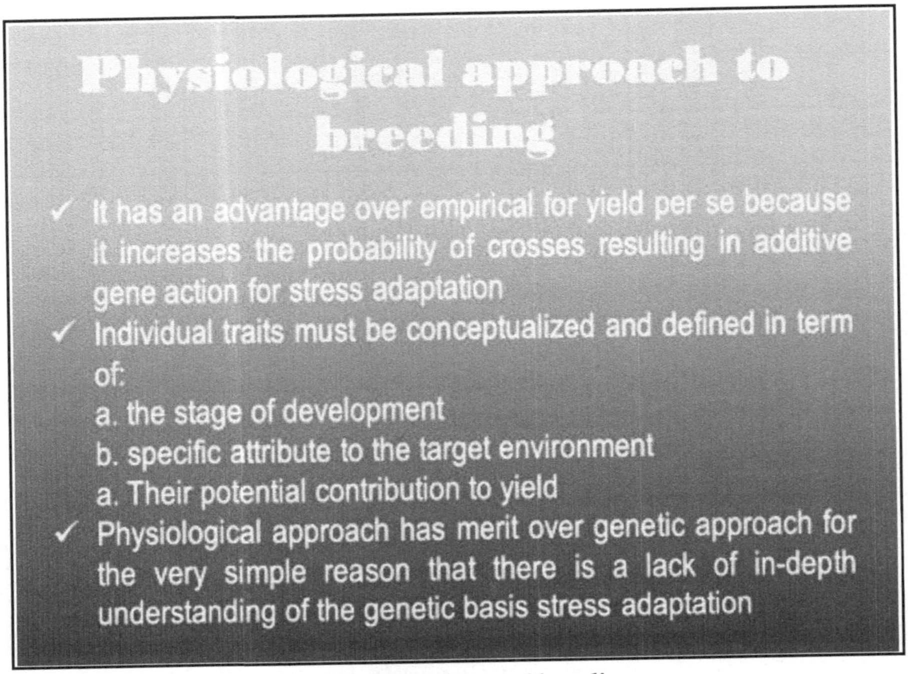

Fig. 4.23: Physiology and breeding
Source: Based on review of literature

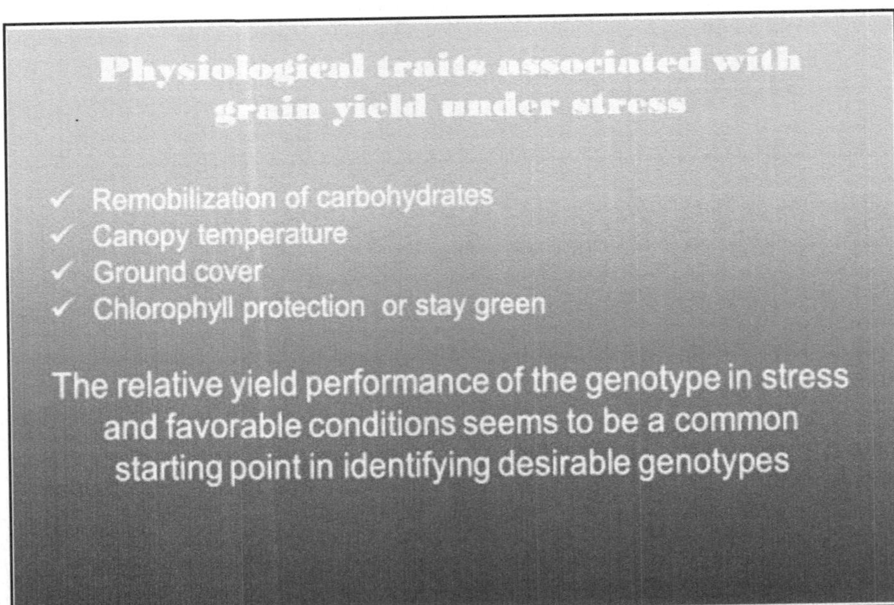

Fig. 4.24: Physiological traits associated with grain yield
Source: Based on review of literature

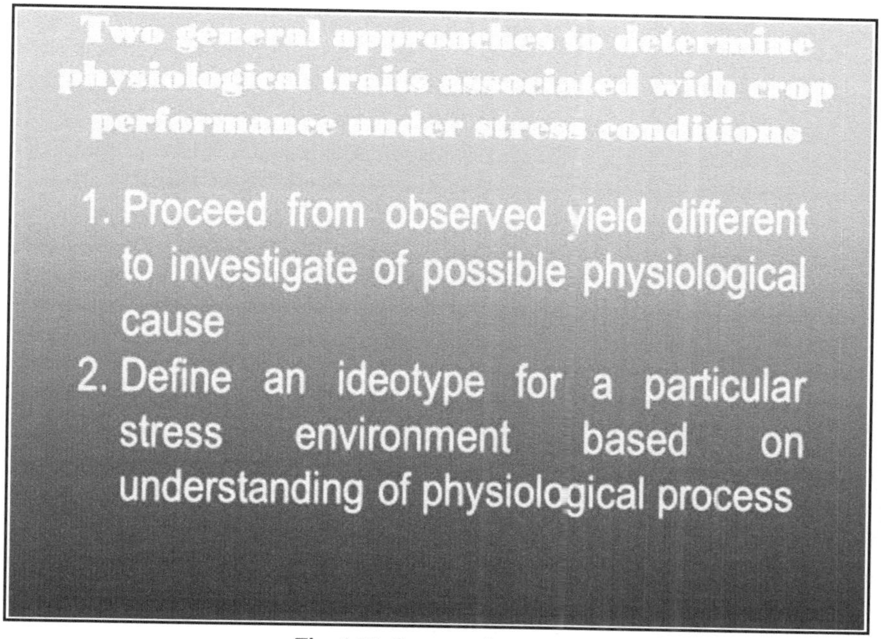

Fig. 4.25: Crop performance
Source: Based on review of literature

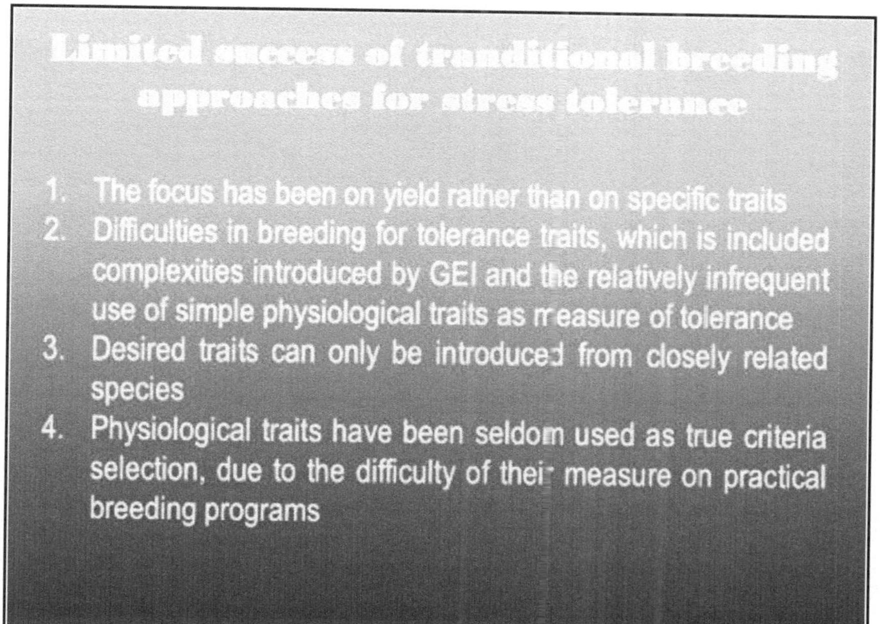

Fig. 4.26: Traditional breeding approaches
Source: Based on review of literature

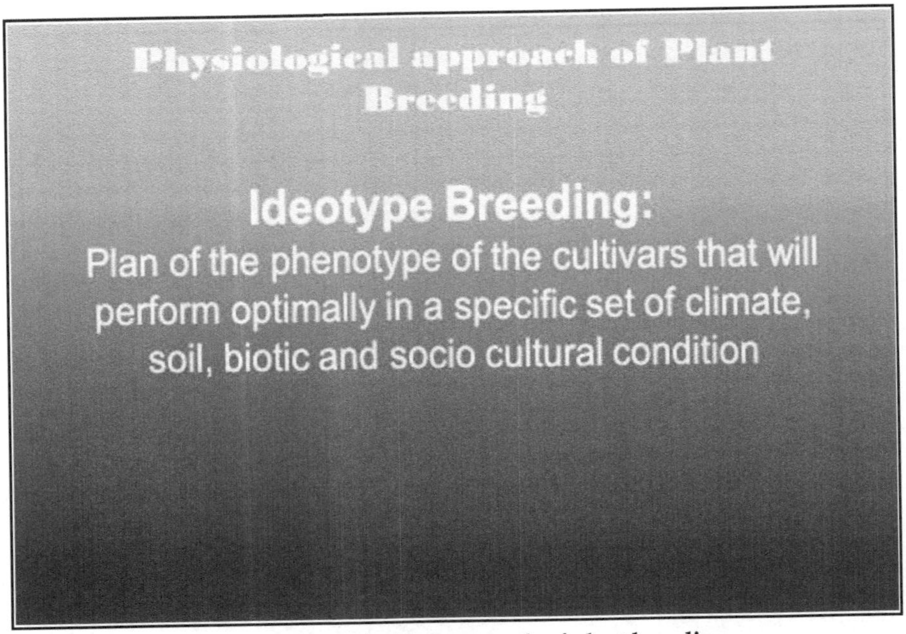

Fig. 4.27: Physiological approach of plant breeding
Source: Based on review of literature

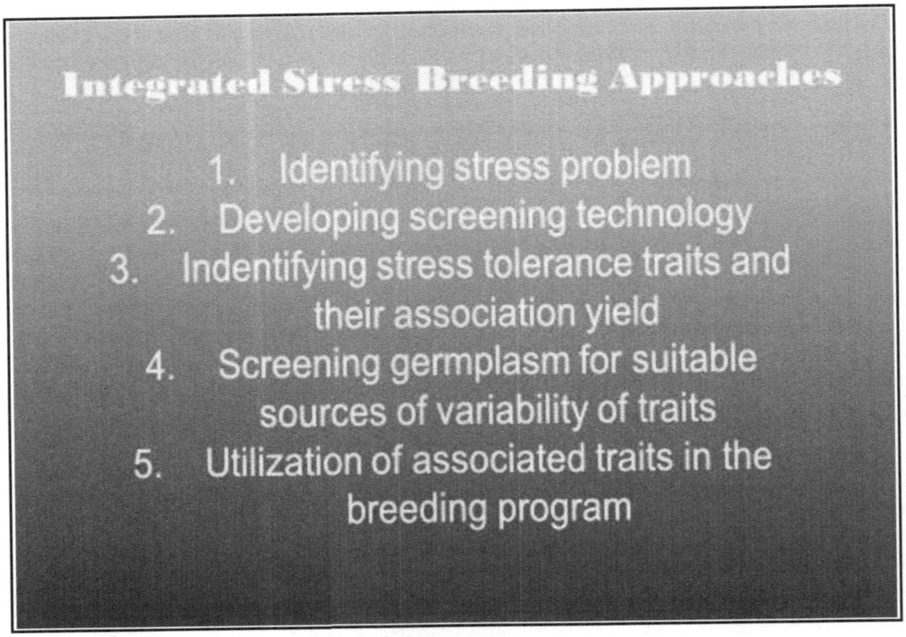

Fig. 4.28: Integrated stress breeding approaches
Source: Based on review of literature

CONCLUSION

Stress, either physiological or biological, is an organism's response to a stressor such as an environmental condition. Stress is the body's method of reacting to a condition such as a threat, challenge or physical and psychological barrier. Stimuli that alter an organism's environment are responded to by multiple systems in the body. The autonomic nervous system and hypothalamic-pituitary-adrenal (HPA) axis are two major systems that respond to stress.The sympathoadrenal medullary (SAM) axis may activate the fight-or-flight response through the sympathetic nervous system, which dedicates energy to more relevant bodily systems to acute adaptation to stress, while the parasympathetic nervous system returns the body to homeostasis. The second major physiological stress, the HPA axis regulates the release of cortisol, which influences many bodily functions such as metabolic, psychological and immunological functions. The SAM and HPA axes are regulated by several brain regions, including the limbic system, prefrontal cortex, amygdala, hypothalamus, and striaterminalis.

REFERENCES

https://en.wikipedia.org/wiki/Cellular_stress_response

https://en.wikipedia.org/wiki/Stress_(biology)

https://en.wikipedia.org/wiki/Bacterial_stress_response

https://en.wikipedia.org/wiki/Unfolded_protein_response

https://en.wikipedia.org/wiki/Integrated_stress_response

https://en.wikipedia.org/wiki/Heat_shock_response

https://en.wikipedia.org/wiki/Stringent_response

https://en.wikipedia.org/wiki/Acute_stress_reaction

https://en.wikipedia.org/wiki/Fear_processing_in_the_brain

Pages: 66-80

Current Research in Biochemistry and Molecular Biology
Edited by: Dr. Prasann Kumar and Dr. Pawan Kumar 'Bharti'
ISBN: 978-93-88854-33-7
Edition: **2020**
Published by: **Discovery Publishing House Pvt. Ltd., New Delhi (India)**

CHAPTER
5

The Plant Cells

Prasann Kumar[1,2*] Johnson Yumnam[1]

GRAPHICAL ABSTRACT

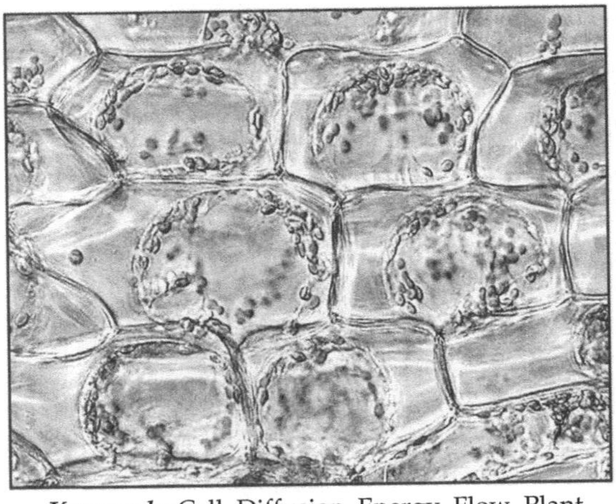

Keywords: Cell, Diffusion, Energy, Flow, Plant

INTRODUCTION

- 1838 – Matthias Schleiden – stated all plants composed of cells
- 1839 – Theodor Schwann – stated all animals also composed of cells – thus claimed all living things composed of cells
- 1858 – Rudolf Virchow – all cells come from preexisting cells

[1] Department of Agronomy, School of Agriculture, Lovely Professional University, Jalandhar - 144 411 (Punjab) (India)
[2] Divison of Research and Development, Lovely Professional University, Jalandhar - 144 411 (Punjab) (India)

Fig. 5.1: Robert Hooke
Source: based on review of literature

Fig. 5.2: Hooke's Microscope
Source: based on review of literature

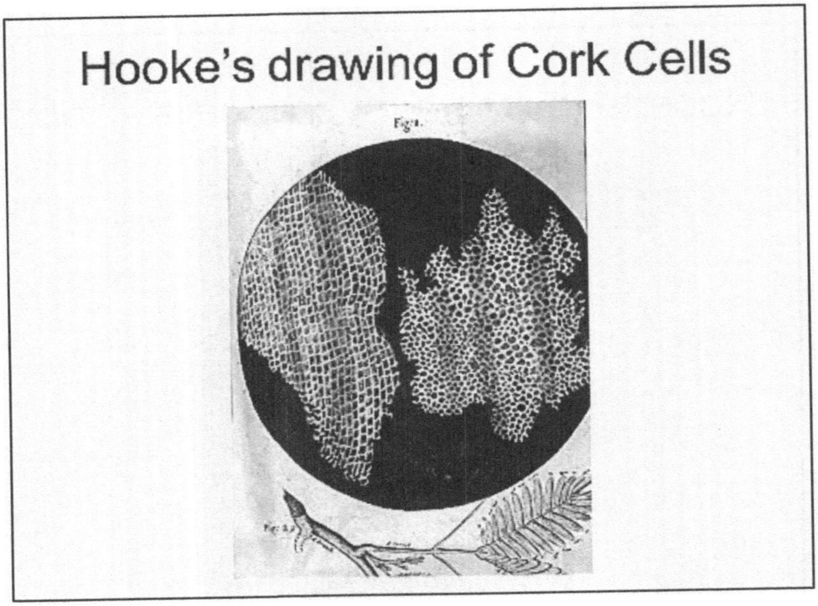

Fig. 5.3: Cork Cells
Source: based on review of literature

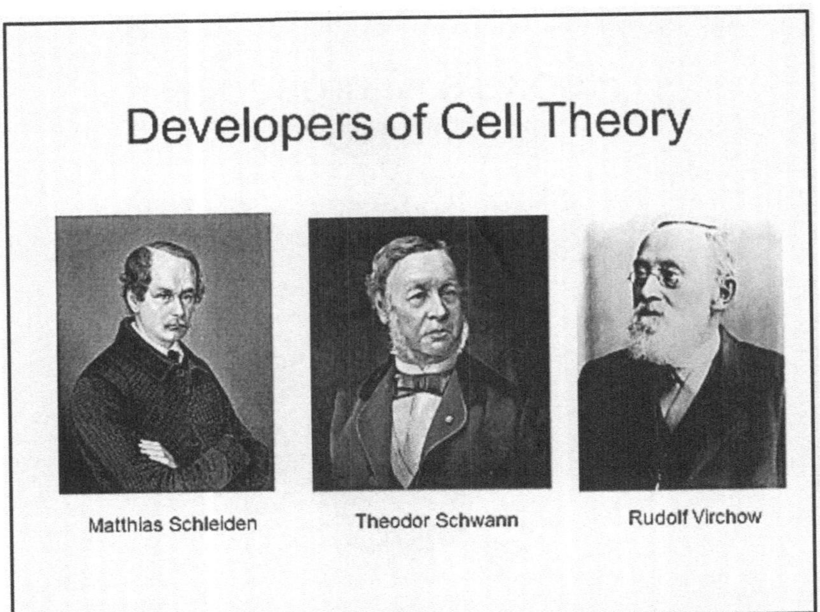

Fig. 5.4: Developers of cell theory
Source: based on review of literature

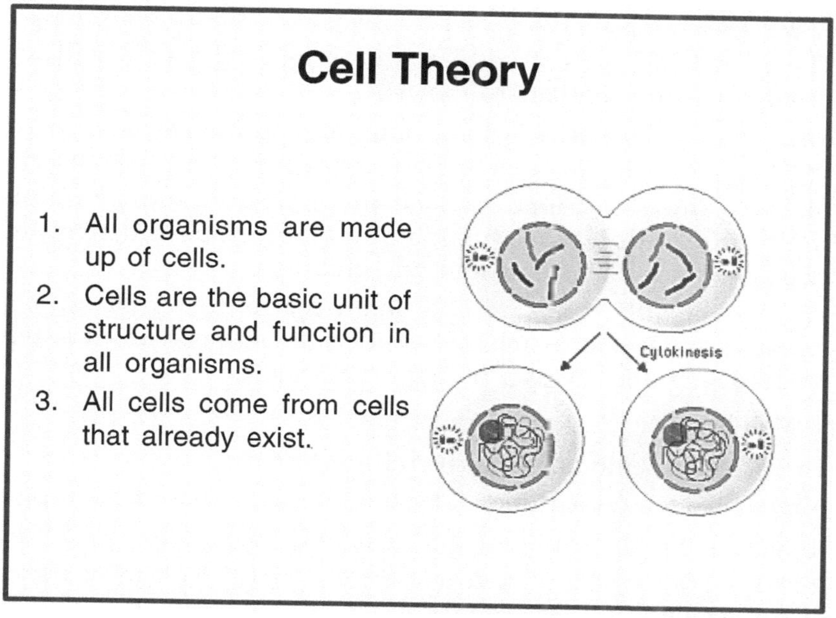

Fig. 5.5: Cell theory
Source: based on review of literature

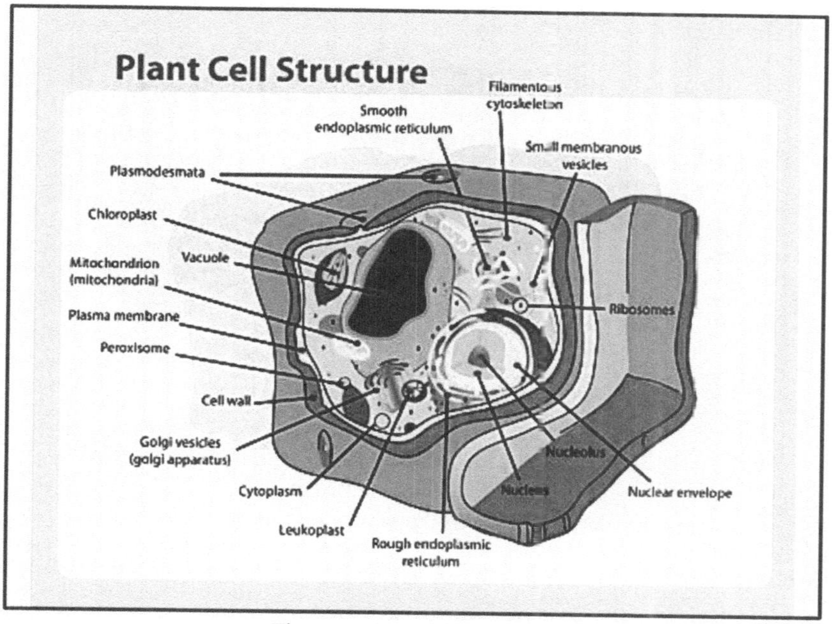

Fig. 5.6: Plant cell structure
Source: based on review of literature

The Plant Cell

- The Plant Cell consists of a more or less rigid cell wall and the protoplast - the contents of the cell
- The protoplast consists of the cytoplasm and a nucleus
- The cytoplasm includes distinct membrane-bound organelles such as plastids and mitochondria; systems of membranes (endoplasmic reticulum anddictyosomes); nonmembranous entities such as ribosomes, actin filaments and microtubules
- The rest of the cytoplasm is a liquid matrix in which the nucleus, various entities and membrane systems are suspended - it is typically referred to as the cytosol or ground substance

Plasma Membrane

The plasma membrane has several functions

1. It mediates the transport of substances into and out of the protoplasm
2. It coordinates the synthesis and assembly of cellulose microfibrils
3. It relays hormonal and environmental signals involved in the control of cell growth and differentiation

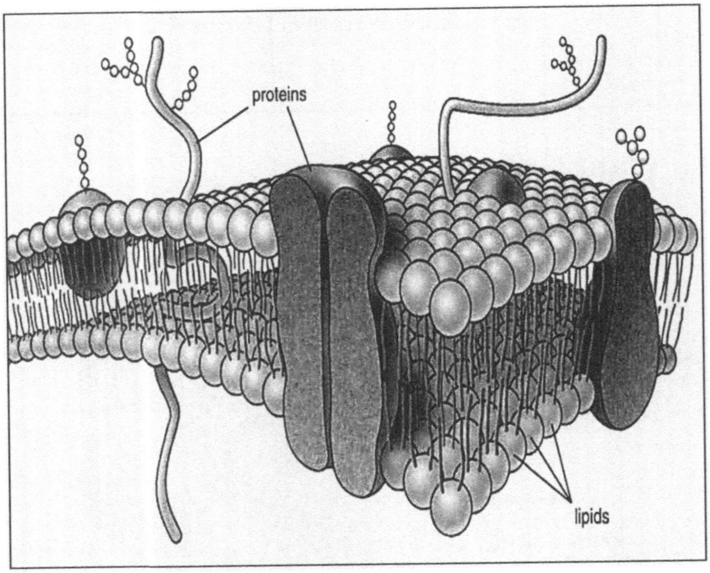

Fig. 5.7: Plasma membrane
Source: Based on review of literature

Cell Nucleus

The nucleus is usually the most prominent structure in the protoplast of eukaryote cells.

1. It controls the ongoing activities of the cell by determining which protein molecules are produced by the cell and when they are produced
2. It stores genetic information, passing it onto daughter cells during cell division

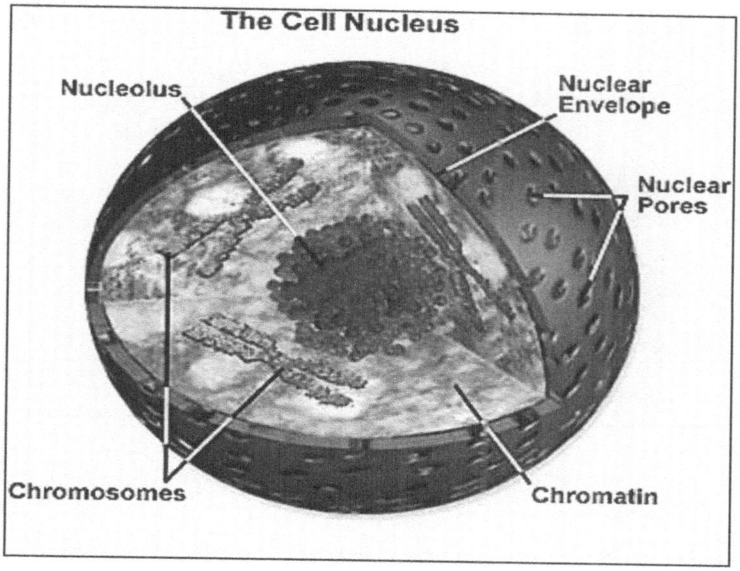

Fig. 5.8: The cell nucleus
Source: based on review of literature

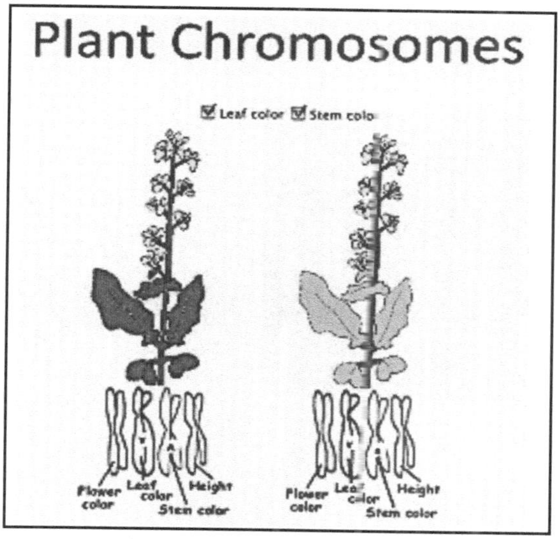

Fig. 5.9: Plant chromosomes
Source: based on review of literature

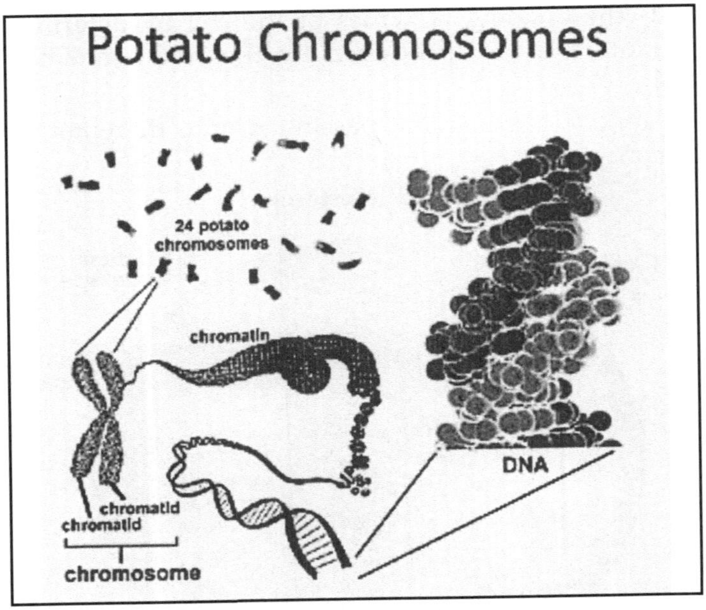

Fig. 5.10: Potato chromosomes
Source: based on review of literature

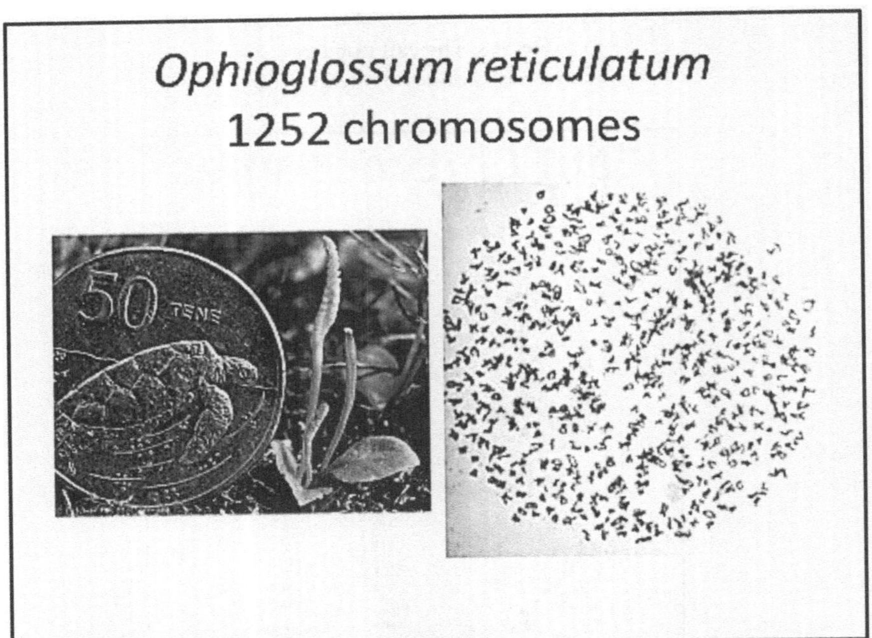

Fig. 5.11: *Ophioglossumreticulatum*
Source: based on review of literature

Plastids

- Plastids are a characteristic component of plant cells
- Plastids are classified and named based on the kinds of pigments they contain
- Each plastid is surrounded by two membranes and internally the plastid has a system of membranes which form flattened sacs called thylakoids and a ground (fluid) substance called stroma

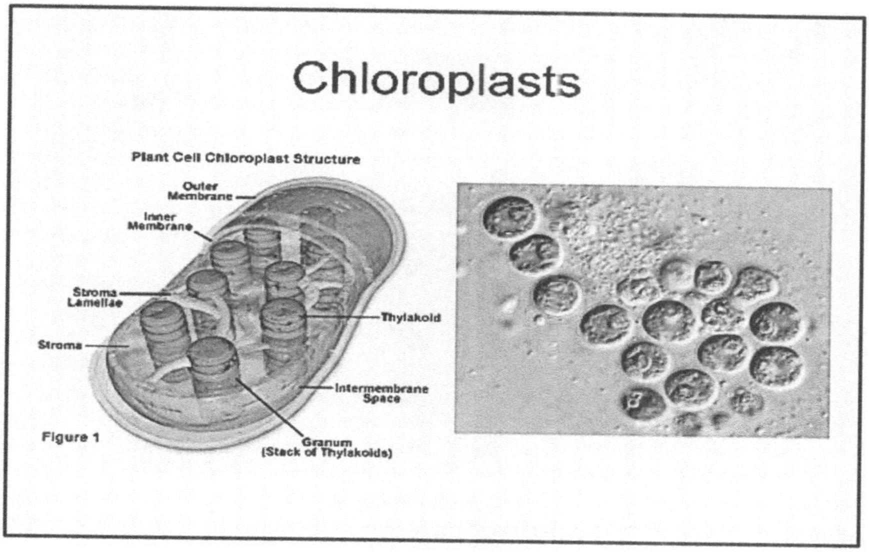

Fig. 5.12: Chloroplast
Source: based on review of literature

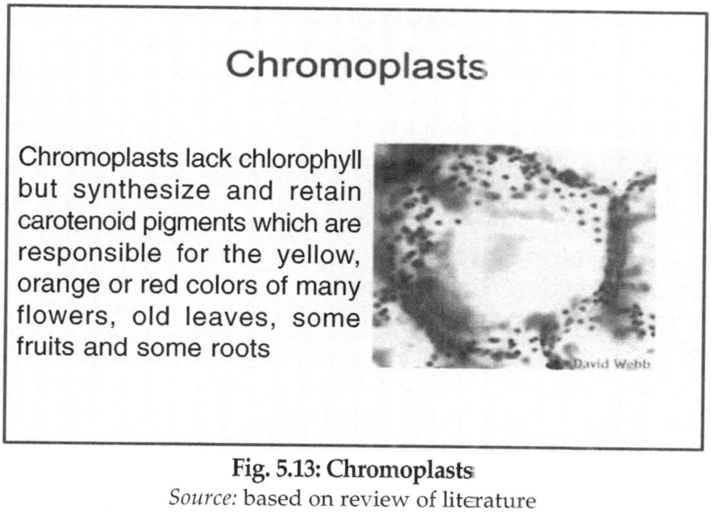

Fig. 5.13: Chromoplasts
Source: based on review of literature

Leucoplasts

- Leucoplasts are nonpigmented plastids some of which synthesize starch while others produce oils or proteins
- Upon exposure to light they may develop into chloroplasts

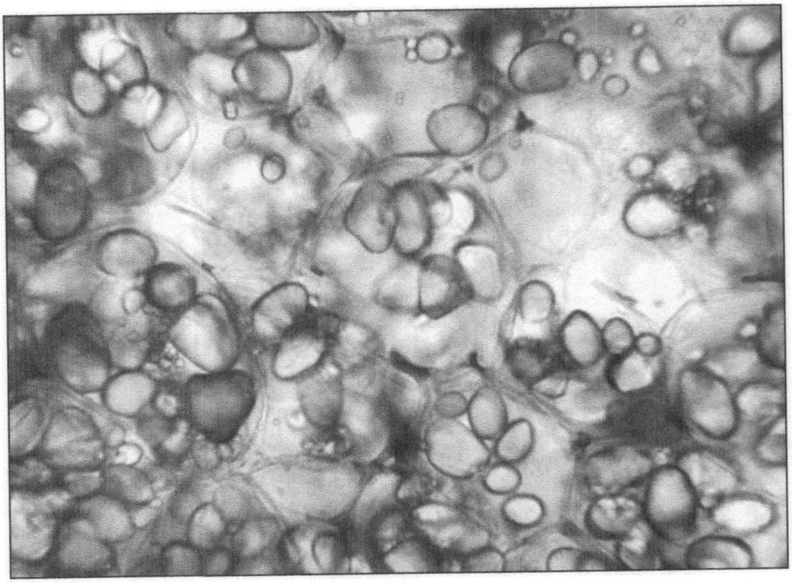

Fig. 5.14: Leucoplast
Source: based on review of literature

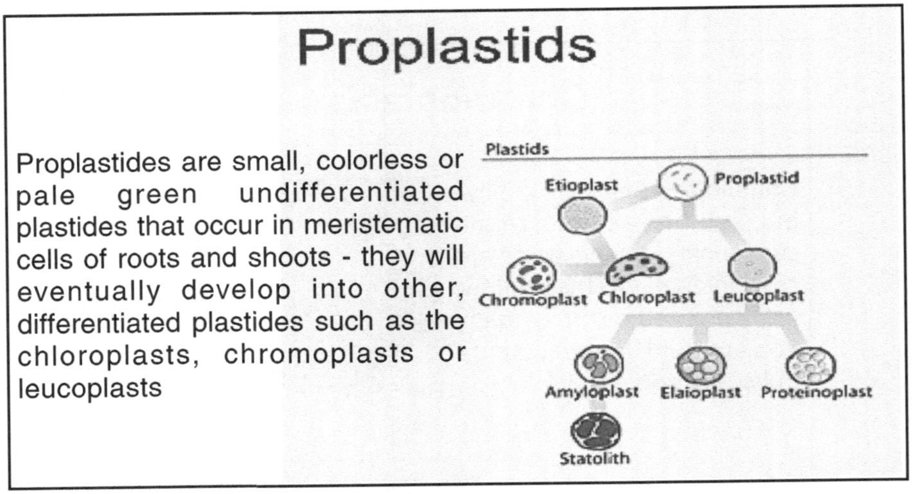

Fig. 5.15: Proplastids
Source: based on review of literature

Mitochondria

- Mitochondria are another organelle bounded by two membranes
- The inner membrane is folded into many pleats called cristae
- Mitochondria are the sites of cellular respiration - converting organic molecules to ATP the main immediate energy source for living eukaryote cells - plant cells may have hundreds to thousands of mitochondria.

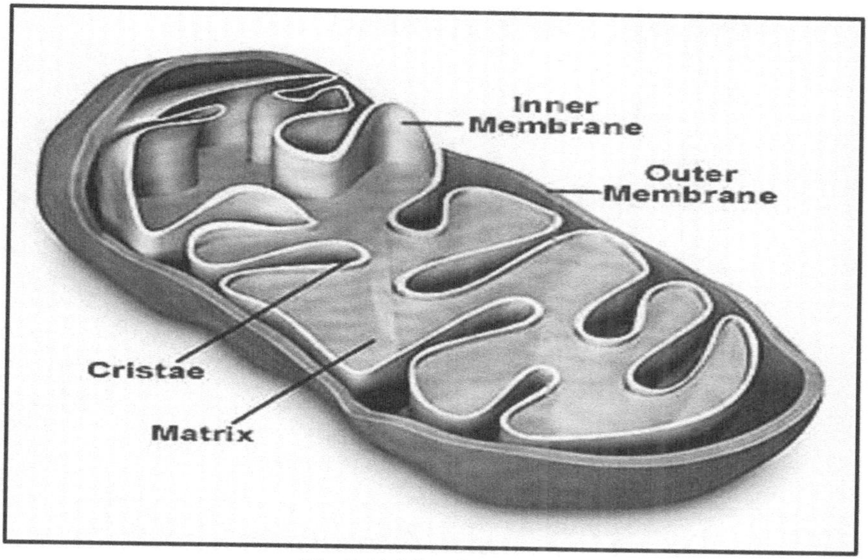

Fig. 5.16: Mitochondria
Source: based on review of literature

Vacuoles

- Vacuoles are membrane bound organelles filled with cell sap
- The membrane is referred to as the tonoplast
- Different kinds of vacuoles may have different functions within the same cell
- Along with water based cell sap, vacuoles typically contain salts, sugars and some dissolved proteins

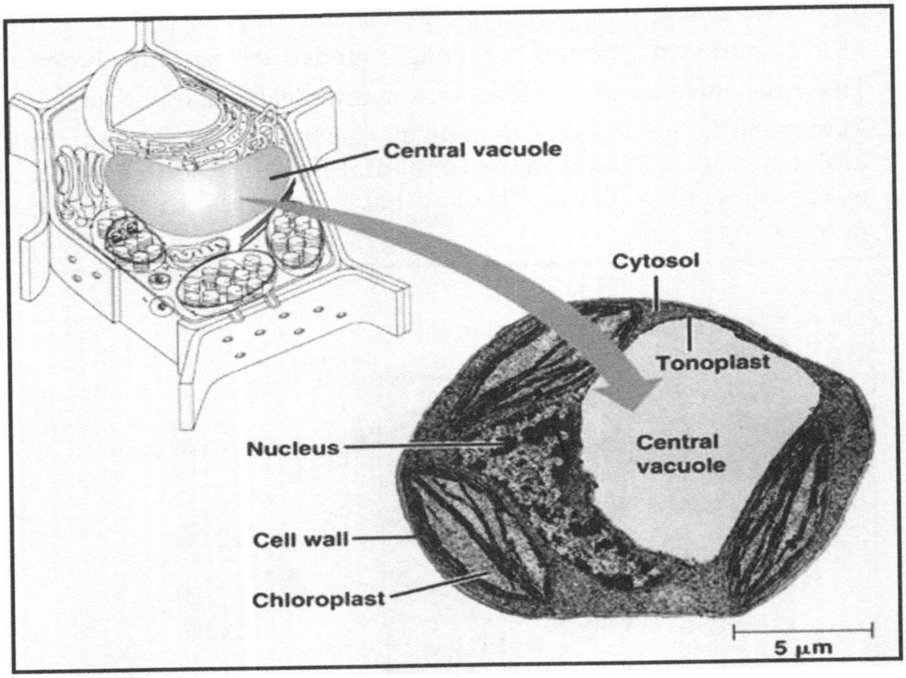

Fig. 5.17: Vacuoles
Source: based on review of literature

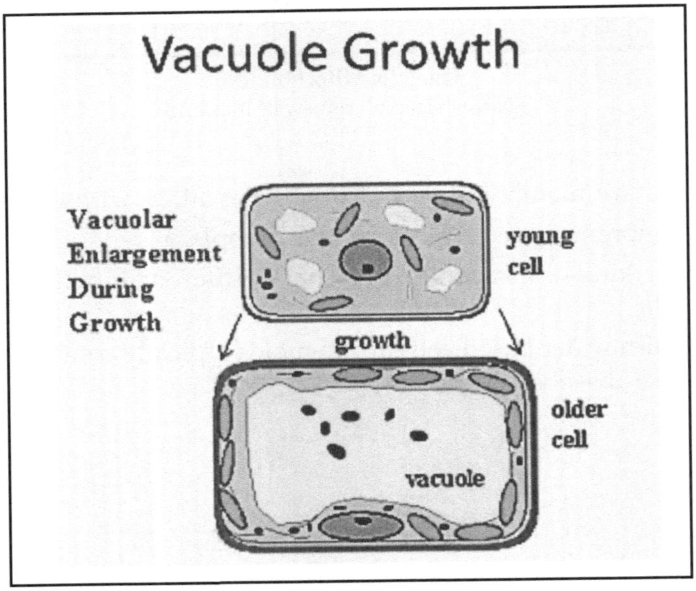

Fig. 5.18: Vacuole growth
Source: based on review of literature

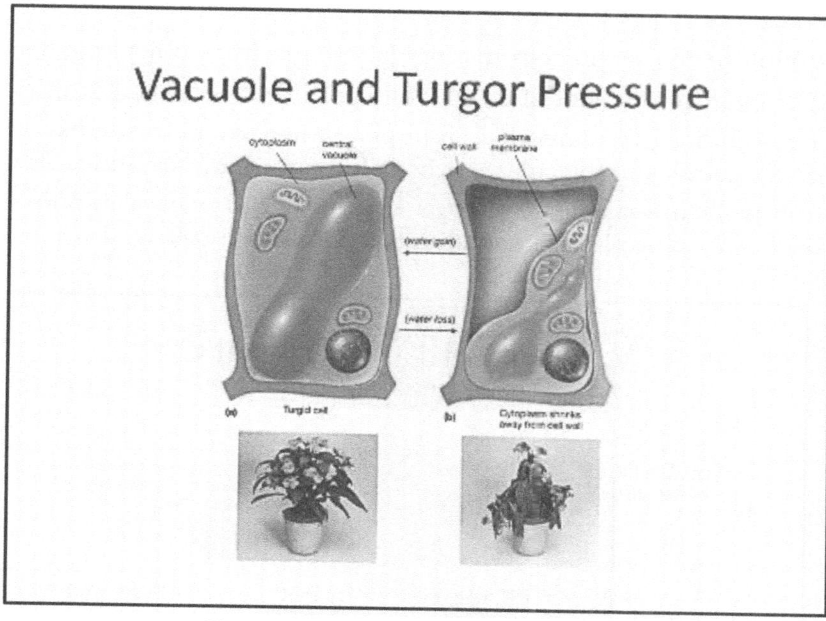

Fig. 5.19: Vacuole and Turgor Pressure
Source: based on review of literature

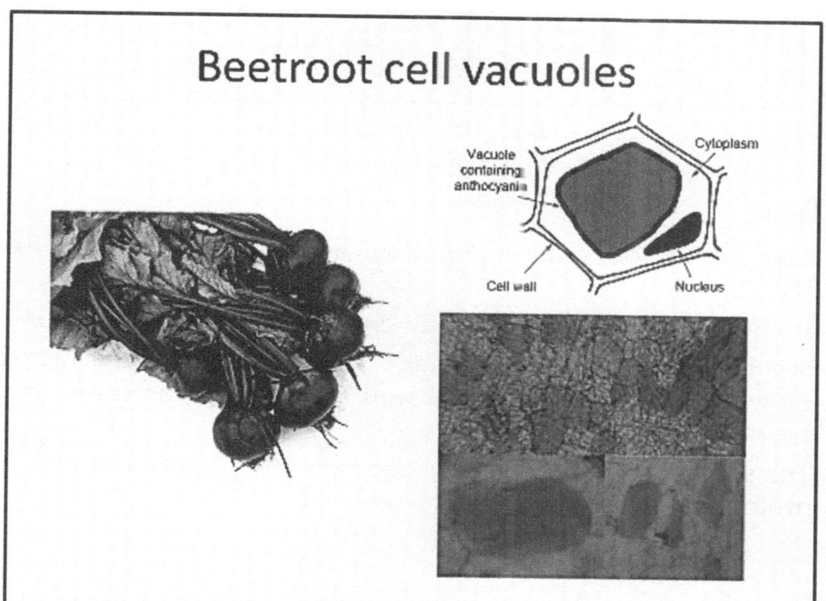

Fig. 5.20: Beetroot cell vacuoles
Source: based on review of literature

Cell Walls

- Cellulose cell walls help distinguish plants from other organisms
- The main component of a cell wall is cellulose arranged in microfibers
- The cellulose framework is interpenetrated by a cross-linked matrix of noncellulose molecules - primarily hemicelluloses and pectins
- Cell walls are layered - there is a primary cell wall, a middle lamella between two cells and sometimes a secondary cell wall

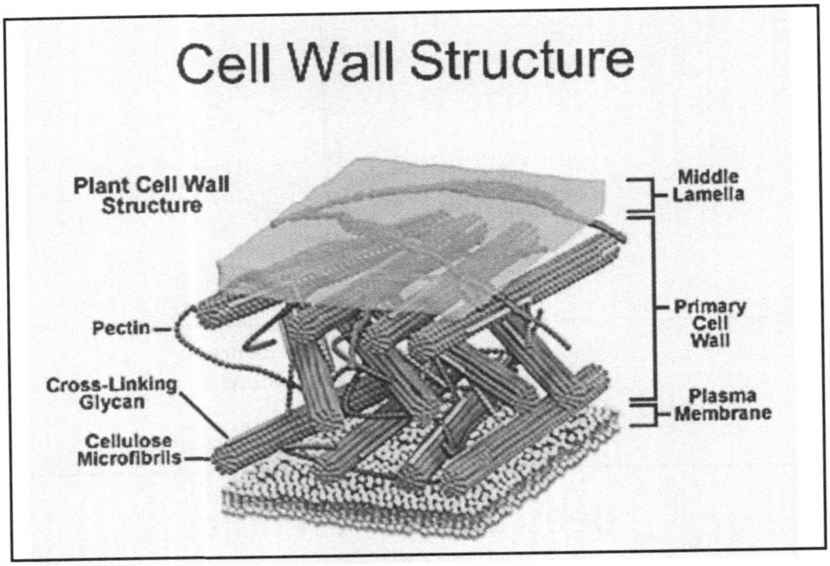

Fig. 5.21: Cell wall structure

Source: based on review of literature

Cell Walls

- The primary cell wall is deposited before and during growth of the cell
- Actively dividing cells typically only have primary cell walls
- Secondary cell walls are usually formed after the cell has stopped growing and the primary cell wall is no longer increasing in surface area
- The secondary cell wall forms between the primary cell wall and the protoplast

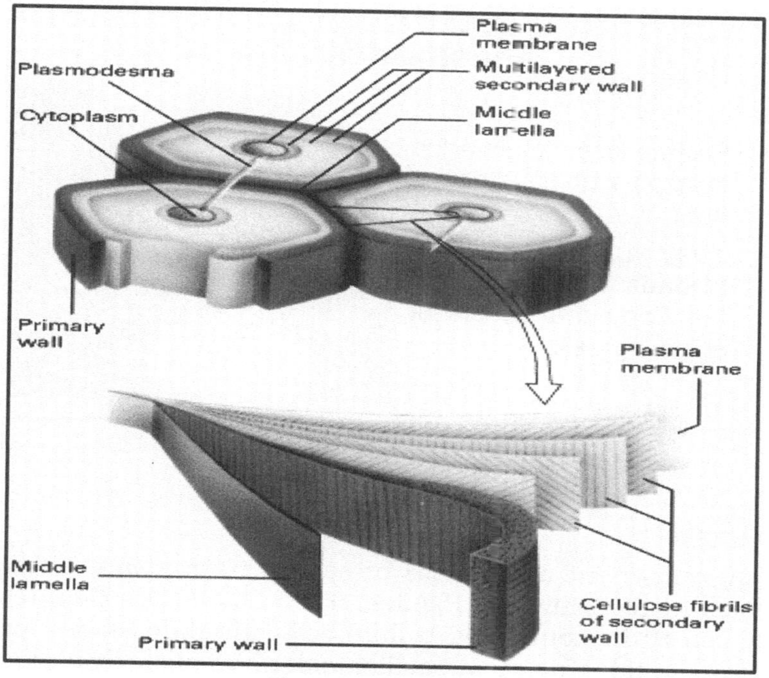

Fig. 5.22: Cell walls
Source: based on review of literature

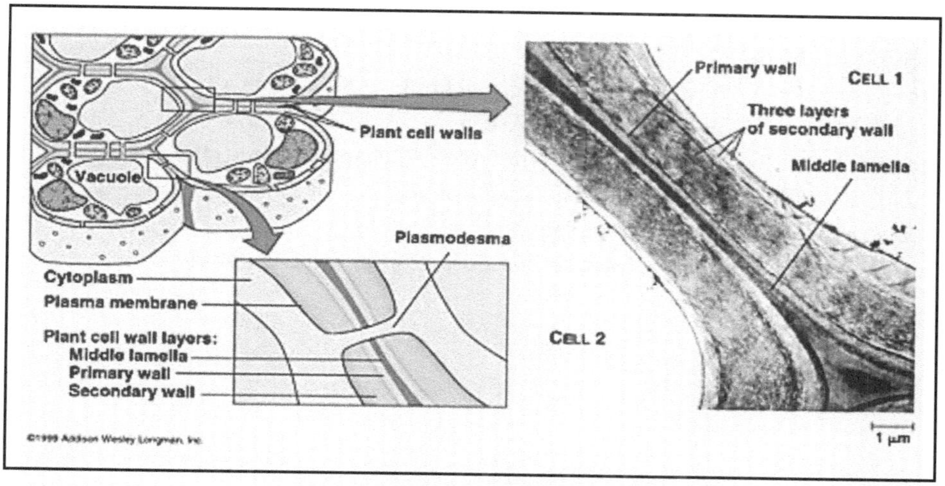

Fig. 5.23: Cell wall infrastructure
Source: based on review of literature

Plasmodesmata

- Plasmodesmata allow the transport of substances from one cell to the next
- They are cytoplasmic threads which connect the living protoplasts of adjoining cells

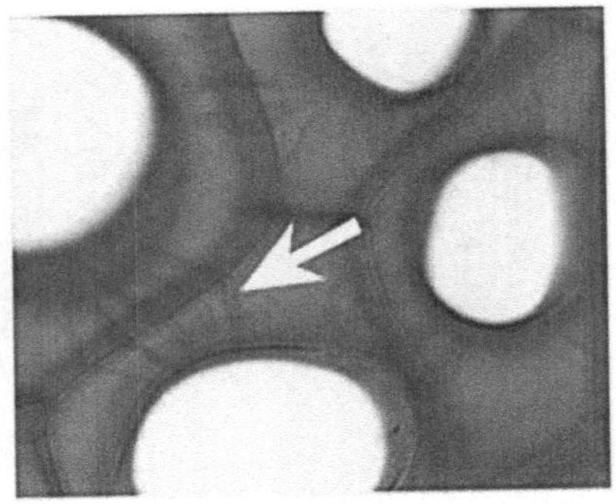

Fig. 5.24: Plasmodesmata

Source: based on review of literature

CONCLUSION

Plant cells are eukaryotic cells present in green plants, photosynthetic eukaryotes of the kingdom Plantae. Their distinctive features include primary cell walls containing cellulose, hemicelluloses and pectin, the presence of plastids with the capability to perform photosynthesis and store starch, a large vacuole that regulates turgor pressure, the absence of flagella or centrioles, except in the gametes, and a unique method of cell division involving the formation of a cell plate or phragmoplast that separates the new daughter cells.

REFERENCES

https://en.wikipedia.org/wiki/Plant_cell

www.plantcell.org/

https://micro.magnet.fsu.edu/cells/plantcell.html

https://byjus.com › Biology › Biology Article

https://courses.lumenlearning.com/wm-biology2/chapter/plant-cells/

https://www.thoughtco.com › ... › Science › Biology › Cell Biology

https://biologydictionary.net › Botany

https://www.nature.com/.../plant-cells-chloroplasts-and-cell-walls-14053956

Pages: 81-95

Current Research in Biochemistry and Molecular Biology
Edited by: **Dr. Prasann Kumar and Dr. Pawan Kumar 'Bharti'**
ISBN: 978-93-88854-33-7
Edition: **2020**
Published by: **Discovery Publishing House Pvt. Ltd., New Delhi (India)**

CHAPTER 6

Biochemistry of Methane Oxidation and Technologies for Mitigation

Anitha, T.*, V. Balamurugan[1], K.R.Vijayalatha[2] E. Parameswari[3] and V. Davamani[3]

INTRODUCTION

Agriculture releases to the atmosphere significant amounts of CO_2, CH_4 and N_2O. Carbon dioxide is released largely from microbial decay or burning of plant litter and soil organic matter. Methane is produced when organic materials decompose in oxygen-deprived conditions, notably from fermentative digestion by ruminant livestock, stored manures and rice grown under flooded conditions. Nitrous oxide is generated by the microbial transformation of nitrogen in soils and manures, and is often enhanced where available N exceeds plant requirements, especially under wet conditions. Agricultural greenhouse gas (GHG) fluxes are complex and heterogeneous, but the active management of agricultural systems offers possibilities for mitigation. Many of these mitigation opportunities use current technologies and can be implemented immediately.

Methane absorbs infrared terrestrial radiation, thus trapping heat and contributing to global warming . It also participates in chemical reactions leading to production of tropospheric ozone and stratospheric water vapour. On a mass basis, the global warming potential of methane on a 20-yr time horizon is estimated to be 62 times that of carbon dioxide

Horticultural College &Research Institute, Tamil Nadu Agricultural University, Coimbatore, (India)
[1] RVS College of Horticulture, Sempatti (India)
[2] Information & Training Centre, Tamil Nadu Agricultural University, Chennai (India)
[3] Dept.of Environmental Sciences, Tamil Nadu Agricultural University, Coimbatore (India)

(Houghton *et al.* 1994). Measurements made with ice cores indicate that the concentration of this gas has been increasing rapidly since the start of the industrial age, currently at a rate of about 0.8% annually. The current atmospheric methane concentration is about 1.7 parts per million (vol/vol). The major natural sources of methane include enteric fermentations in ruminants and some insects, and the anaerobic decomposition of organic matter in waterlogged soils (Lelieveld *et al.* 1993). Anthropogenic sources include coal burning, leakage of natural gas from pipelines, burning of plant matter in the tropics, and municipal landfill sites. Including landfill sites, soils are estimated to account for about 45% of global methane production. The major sink for atmospheric methane is through chemical reaction with hydroxyl radical in the troposphere. However, oxidation of methane by soils is also a significant sink, representing about 10% of the total sink. Methane oxidizing microorganisms at oxic/anoxic interfaces play an important role in limiting methane emissions from soils. The global methane budget has been reviewed extensively (Cicerone and Oremland 1988; Bouwman 1990; Khalil and Shearer 1993).

MICROBIAL PRODUCTION AND CONSUMPTION OF METHANE

Methane and the Carbon Cycle Methane plays a critical role in the global carbon cycle because it is at the bottom of the redox scale. The carbon atom found in the methane molecule is fully reduced; it cannot accept further electrons, but is a potential electron donor. At the other extreme of the redox scale lies carbon dioxide, the most oxidized form of carbon found in the cycle. Carbon dioxide cannot donate electrons but is a potential electron acceptor. Carbon dioxide generally enters the carbon cycle by photosynthetic fixation to glucose. Carbon atoms are then converted into the myriad of other organic molecules found in nature, varying in size and complexity but all intermediate in redox potential between carbon dioxide and methane. Carbon atoms are shuffled around these organic molecules by biosynthetic and biodegradative reactions which organisms use to acquire the energy and material needed to generate and maintain life. Under anaerobic conditions, organic materials may be converted by fermentative microbial communities to small organic acids, alcohols and methylated amines. Anaerobic fermentations can also produce substantial quantities of hydrogen gas. Under highly reducing conditions in the absence of other potential electron acceptors such as nitrate, sulfate, or ferric iron, these substrates can be converted to methane. Some methane-producing bacteria are able to produce methane by coupling the reduction of carbon dioxide to hydrogen oxidation, others by further reducing the small organic substrates fermentatively. In either case, methanogens are able to derive energy from this process.

Under anaerobic conditions methane is inherently stable and found in pockets of natural gas dating from geological times. However, in the presence of oxygen, methane is oxidized to carbon dioxide by bacteria which use this gas as the sole source of carbon and energy. The oxidation of methane to carbon dioxide completes the carbon cycle.

Methanogens Methane-producing bacteria (methanogens) are a phylogenetically diverse but coherent group within the domain Archaea (Woese *et al.*, 1990). This domain includes the most ancient of microorganisms including extreme halophiles and thermophiles. Methanogens have several features unique to them in the microbial world including novel cofactors involved in the methane-producing pathway, and unusual membrane lipids. Methanogens are extremely sensitive to oxygen and reactive oxygen species and methane production (methanogenesis) in soils only occurs under anaerobic, highly reducing conditions in the absence of nitrate, sulfate or ferric iron. Thus, anaerobic soils, such as rice paddies and wetlands, that are rich in organic matter, can be significant methane sources. Methanogens can also be found in a number of other environments including some marine sediments, the digestive tract of many animals and insects, and anaerobic sewage digesters. Most methanogens are mesophilic, able to function in a temperature range of about 20-40° C, but some thermophilic isolates have been described. Methanogens are very responsive to temperature changes within their functional temperature range. Most methanogens grow in the pH range of 6.0-8.0, but methanogenesis in peat suggests that some methanogens can function under acidic conditions. Methanogens are obligately methanogenic and cannot use other heterotrophic substrates. These organisms derive energy from the reduction of more oxidized forms of carbon atoms to methane. The substrate range available for methanogenesis is extremely narrow. Many methanogens reduce carbon dioxide using hydrogen as electron donor.

Some methanogens can metabolize small molecules such as methanol, acetate or methylamines, to form methane and carbon dioxide. Methanogens are metabolically highly specialized, difficult to isolate, and fastidious to work with. Some of them can fix dinitrogen gas. Methanogens complete the last step in the anaerobic decomposition of organic matter in most environments. Methane is the final product of a large and complex community of organisms breaking organic materials down into the simple methanogenic substrates. Because they are dependent on other organisms for provision of substrate and the establishment of reducing conditions, methanogens can only function as members of microbial communities. Methanogenesis is frequently rate-limited by the activities of the other members of the community, and particularly by how rapidly hydrogen or acetate is made available. The study of methanogen ecology is now facilitated by the recent development of methanogen-specific nucleic acid

(16s rRNA) probes which allow their study in situ without the need for isolation. The physiology, biochemistry, and ecology of methanogens has been recently reviewed (Garcia 1990; Boone 1991; Jones 1991).

METHANOTROPHS

Methane is the most reduced form of carbon and cannot itself be transformed without the provision of an electron acceptor. Methane-oxidizing bacteria (methanotrophs) are ubiquitous and can be isolated from all types of soils. Methanotrophs are phylogenetically and physiologically diverse. They are divided into two main groups based on a number of properties including the pathway of carbon assimilation, and structure of membrane lipids. Almost all isolates examined to date are obligately methanotrophic and cannot use other substrates. Some methanotrophs fix carbon dioxide autotrophically and some can fix dinitrogen gas under microaerobic conditions. As with the methanogens, methanotrophs prefer the pH in the neutral range, and are generally mesophilic and relatively unresponsive to temperature changes in their functional temperature range. Methane is oxidized to carbon dioxide through the sequential intermediates methanol, formaldehyde, and formate. Methanotrophs derive energy from this oxidation pathway and utilize the intermediate formaldehyde as their sole or primary carbon source for growth. Oxygen is required as a terminal electron acceptor, and is also an obligate reagent in the first reaction of the methane oxidation pathway catalyzed by the enzyme methane monooxygenase (MMO). This requirement for oxygen to "prime" the methane oxidation pathway explains why methane is not consumed under other redox conditions in the soil, for example under denitrifying conditions. Although circumstantial evidence suggests that anaerobic oxidation of methane can occur in aquatic sediments, no isolates have to date been described, and the general significance of this activity in soils is doubtful (Alperin and Reeburgh 1985; Oremland *et al*. 1987). The MMO enzyme also requires a reducing agent provided for by a cofactor which transfers electrons liberated by the oxidation reactions further on down the pathway. Thus, soils porous enough to permit the diffusion of atmospheric oxygen have the potential to consume methane. Methanotrophs resemble the chemoautotrophic ammonia-oxidizing nitrifiers in many respects. Ammonia is oxidized by MMO, analagous to the reaction catalyzed by ammonia monooxygenase (AMO), and AMO can likewise oxidize methane to methanol. The substrate range of these two enzymes is similar, both hydroxylating various aliphatic and aromatic molecules. They are sensitive to many of the same inhibitors. The half saturation constants (Km) for methane is much lower in the methanotrophs than nitrifiers, and that for ammonium much higher in the methanotrophs than the nitrifiers. The physiology, biochemistry and ecology of methane-oxidizing bacteria have been recently reviewed. Discrepancies between the kinetic properties of characterized methanotrophs and those of soils suggest that the methanotrophic isolates characterized to date are not the organisms that are consuming atmospheric methane concentrations in situ. Soils that are sinks for atmospheric methane have a much higher apparent affinity for this gas than do bacterial isolates or purified MMO. Typical Km for bacteria and environmental samples range from about 0.8 to 160 μM. The dissolved methane concentrations in oxic soil water exposed to atmospheric methane at ambient temperatures is in the low nanomolar range, three orders of magnitude lower than the Km. This concentration is apparently much too low to support the growth of methanotrophs.

PRODUCTION AND CONSUMPTION OF METHANE BY SOILS

The ability of soils to produce or consume methane is widespread geographically, and in terms of land use and ecological type. Soils ranging from tropical forest to tundra can consume atmospheric methane, typically at rates ranging from a few to a fraction of an mg m^{-2} d^{-1}. Wetlands and paddy soils can produce methane at rates ranging from several to a few hundred mg m^{-2} d^{-1}. Factors Affecting Methane Fluxes

(i) Soil moisture

Soils probably generally harbour both methanogens and methanotrophs. An agricultural Humisol incubated in the laboratory produced methane under anaerobic conditions, and consumed it under aerobic conditions. In many terrestrial and wetland ecosystems methanogens and methanotrophs are simultaneously active. Methane emission occurs when the activity of the methanogens dominates, and methane consumption is prominent when the methanotrophs dominate. The interplay of the two processes can be readily seen in peat bogs. As the methane diffuses upwards into the aerated soil layer overlying the water table, it is oxidized by methanotrophs. In vertically stratified systems such as peats, landfills, and aquatic sediments, methanotrophic activity is normally at its maximum at the oxic-anoxic interface where oxygen diffuses from above and methane from below (Amaral 1995). Methanogenesis in waterlogged bogs is highest near the peat surface where labile carbon from plant material is available (Moore and Knowles 1990). Methane diffuses about 104 times more rapidly in air than it does in water and methane diffusion can become rate limiting at higher moisture contents. There was a strong negative linear correlation between soil water content and methane uptake. Dunfield *et al.* (1995) measured methane uptake in laboratory incubations of an agricultural Humisol. In soil cores gradually saturated with water the rate of methane uptake did not decrease until the air filled porosity (φg) fell below 0.2-0.25 (120-130% water). It was suggested that, in this soil, the rate of methane uptake was limited by the rate of diffusion in the soil matrix air. The significance of diffusional limitation to the kinetics of methane oxidation will depend on soil structure and porosity, soil moisture, and the methane-oxidizing potential. Well-drained soils which would normally be expected to behave as weak methane sinks may produce methane in situ when saturated. An Orthic Black Chernozemic loam near Saskatoon Saskatchewan emitted methane at rates of 7.8-10.5 mg m–2 d–1 in the spring following snowmelt. Significant rates of methane emission only occurred at lower slope positions. Methane emissions of 0.64 mg m–2 d–1 also occurred in July following a heavy rainfall. In contrast, water can stimulate biological activity and methane oxidation in very dry soils. Rates of methane uptake by a desert soil increased by as much as 250% 48 h following precipitation.

(ii) Eh, pH, and temperature

The threshold for methanogenesis to be –150 mV with the rate increasing rapidly as Eh was further reduced. Laboratory incubations of fen and bog soil samples ranging in pH from 2.9 to 6.1 under either anaerobic or aerobic conditions showed no association between either methane production or consumption, and pH. Aerobic and anaerobic incubations of peat samples (native pH range 3.7-6.1) buffered to pH values ranging from 3.5 to 8.0 indicated that both methane consumption and production had pH optima generally 0.5-2 units above the native pH (Dunfield *et al.* 1993). Methane fluxes were similar in limed and control plots of a hardwood forest (Yavitt *et al.* 1995). Methanogenesis is much more responsive to temperature than is methane oxidation. Laboratory incubations of peat in the presence or absence of oxygen revealed a Q10 of 1.4-2.1 for methane consumption, and a Q10 of 5.6-16 for methane production in the temperature range of 0-35°C (Dunfield *et al.* 1993). The temperature optimum for both processes was about 25°C. The authors suggest that the difference in temperature sensitivity would result in methane emissions decreasing at lower temperatures. Since methane-consuming bacteria are relatively insensitive to temperature fluctuations in the mesophilic range, there is little diurnal variation in soils that are methane sinks. Methane consumption varied by only 10% over a 24-h period on a grassland site (Mosier *et al.* 1991).

METHANE TRANSPORT TO THE ATMOSPHERE

The mechanisms of methane transport from soils to the atmosphere are molecular diffusion, ebullition, and plant-mediated transport. These mechanisms will influence the spatial and temporal variability of methane emissions and consideration should be given to the likely dominant transport mechanism when developing sampling strategies. The significance of moisture content on limiting molecular diffusion has already been discussed. Plants in wetlands can attenuate methane emissions by transporting and releasing oxygen in the rootzone. Conversely, plants can enhance methane emissions by providing methanogenic substrates in root exudates, and serving as conduits for methane, bypassing aerobic methanotrophic zones through which the gas would otherwise diffuse and be consumed. More than 95% of the methane emitted from a rice paddy was transported through the plants, effectively bypassing the methane-oxidizing aerobic zone and reducing its efficacy as a methane "buffer" (Banker *et al.* 1995). Whiting and Chanton (1992) found a linear relationship between methane emission rates and aboveground biomass in Carex-dominated fens in northern Quebec and the Experimental Lakes Area of Ontario. A comparison of emission rates in plots following the removal of vegetation suggested that plant-dependent transport accounted for over 90% of the methane emitted. Furthermore, methane emissions also correlated strongly with daily net ecosystem exchange (i.e. the difference between CO2 fixed photosynthetically and that respired by the plants and soil) suggesting that carbon in root exudates was supporting methanogenesis. Episodic emission events can result in large temporal variability. For example, the lowering of the water table in the hot month of August resulted in the release of a large quantity of stored methane to the atmosphere representing 18-65% of the seasonal methane emission (Moore *et al.* 1990). Methane can accumulate in bogs in pockets and occlude water flow until released in episodic ebullition events (Reynolds *et al.* 1992; Buttler *et al.* 1994).

Anthropogenic Effects on Soil Methane Uptake and Production Changes in soil moisture due to flooding or drainage of land can drastically influence methane fluxes. Flooding of soil for rice cultivation or as a consequence of hydroelectric dam construction tend to increase methane emissions (Duchemin *et al.* 1995). In contrast, drainage of peatlands converts the site from a methane source to sink (Roulet *et al.* 1993). Cultivation of drained soils disrupts methane uptake. Methane consumption was lower in soil cropped to wheat than in a fallow field. Methane uptake in cultivated soils was one quarter that in corresponding semideciduous tropical forest soils in Panama. Methane uptake was undetectable in a cultivated soil adjacent to a mixed forest that was a weak methane sink in Ottawa, Canada. Soil compaction of a well-drained sandy loam by tractor traffic reduced methane uptake by one half, presumably because of more limited diffusion (Hansen *et al.* 1993). Some agrochemicals inhibit methane oxidation in laboratory incubations of pure cultures and soils. The significance of this in agricultural field soils is as yet unknown. Compounds which inhibit methanotrophs include the nitrification inhibitor nitrapyrin (N-serve) the herbicide bromoxynil, and insecticide methomyl (Topp 1993). Numerous studies have shown that the application of nitrogenous fertilizer to soils frequently inhibits methane oxidation (Hansen *et al.* 1993 and Dunfield *et al.* 1995). Two mechanisms to explain the inhibitory effect of nitrogen have been proposed based on what is known about the biochemistry of methane oxidation. Firstly, studies with pure cultures of methanotrophs show that ammonia is a competitive inhibitor of methane monooxygenase. MMO oxidizes ammonia to hydroxylamine, which is then oxidized to nitrite with the simultaneous production of nitrous oxide. Secondly, it has been proposed that the nitrite produced by methanotrophic nitrification is toxic to the organisms, possibly because it inhibits the last enzyme in the methane oxidation pathway, formate dehydrogenase. Inhibition of formate oxidation could starve MMO of the reductant required to metabolize methane. Estimates suggest that 25-40% of the carbon deposited in landfills can be converted to methane and carbon dioxide. The major source of methane is cellulose. Methane oxidation in the soil surface at the oxicanoxic interface can limit or prevent methane emissions.

TECHNIQUES FOR MEASURING METHANE FLUXES

Techniques for measuring methane fluxes at the earth's surface are chosen depending on the goal of the study and on the resources available. Important criteria for the choice include the spatial and temporal coverage required, and the expected magnitude of the methane flux. The accuracy of the methane flux measurement depends on the resolution and precision of the sensors used to determine the methane concentration, and on the sampling intensity. The fluxes from soil core incubations give a relative measure of gas exchange between treatments. Dunfield *et al.* (1995) showed a good agreement between soil core incubations and field flux measurements using chambers. Fick's first law of diffusion can be used to estimate methane fluxes using in situ determinations of the methane concentration in the soil profile (e.g. Whalen *et al.* 1992; Koschorreck and Conrad 1993; Dunfield *et al.* 1995). Gas samples from various soil depths are generally taken using a syringe attached to a thin probe and then subjected to gas chromatographic analysis. Sampling causes minimal soil disturbance. A major limitation of this method is that it requires the experimental determination of the soil diffusivity, a difficult undertaking, particularly at high soil moisture content. The soil diffusivity coefficient is often determined by tracer equilibration approach using argon. Another approach consists of placing closed chambers on the soil surface to isolate a fraction of a square metre of soil area. The flux is proportional to the initial rate of change of the methane concentration in the chamber headspace. Soil disturbance can be minimized by inserting a circular "collar" into the soil permanently at the start of the sampling season. To determine methane flux a cover is affixed to the top of the collar for the measuring period, usually less than one hour. The cover is usually equipped with a vent tube to maintain the chamber headspace at atmospheric pressure during the sampling period. In "static" chambers, headspace air samples are periodically withdrawn through a rubber septum built into the cover by means of a needle affixed to either 1-50 mL syringes or evacuated vials, and subjected to gas chromatographic analysis. The "dynamic" closed chamber system, a variant on the preceding setup, is preferred when a methane analyzer can be connected by a closed loop to the chamber. Air is circulated between the chamber and the analyzer, where the methane concentration is quantified continuously. Very small fluxes can be detected using the closed chamber technique by reducing the chamber height, and increasing the sampling period. The closed chamber technique requires little capital investment, but is labour intensive if some measure of spatial and temporal variability is required. More details on closed chamber measurements are presented in this issue by Rochette *et al.* (1997). Open chambers are rarely used for measuring methane fluxes because they require a much more sophisticated setup, including the analysis in real-time of methane concentration differences between the inlet and outlet of the chamber. These chambers have a continuous flow of air in the headspace, which should reach a steady-state methane concentration difference from ambient air. The flux is proportional to the difference of methane concentration between the outlet and the inlet of the chamber and the air flow rate through it divided by the soil area enclosed by the chamber. The chamber has to be designed for avoiding pressure differential, which would bias the flux. The main advantage of open chambers is the possibility to control ambient conditions such as methane concentration, humidity, temperature, etc. Micrometeorological techniques have several advantages compared with chamber techniques. The most important is that they integrate the methane fluxes over much larger areas and, with tower-based systems, continuous measurements can be made. The measurements are taken in situ without interfering significantly with the studied environment. The detection limit of the methane analyzers needs to be much higher than for chamber techniques. It requires fast-response sensors having a response time of about 0.1 s. This short time is required to measure the fluctuations of vertical wind velocity and methane concentration, which are averaged over time for tower-based systems, and over space for aircraft-based systems. Several recent comprehensive descriptions of the theoretical basis and precautions to be taken for performing micrometeorological measurements are available. In cases where a fast-response analyzer is not available, or when the analysis must be done after completing the sampling, the relaxed eddy-accumulation (REA) technique, offers an interesting alternative. REA has a theoretical basis similar to that of EC. Air is sampled using fast-response valves in two distinct reservoirs conditionnally to the vertical wind velocity (updraft or downdraft). The flux is then proportional to the difference of methane concentration between the upward and downward moving air accumulated over a given time or space. Preliminary measurements were carried out from a tower located in old black spruce site during the Boreal Ecosystems Atmosphere Study (BOREAS) with a conditional sampler developed by Pattey *et al.* (1993) and with an aircraft using the system developed by MacPherson and Desjardins (1991). The methodology for analysing the samples on site needed improvements to reduce the impact of ambient conditions on the measurement precision. The difference in methane concentration between updraft and downdraft samples is usually very small concentration difference of 1 ppbv is equivalent to a flux of about 10 mg m^{-2} d^{-1}. The best precision is achieved when the updraft and downdraft samples are analyzed using the same instrument. Gradient techniques are the traditional way of measuring fluxes with slow-response sensors. The methane flux is proportional to the mean vertical concentration gradient of methane multiplied by an eddy diffusivity coefficient, K. The coefficient K can be computed from several techniques such as the wind profile, the bowen-ratio/energy balance or the eddy-covariance technique. This technique cannot be used within canopie and precautions should also be taken for locating high enough the lowest level of vertical profile above rough surfaces such as forest stands (Cellier, 1986). It should be located above the canopy, at about 100 times the roughness length. This approach was used in northern wetlands where average methane fluxes were 15 mg m^{-2} d^{-1}, in rice paddies for mean emissions about 500 mg m^{-2} d^{-1} and also during BOREAS by several teams. Recently, fast-response closed-path analyzers based on absorption of a specific infrared laser line by methane molecules have been developed. The laser intensity absorption follows the Beer-Lambert law of attenuation and is a function of the absorption cross section, the path length and of the concentration of methane molecules. In the tunable diode laser trace gas analyzer (TGAS) developed by the University of Guelph and commercialized by Campbell Scientific, the laser beam absorption is measured simultaneously in a 155-cm-long sample cell, and in a 5-cmlong reference cell filled with 2% methane in nitrogen maintained at about 8 kPa. The number of molecules in the sample cell is equal to the known number of molecules in the reference cell multiplied by the ratio of path-lengths between the reference and sample cell, and multiplied by the ratio of the wavelength integrated absorbance between the sample and the reference cell. Both cells are maintained at low pressure to limit pressure broadening of the methane absorption line. With such TDL, high-resolution measurements can be obtained. For example, the mean root square error of the TGAS was 0.1 ppbv for measuring 30-min averaged methane gradients (Simpson, 1993). The operating temperature of the TGAS diode laser is in the range of 90 K, which is maintained with liquid nitrogen. The tunable diode laser (TDL) developed by Unisearch (Hastie *et al.* 1983) uses a compressor to cool the diode laser rather than a liquid nitrogen cooled Dewar. Most TDLs are very sensitive to vibration. For ground-based operation, a vibrationfree environment can be relatively easily maintained, while for airborne operation the noise level is considerably higher. Only the NASA Electra aircraft equipped with a TDL having a 10-m folded optical path has reported methane fluxes measured by eddy-covariance (Ritter *et al.* 1992). However, most of the flux instrumented aircrafts would not be able to fly with such a big and heavy sensor. The closest alternative to EC for measuring turbulent methane flux in the mixed layer with an aircraft is to sample using the REA technique and analyze afterwards the air samples in differential mode using either a ground-based TDL or gas chromatograph fitted with a flame ionization detector (GC-FID). A GC-FID having a column with Pt catalyst to remove non-methane hydrocarbons by combustion has been described by Tohjima and Wakita (1994). It has a detection limit of 4 ppb and a response time of about 10 s. This GC-FID then can be used to measure successive series of samples of the concentrations associated with updrafts and downdrafts for computing the flux by REA. The detection limit should still be improved for measuring small fluxes of less than 40 mg m^{-2} d^{-1}.

SPATIAL AND TEMPORAL VARIABILITY OF METHANE FLUXES

The spatial variability of CH4 fluxes is usually very high. The coefficient of variation for tundra soil is typically 50 to 100% (Whalen and Reeburgh 1988). The spatial variability found in wetland methane emissions is apparently largely due to the effect of water table height. The rate was influenced heavily by the mean seasonal water table position. Roulet *et al.* (1993) compared peatlands that had been drained with undrained control sites near Cochrane in northern Ontario. They found that sites with water table levels lowered by as little as 10 cm below the level in control sites became methane sinks, whereas control sites were weak sources. The water table threshold below which the sites went from sources to sinks was between –0.25 and –0.3 m. The main effect of lowering the water table was to eliminate the subsurface methanogenic zone. Lessard *et al.* (1994) computed the number of measurements required to estimate methane uptake from a forest floor within 10% (α = 0.05) using the closed chamber method. For very small fluxes (–0.09 mg m–2 d–1), more than 1000 sites would have been required, while for uptake fluxes averaging at 0.58 mg m–2 d–1 (SD 0.19 mg m–2 d–1), 137 sites would have been needed. Such a high number of observations cannot realistically be done. The spatial variability of methane fluxes can perhaps be determined more easily using micrometeorological techniques. Edwards *et al.* (1995) did extensive methane flux measurements by the aerodynamic-gradient technique using a TDL from a tower located in the old aspen stand of the BOREAS southern site. The site was a heterogeneous mix of wet and dry areas. They found an upward flux of 2.07 ± 0.43 mg m^{-2} d^{-1} as seasonal average from data collected between mid-April to mid-September 1994. It had been expected that this boreal forest stand was a small sink rather than a source. From other measurements taken at different wet and dry sites around the tower, they generally found consumption at the dry sites and emissions at the wet ones i.e. between 9 and 86 mg m–2 d–1 at a beaver bond site (Edwards *et al.* 1995). As the exact values are not available yet (Edwards *et al.* 1995), speculation can only be made on what did happen during the spatial integration. If we consider that the tower-based flux system was integrating 95% of dry area having a mean consumption of 0.09 mg m–2 d–1 and 5% of wet area releasing an average methane flux of 43 mg m–2 d–1, we obtain their seasonal average value of 2.07 mg m–2 d–1. In this case the forest stand is no longer a sink but rather a small source of methane. This result illustrates the importance of the spatial integration and the uncertainties in the large scale integration estimates based on point-measurements. Therefore, forest sink estimates in global methane budgets are likely overestimated (Edwards, G.C. 1995, personal communication). Ritter *et al.* (1992) did a survey flight over Alaska's Yukon-Kuskokwim Delta, from which they were able to extrapolate a contour-plot of methane flux superimposed to the land cover types. It showed the kind of spatial flux variations that can be obtained at the regional scale. No uptake was observed during the freeze period (January to March) and maximum uptake between July to September coincided with warmer soil temperatures. The soil temperature effect on the methane flux was weaker when diffusion controlled the emissions. The two seasonal cycles he studied, exhibited a 6.5% difference, showing how similar they were. Variations in water table depth also contribute to the temporal variability of methane fluxes in wetlands. Throughout most of the year the peat swamp emitted methane. However, in late summer and the fall when the water table was at its lowest the site was a sink for atmospheric methane.

Gobal and Regional Estimates of Agricultural GHG Mitigation Potential

The per-area/per-animal values for mitigation potential for each climate region, were used to scale-up to regions and to the world by multiplying by the appropriate area under each climate in each region. The regions, climate zones within each region, areas of crop, crop mix and grassland in each climate zone in each region, area of cultivated organic soils within each climate zone in each region, the area of degraded land in each climate zone in each region and the total area of rice cultivation for each region were derived from the FAO Global Agro-Ecological Zones FAO Digital Soils Map of the World and FAO statistical databases as follows

Areas of each region: Area of each region in the FAO AEZ database

(a) *Areas of climate zones within each region.* Geographic information system (GIS) overlay of FAO AEZ regions with climate regions defined as follows: 'warm' for use with the mitigation factors is defined by

'tropical' and 'subtropical' categories of the thermal climate dataset and 'cool' is defined by the 'temperate' categories of the thermal climate dataset. Boreal climates were excluded as little agriculture takes place in these zones. 'Dry' climates are defined by areas with 'severe moisture constraints or moisture constraints' in the climate constraints dataset with all other areas defined as 'moist'. The GIS overlay gives the areas in region in the cool-dry, cool-moist, warm-dry and warm-moist climate categories used

(b) *Areas of crop, crop mix and grassland in each climate zone within each region in 2030*. The areas under these land uses in 2030 were projected by taking the proportional change in each area in 2030 in each region as projected by the IMAGE v. 2.2 model for the four IPCC Special Report on Emissions Scenarios (SRES) scenarios. The area defined as 'mixture including crops' was added 50:50 to 'crops' and 'grassland' areas from the 'dominant land cover' dataset of FAO AEZ. This proportional change was then applied to the current areas of crops and grassland areas using a GIS overlay of the regional and climate data described above. This was done to normalize the areas between IMAGE v. 2.2 and FAO AEZ, since differences in classification between the two schemes could lead to misleading changes in land use.

(c) *Areas of cultivated organic soils in each climate zone within each region*. GIS overlay of areas under crops of the dominant land cover dataset of FAO AEZ and the FAO soils database, with organic soils defined by soil carbon contents greater than 30 kg m^{-2} to 100 cm depth.

(d) *Area of degraded land in each climate zone within each region*. GIS overlay of areas under crops from the dominant land cover dataset of FAO AEZ with the 'severe fertility constraints' and 'unsuitable for agriculture' categories of the 'soil fertility constraints' dataset of the FAO AEZ database.

(e) *Areas of rice cultivation within each region in 2030*. The proportional changes in rice area for each region, as projected by the IMPACT model for 2020 (the closest year to 2030 for which data were available), were used to project changes in harvested rice area for each region using 2004 areas given in the FAOSTAT database.

REFERENCES

Amaral, J.A. and Knowles, R. 1995. Growth of Methanotrophs in Methane and Oxygen Counter Gradients. FEMS Microbiol. Letts. 126: 215-220.

Bartlett, K. and Harriss, R.C. 1993. Review and Assessment of Methane Emissions from Wetlands. Chemosphere 26: 272-276.

Boone, D.R. 1991. Ecology of Methanogenesis. Pages 57-70.

Bouwman, A.F. 1990. Soils and the Greenhouse Effect. John Wiley and Sons, Chichester, UK.

Cicerone, R.J. and Oremland, R.S. 1988. Biogeochemical Aspects of Atmospheric Methane. Global Biogeochem. Cycles 2: 299-327.

Hansen, S, Maehlum, J.E. and Bakken, R.R. 1993. N2O and CH4 Fluxes in Soil Influenced by Fertilization and Tractor Traffic. Soil Biol. Biochem. 25: 621-630.

Hastie, D.R., Mackay, G.I., Iguchi, T., Ridley, B.A. and Schiff, H.I. 1983. Tunable Diode Laser Systems for measuring Trace Gases in Tropospheric Air. Environ. Sci. Technol. 17: 352A-364.

Guelph, ON. Striegl, R.G., McConnaughey, T.A., Thorstenson, D.C., Weeks, E.P. and Woodward, J.C. 1992. Consumption of Atmospheric Methane by Desert Soils. Nature 357: 145-147.

Lelieveld, J., Crutzen, P.J. and Bruhl, C. 1993. Climate Effects of Atmospheric Methane. Chemosphere 26: 739-768.

Mancinelli, R.L. 1995. The Regulation of Methane Oxidation in Soil. Ann. Rev. Microbiol. 49: 581-605.

Moore, T.R. 1993. Methane Production and Consumption in Temperate and Subarctic Peat Soils — Response to Temperature and pH. Soil Biol. Biochem. 25: 321-326.

Moore, T.R. and Knowles, R. 1990. Methane Emissions from Fen, Bog and Swamp Peatlands in Quebec. Biogeochem. 11: 45-61.

Oremland, R.S., Miller, L.G. and Whitticar M.J. 1987. Sources and Flux of Natural Gases from Mono Lake, California. Geochim. Cosmichim. Acta. 51: 2915-2929.

Pherson, J.I. and Pattey, E. 1993. Measurements of Greenhouse Gas Fluxes using Air Craft and Tower-based Techniques. Pages 45-62.

Reynolds, W.D., Brown, D.A., Mathur, S.P. and Overend, R.P. 1992. Effect of *in-situ* Gas Accumulation on the Hydraulic Conductivity of Peat. Soil Sci. 153: 397-408.

Rochette, P., Topp, E., Pattey, E., Desjardins, R.L. and Beaumont, G. 1994. Methane and Carbon Dioxide Fluxes from Poorly Drained Adjacent Cultivated and Forest Sites. Can. J. Soil Sci. 74: 139-146.

Roulet, N. and Knowles, R. 1990. Spatial and Temporal Variations of Methane Flux from Subarctic/Northern Boreal Fens. Global Biogeochem. Cycles 4: 29-46.

Ritter, J.A., Barrick, J.D., Sachse, G.W., Gregory, G.L., Woerner, M.A., Watson, C.E., Hill, G.F. and Collins, J.E. 1992. Airborne Flux Measurements of Trace Species in an Arctic Boundary Layer. J. Geophys. Res. 95: 16601-16625.

Rochette, P., Ellert, B., Gregorich, E.G., Desjardins, R.L., Pattey, E., Lessard, R. and Johnson, B.G. 1997. Description of a Dynamic Closed Chamber for measuring Soil Respiration and its Comparison with other Techniques. Can. J. Soil Sci. 77: 195-203.

Roulet, N.T. and Savage, K. 1993. Micro Topography and Methane Flux in Boreal Peatlands, Northern Ontario, Canada. Can. J. Bot. 71: 1056-1063.

Roulet, N.T., Ash, R., Quinton, W. and Moore, T.R. 1993. Methane Flux from Drained Northern Peatlands: Effect of a Persistent Water Table Lowering on Flux. Global Biogeochem. Cycles 7: 749-769.

Seiler, W., Holzapfel-Pschorn, A., Conrad, R. and Scharffe, D. 1984. Methane Emission from Rice Paddies. J. Atmos. Chem. 1: 241-268.

Tohjima, Y. and Wakita, H. 1994. Development of a Continuous measurement System and Area Distribution of Methane in some Source Areas. Appl. Geochem. 9: 141-146.

Topp E. 1993. Effects of Selected Agrochemicals on Methane Oxidation by an Organic Agricultural Soil. Can. J. Soil Sci. 73: 287-91.

Topp, E. and Knowles, R. 1984. Effects of Nitrapyrin [2-chloro6-(trichloromethyl) pyridine] on the Obligate Methanotroph *Methylosinus trichosporium* OB3b. Appl. Environ. Microbiol. 47: 258-262.

Topp, E. and Hanson, R.S. 1991. Metabolism of Radioact.vely Important Trace Gases by Methane-oxidizing Bacteria. Pages 71-90.

Topp, E., Archambault, C. and Knowles, R. 1995. Effect of Nitrogen Fertilizers and Moisture Content on CH4 and N2O Fluxes in a Humisol: Measurements in the Field and intact Soil Cores. Biogeochemistry 29: 199-222.

Whalen, S.C. and Reeburgh, W.S. 1988. A Methane Flux Time Series for Tundra Environments. Global Biogeochem. Cycles 2: 399-409. Whalen, S.C.

Whiting, G.J. and Chanton, J.P. 1992. Plant-dependent CH4 Can. J. Soil. Sci. Downloaded from www.nrcresearchpress.com by 157.51.136.88 on 03/28/19 For Personal use only. 178 CANADIAN JOURNAL OF SOIL SCIENCE Emission in a Subarctic Canadian fen. Global Biogeochem. Cycles 6: 225-231.

Woese, C.R., Kandler, O. and Wheels, M.L. 1990. Towards a Natural System of Organisms: Proposal for the Domains Archaea, Bacteria, and Eucarya. Proc. Natl. Acad. Sci. USA 87: 4576-4579.

Yavitt, J.B., Fahey, T.J. and Simmons, J.A. 1995. Methane and Carbon Dioxide Dynamics in a Northern Hardwood Ecosystem. Soil Sci. Soc. Am. J. 59: 796-804.

Pages: 96-110

Current Research in Biochemistry and Molecular Biology
Edited by: Dr. Prasann Kumar and Dr. Pawan Kumar 'Bharti'
ISBN: 978-93-88854-33-7
Edition: **2020**
Published by: **Discovery Publishing House Pvt. Ltd., New Delhi (India)**

CHAPTER
7

Isolation of Secondary Metabolites
An Overview

Prasann Kumar[1,2*], Shipa Rani Dey[1]

GRAPHICAL ABSTRACT

Keywords: Isolation, Products, Metabolites, Overview

INTRODUCTION

What is natural products?
Products of natural origins
Natural products include:

[1]Department of Agronomy, School of Agriculture, Lovely Professional University, Jalandhar - 144 411 (Punjab) (India)
[2] Divison of Research and Development, Lovely Professional University, Jalandhar - 144 411 (Punjab) (India)

1. An entire organism (e.g., a plant, an animal, or a microorganism)
2. Part of an organism (e.g., leaves or flowers of a plant, an isolated animal organ)
3. An extract of an organism or part of an organism, and exudates
4. Pure compounds (e.g., alkaloids, coumarins, flavonoids, glycosides, lignans, steroids, sugars, terpenoids, etc.) isolated from plants, animals, or microorganisms

- Natural products refers to secondary metabolites, small molecules (molwt<2000 amu) produced by an organism that are not strictly necessary for the survival of the organism.
- Concepts of secondary metabolism include products of overflow metabolism as a result of nutrient limitation, shunt metabolism produced during idiophase, defense mechanism regulator molecules, etc.
- Natural products can be from any terrestrial or marine source: plants (e.g., paclitaxel [Taxol] from *Taxusbrevifolia*), animals (e.g., vitamins A and D from cod liver oil), or microorganisms (e.g., doxorubicin from *Streptomyces peucetius*).

Strategies for research in the area of natural products

1. Older strategies:
   (a) Focus on chemistry of compounds, but not on activity
   (b) Straightforward isolation and identification of compounds followed by biological activity testing (mainly *in vivo*)
   (c) Chemotaxonomic investigation
   (d) Selection of organisms primarily based on ethnopharmacological information, folkloric reputations, or traditional uses
2. Modern strategies:
   (a) Bioassay-guided isolation and identification of active compounds (lead) (mainly *in vitro*)
   (b) Production of natural products libraries
   (c) Production of active compounds in cell or tissue culture, genetic manipulation, natural combinatorial chemistry, and so on.
   (d) More focused on bioactivity.
   (e) Introduction of the concepts of dereplication, chemical fingerprinting, and metabolomics.
   (f) Selection of organisms based on ethnopharmacological information, folkloric reputations, or traditional uses, and also those randomly selected.

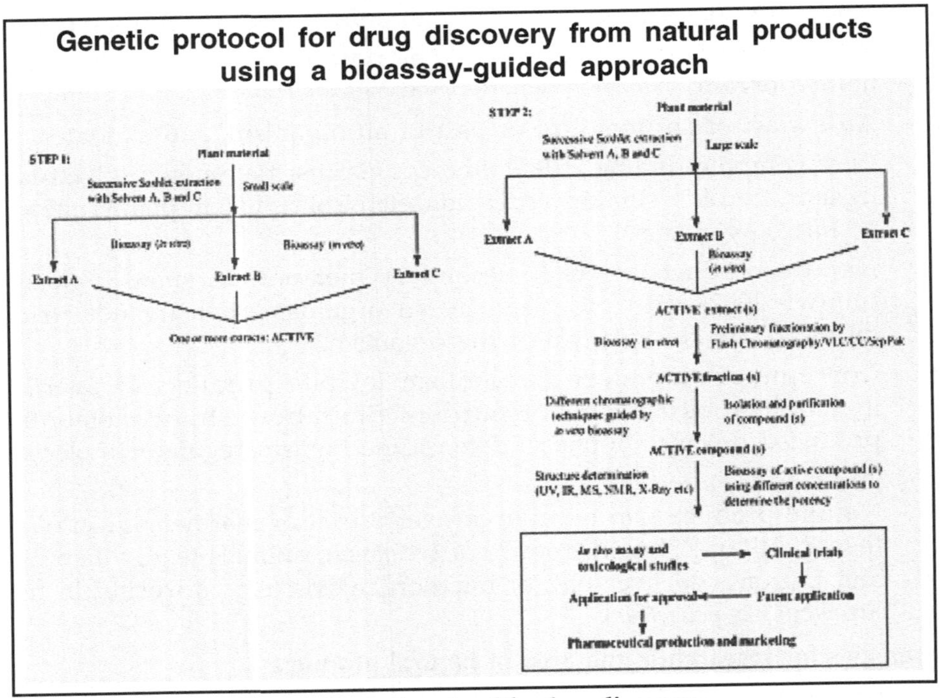

Fig. 7.1: General protocol for drug discovery

Source: based on review of literature

Natural products can contribute to the search for new drugs in three different ways by:

1. Acting as new drugs that can be used in an unmodified state (e.g., vincristine from *Catharanthusroseus*).
2. Providing chemical "building blocks" used to synthesize more complex molecules (e.g., diosgenin from *Dioscorea floribunda* for the synthesis of oral contraceptives).
3. Indicating new modes of pharmacological action that allow complete synthesis of novel analogs (e.g., synthetic analogs of penicillin from *Penicilliumnotatum*).

Natural products as one of the major sources of new drugs, because:

1. Incomparable structural diversity
2. Many of them are relatively small (<2000 Da)
3. "drug-like" properties (i.e., they can be absorbed and metabolized).

Extraction

- Process of isolation of soluble material from an insoluble residue (liquid or solid) by treatment with a solvent (menstruum) on the basis of the physical nature of crude drug (liquid or solid) to be extracted.

- Extraction process may be liquid—liquid extraction or solid—liquid extraction.
- Extraction process is controlled by mass transfer (transfer of mass of soluble material from a solid to a fluid.

Important factors which influence the effectiveness of extraction

- Temperature
- Particle size of the grounded drug
- Polarity of the solvent

Choice of extraction procedure depends on:

- Nature of the source material and
- Compounds to be isolated

Prior to choosing a method, it is necessary to establish the target of the extraction

Targets of extraction

1. An unknown bioactive compound
2. A known compound present in an organism
3. A group of compounds within an organism that are structurally related
4. All secondary metabolites produced by one natural source that are not produced by a different "control" source, e.g., two species of the same genus or the same species grown under different conditions.
5. Identification of all secondary metabolites present in an organism for chemical fingerprinting or metabolomics study.

It is also necessary to seek answers to the questions related to the expected outcome of the extraction. These include:

1. Is this extraction for purifying a sufficient amount of a compound to characterize it partially or fully? What is the required level of purity?
2. Is this to provide enough material for confirmation or denial of a proposed structure of a previously isolated compound?
3. Is this to produce as much material as possible so that it can be used for further studies, e.g., clinical trial?

Typical extraction process for plant materials

1. Drying and grinding of plant material or homogenizing fresh plant parts (leaves, flowers, etc.) or maceration of total plant parts with a solvent
2. Choice of solvents (Eluotropic series)
   (a) Polar extraction: water, methanol, ethanol, acetone
   (b) Medium polarity extraction: ethyl acetate (EtOAc), chloroform, dichloromethane
   (c) Non-polar extraction: cyclohexane, *n*-hexane, pet-ether, and so on.

Non-polar extraction is done for defatting

3. Choice of extraction method
    (a) Maceration
    (b) Percolation
    (c) Boiling
    (d) Soxhlet
    (e) Supercritical fluid extraction
    (f) Sublimation

Steam distillation

- Maceration is carried out at room temperature by soaking the material with the solvent with eventual stirring. It has the advantage of moderate extraction conditions but suffers from high solvent consumption, long extraction times and low extraction yields.
- Extraction yield is improved by percolation, i.e. packing the pre-soaked plant material in a container which allows the constantly controlled removal of the extract via a valve at the bottom and adding fresh solvent from the top.
- Soxhlet extraction is a popular method for extraction due to its reduced solvent consumption; however, thermo-labile compounds might be degraded during the extraction process.

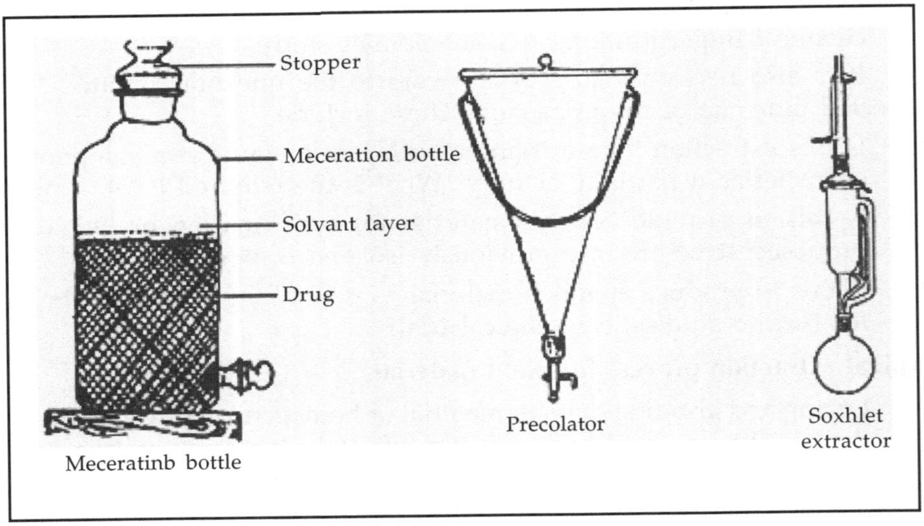

Fig. 7.2: Process of extraction
Source: based on review of literature

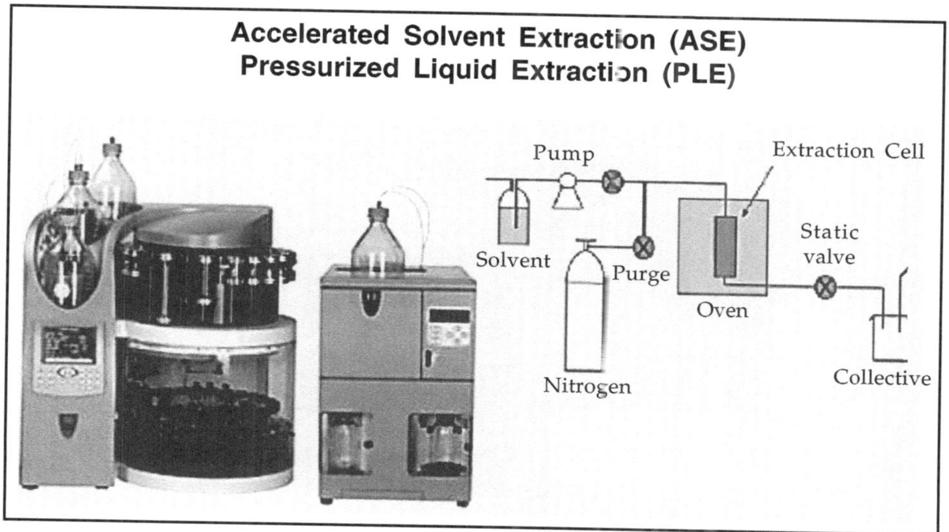

Fig. 7.3: ASE and PLE
Source: based on review of literature

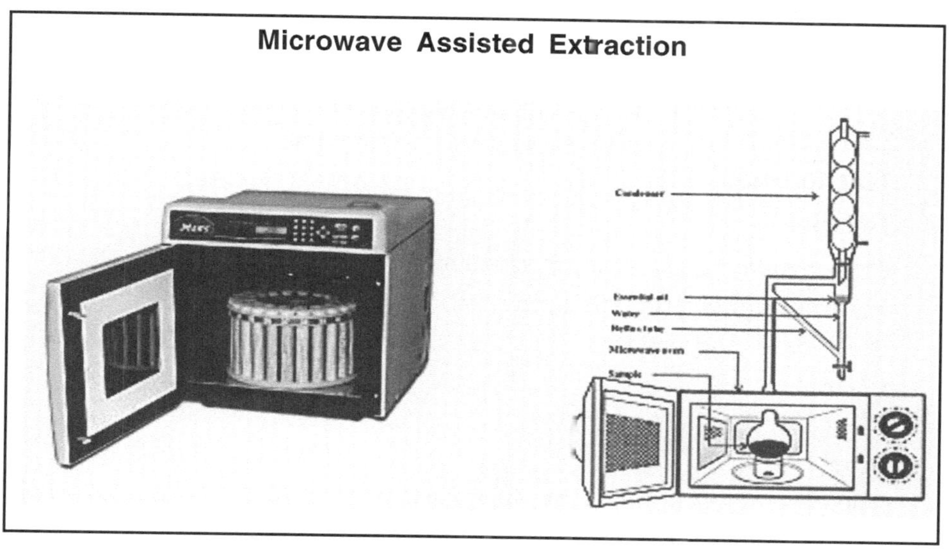

Fig. 7.4: Microwave Assisted Extraction
Source: based on review of literature

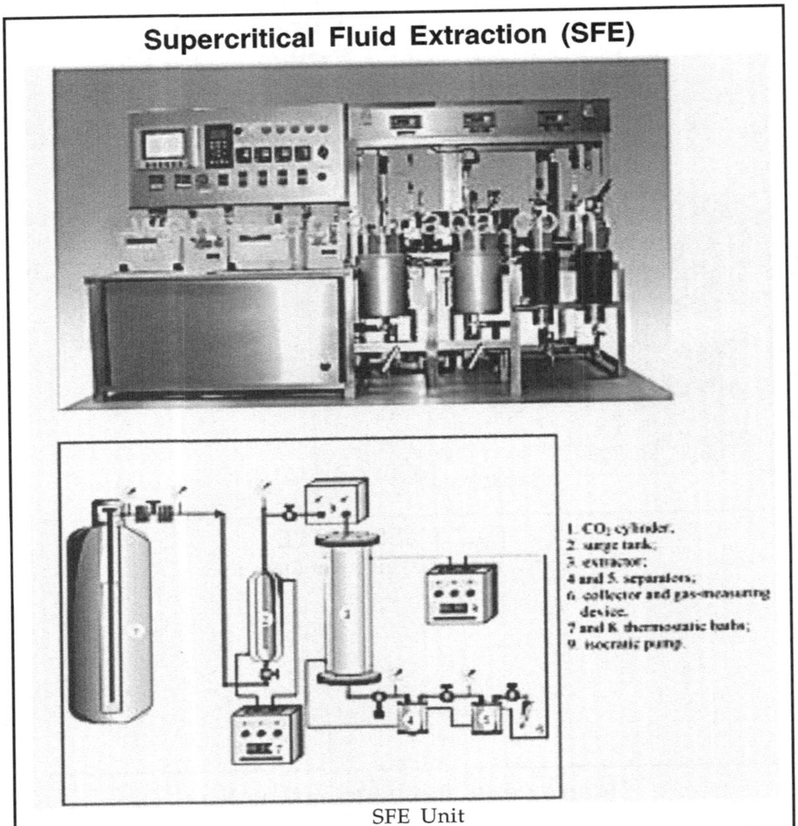

SFE Unit

Fig. 7.5: Supercritical Fluid Extraction (SFE)

Source: based on review of literature

- **Fractionation**
- **Isolation**
- *Determination of physical properties of the extracts*

1. Hydrophobicity or hydrophilicity
2. Acid–base properties
3. Charge
4. Heat stability
5. Size
6. The chromatographic techniques used in the isolation of various types of natural products.

A. Classical or older chromatographic techniques

1. Thin-layer chromatography (TLC)
2. Preparative thin-layer chromatography (PTLC)

3. Open-column chromatography (CC)
4. Flash chromatography (FC)

B. Modern chromatographic techniques

1. High-performance thin-layer chromatography (HPTLC)
2. Multiflash chromatography (e.g., Biotage)
3. Vacuum liquid chromatography (VLC)
4. Solid-phase extraction (e.g., Sep-Pak)
5. Droplet countercurrent chromatography (DCCC)
6. High-performance liquid chromatography (HPLC)
7. Hyphenated techniques (e.g., HPLC-PDA, LC-MS, LC-NMR, LC-MS-NMR)

Isolation of microbial natural products: spirocardins A and B from *Nocardia sp*

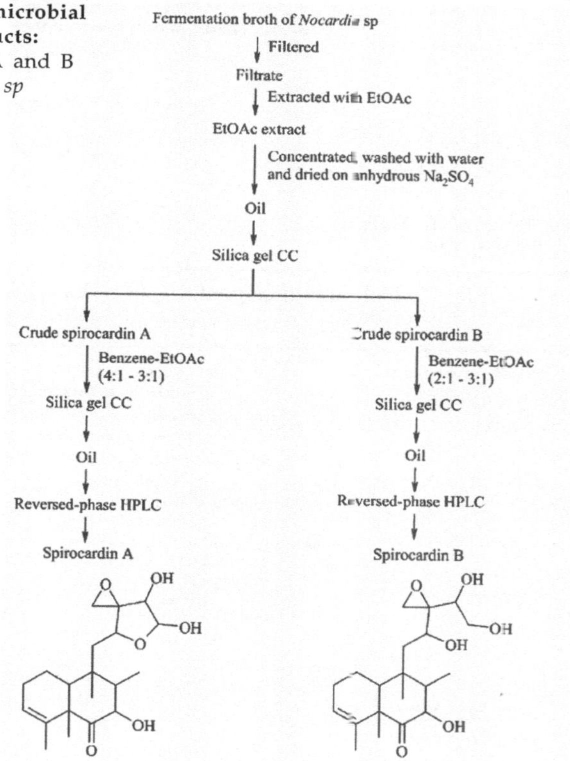

Nakajima, M. *et. al.* J. Antibiot, 1989, 42, 1741-1748

Fig. 7.6: Isolation of microbial natural products (spirocardins A and B from *Nocardia* sp.)

Source: based on review of literature

Isolation of microbial natural products: cispentacin from *Bacillus cerneus*

Fermentation broth of *Bacillus cereus*

↓ **Centrifuged**

Supernatant

↓ **Extracted with EtOAc**

Cation exchangte column (Amberlite IR 120)

↓

Cation exchange column (Dowex 50WX8)

↓

Activated charcoal CC

↓

Cispentacin (96% pure)

↓

Recrystallization
(from acetone-ethanol-water)

↓

Cispentacin (>98% pure)

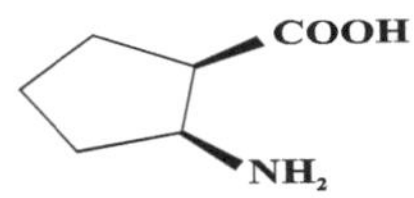

Konishi, N. *et. al.* J. Antibiot, 1989, 42, 1749-1755

Fig. 7.7: Isolation of cispentacin from Bacillus cereus)

Source: based on review of literature

Isolation of microbial natural products: phytoecdysteroids from *Limnanthes douglasii*

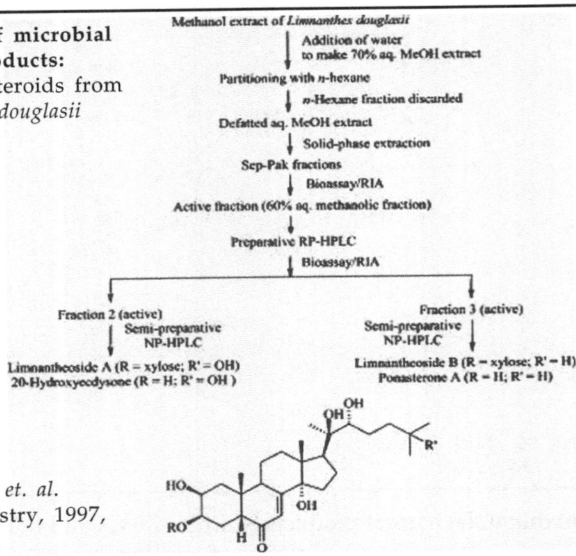

Saiket, S.D. *et. al.* Phytochemistry, 1997, 44, 513-521

Fig. 7.8: Isolation of phytoecdysteroids from *Limnanthes douglasii*

Source: based on review of literature

Isolation of microbial natural products:
moschatine, a steroidal glycoside from *Centaurea moschata*

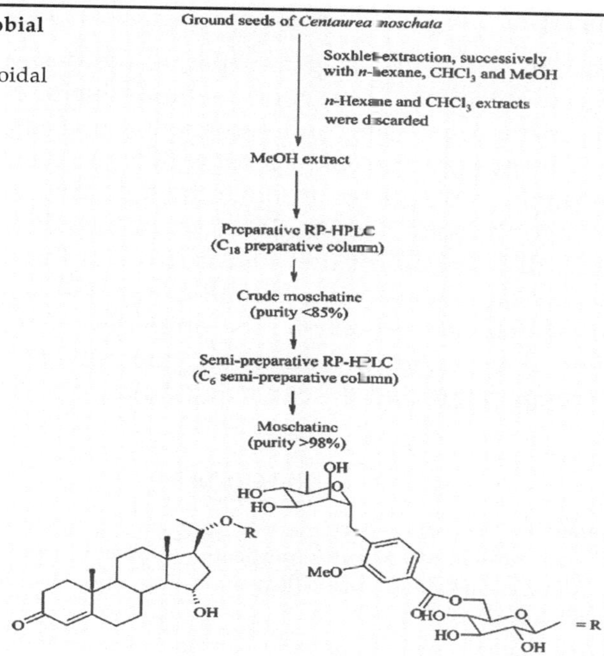

Saiket, S.D. *et. al.* Phytochemistry, 1998, 48, 1039-1043

Fig. 7.9: Isolation of microbial natural product
Source: based on review of literature

Isolation of microbial natural products:
saponius from *S. salzmanniana*

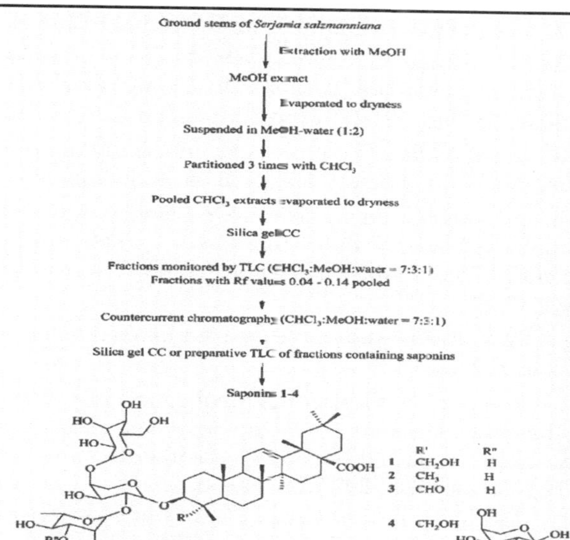

Ekabo, O.A. *et al.*, J. Nat, Prod. 1996, 59, 431-435

Fig. 7.10: Isolation of saponins
Source: based on review of literature

CONCLUSION

Extraction is the first step to separate the desired natural products from the raw materials. Extraction methods include solvent extraction, distillation method, pressing and sublimation according to the extraction principle. Solvent extraction is the most widely used method. The extraction of natural products progresses through the following stages: (1) the solvent penetrates into the solid matrix; (2) the solute dissolves in the solvents; (3) the solute is diffused out of the solid matrix; (4) the extracted solutes are collected. Any factor enhancing the diffusivity and solubility in the above steps will facilitate the extraction. The properties of the extraction solvent, the particle size of the raw materials, the solvent-to-solid ration, the extraction temperature and the extraction duration will affect the extraction efficiency.

REFERENCES

Albuquerque BR, Prieto MA, Barreiro MF, Rodrigues A, Curran TP, Barros L, Ferreira ICFR. Catechin-based Extract Optimization Obtained from *Arbutus unedo* L. fruits using Maceration/Microwave/Ultrasound Extraction Techniques. Ind Crops Prod. 2017; 95: 404-15.

Atanasov AG, Waltenberger B, Pferschy-Wenzig EM, Linder T, Wawrosch C, Uhrin P, Temml V, Wang L, Schwaiger S, Heiss EH, *et al*. Discovery and resupply of Pharmacologically Active Plant-derived Natural Products: A Review. Biotechnol Adv. 2015; 33(8): 1582-614.

Barba FJ, Zhu Z, Koubaa M, Sant'Ana AS, Orlien V. Green Alternative methods for the Extraction of Antioxidant Bioactive Compounds from Winery Wastes and by-products: A Review. Trends Food Sci Technol. 2016; 49: 96-109.

Benmoussa H, Farhat A, Romdhane M, Bouajila J. Enhanced Solvent-free Microwave Extraction of *Foeniculumvulgare* Mill. Essential Oil Seeds using Double Walled Reactor. Arabian J Chem 2016. (in press https://doi.org/10.1016/j.arabjc.2016.02.010).

Bouras M, Grimi N, Bals O, Vorobiev E. Impact of Pulsed Electric Fields on Polyphenols Extraction from Norway Spruce Bark. Ind Crops Prod. 2016; 80: 50-8.

Cai J, Cheng L, Zhao J, Fu Q, Jin Y, Ke Y, Liang X. A Novel Polyacrylamide-based Silica Stationary Phase for the Separation of Carbohydrates using Alcohols as the Weak Eluent in Hydrophilic Interaction Liquid Chromatography. J Chromatogr A. 2017; 1524: 153-9.

Chemat F, Cravotto G. Microwave-assisted Extraction for Bioactive Compounds. Boston: Springer; 2013.

Chemat F, Rombaut N, Sicaire AG, Meullemiestre A, Fabiano-Tixier AS, Abert-Vian M. Ultrasound Assisted Extraction of Food and Natural Products. Mechanisms, Techniques, Combinations, Protocols and Applications. A Review. UltrasonSonochem. 2017; 34: 540-60.

Chen H. Optimization of Microwave-assisted Extraction of Resveratrol from *Polygonumcuspidatum* siebet Zucc by Orthogonal Experiment. Nat Prod Indian J. 2013; 9(4): 138-42.

Chen H, Zhou X, Zhang J. Optimization of Enzyme Assisted Extraction of Polysaccharides from *Astragalusmembranaceus*. CarbohydrPolym. 2014; 111: 567-75.

Chin FS, Chong KP, Markus A, Wong NK. Tea Polyphenols and Alkaloids Content using Soxhlet and Direct Extraction methods. World J Agric Sci. 2013; 9(3): 266-70.

Conde-Hernández LA, Espinosa-Victoria JR, Trejo A, Guerrero-Beltrán JÁ. CO_2-supercritical Extraction, Hydrodistillation and Steam Distillation of Essential Oil of Rosemary (Rosmarinusofficinalis). J Food Eng. 2017; 200: 81-6.

Cragg GM, Newman DJ. Natural Products: A Continuing Source of Novel Drug Leads. Biochim Biophys Acta Gen Subj. 2013; 1830(6): 3670-95.

Cujic N, avikin K, Jankovic T, Pljevljakuic D, Zdunic G, Ibric S. Optimization of Polyphenols Extraction from Dried Chokeberry using Maceration as Traditional Technique. Food Chem. 2016; 194: 135-42.

Dang YY, Li XC, Zhang QW, Li SP, Wang YT. Preparative Isolation and Purification of Six Volatile Compounds from Essential Oil of *Curcuma wenyujin* using High-performance Centrifugal Partition Chromatography. J Sep Sci. 2010; 33(11): 1658-64.

Du G, Zhao HY, Song YL, Zhang QW, Wang YT. Rapid Simultaneous Determination of Isoflavones in Radix Puerariae using High-performance Liquid Chromatography-triple Quadrupole mass Spectrometry with Novel Shell-type Column. J Sep Sci. 2011; 34(19): 2576-85.

Falcão MA, Scopel R, Almeida RN, do Espirito Santo AT, Franceschini G, Garcez JJ, Vargas RMF, Cassel E. Supercritical Fluid Extraction of Vinblastine from *Catharanthusroseus*. J Supercrit Fluids. 2017; 129: 9-15.

Fu M, Zhang L, Han J, Li J. Optimization of the Technology of Ethanol Extraction for Goupi Patch by Orthogonal Design Test. ZhongguoYaoshi (Wuhan, China). 2008; 11(1): 75-6.

Gao M, Wang XL, Gu M, Su ZG, Wang Y, Janson JC. Separation of Polyphenols using Porous Polyamide Resin and Assessment of Mechanism of Retention. J Sep Sci. 2011; 34(15): 1853-8.

Gao X, Han J, Dai H, Xiang L. Study on Optimizing the Technological Condition of Ethanol Percolating Extraction for Goupi Patch. ZhongguoYaoshi. 2009; 12(10): 1395– Li SL, Lai SF, Song JZ, Qiao CF, Liu X, Zhou Y, Cai H, Cai BC, Xu HX. Decocting-induced Chemical Transformations and Global Quality of Du–Shen–Tang, the Decoction of Ginseng Evaluated by UPLC-Q-TOF-MS/MS based Chemical Profiling Approach. J Pharm Biomed Anal. 2010; 53(4): 946-57.19. Zhang WL, Chen JP, Lam KYC, Zhan JYX, Yao P, Dong TTX, TsimKWK. Hydrolysis of Glycosidic Flavonoids during the Preparation of DangguiBuxue Tang: An Outcome of Moderate Boiling of Chinese Herbal Mixture. Evid Based Complement Altern Med. 2014;2014:608721.

Gizir AM, Turker N, Artuvan E. Pressurized Acidified Water Extraction of Black Carrot [*Daucuscarota* ssp. Sativus var. atrorubensAlef.] anthocyanins. Eur Food Res Technol. 2008; 226(3): 363-70.

Guzlek H, Wood PL, Janaway L. Performance Comparison using the GUESS Mixture to Evaluate Counter-current Chromatography Instruments. J Chromatogr A. 2009; 1216(19): 4181-6.

Hou J, He S, Ling M, Li W, Dong R, Pan Y, Zheng Y. A method of Extracting Ginsenosides from Panax Ginseng by Pulsed Electric Field. J Sep Sci. 2010; 33(17-18): 2707-13.

Jin S, Yang M, Kong Y, Yao X, Wei Z, Zu Y, Fu Y. Microwave-assisted Extraction of Flavonoids from *Cajanuscajan* leaves. Zhongcaoyao. 2011; 42(11): 2235-9.

Jovanovic AA, Đordevic VB, Zduniæ GM, Pljevljakuic DS, avikin KP, Godevac DM, Bugarski BM. Optimization of the Extraction Process of Polyphenols from *Thymus serpyllum* L. herb using Maceration, Heat- and Ultrasound-assisted Techniques. Sep Purif Technol. 2017; 179: 369-80.

Kongkiatpaiboon S, Gritsanapan W. Optimized Extraction for High yield of Insecticidal Didehydrostemofoline Alkaloid in *Stemonacollinsiae* Root Extracts. Ind Crops Prod. 2013; 41: 371-4.

Lemos LMS, Oliveira RB, Sampaio BL, Ccana-Ccapatinta GV, Da Costa FB, Martins DTO. Brasiliensic and Isobrasiliensic Acids: Isolation from *Calophyllumbrasiliense* Cambess. and anti-*Helicobacter pylori* Activity. Nat Prod Res. 2016; 30(23): 2720-5.

Li J, Chase HA. Development of Adsorptive (non-ionic) Macroporous Resins and their uses in the Purification of Pharmacologically-active Natural Products from Plant Sources. Nat Prod Rep. 2010; 27(10): 1493-510.

Li J, Gao R, Zhao D, Huang X, Chen Y, Gan F, Liu H, Yang G. Separation and Preparation of Xanthochymol and Guttiferone E by High Performance Liquid Chromatography and High Speed Counter-current Chromatography Combined with Silver Nitrate Coordination Reaction. J Chromatogr A. 2017; 1511: 143-8.

Lim KH, Kam TS. Methyl Chanofruticosinate Alkaloids from *Kopsiaarborea*. Phytochemistry. 2008; 69(2): 558-61.

Li P, Xu G, Li SP, Wang YT, Fan TP, Zhao QS, Zhang QW. Optimizing Ultra Performance Liquid Chromatographic Analysis of 10 Diterpenoid Compounds in Salvia Miltiorrhiza using Central Composite Design. J Agric Food Chem. 2008; 56(4): 1164-71.

Li P, Yin ZQ, Li SL, Huang XJ, Ye WC, Zhang QW. Simultaneous Determination of Wight Flavonoids and Pogostone in Pogostemoncablin by High Performance Liquid Chromatography. J Liq Chromatogr Relat Technol. 2014; 37(12): 1771-84.

Liu T, Sui X, Li L, Zhang J, Liang X, Li W, Zhang H, Fu S. Application of Ionic Liquids based Enzyme-assisted Extraction of Chlorogenic Acid from *Eucommiaulmoides* Leaves. Anal ChimActa. 2016; 903: 91-9.

Liu W, Zhang S, Zu YG, Fu YJ, Ma W, Zhang DY, Kong Y, Li XJ. Preliminary Enrichment and Separation of Genistein and Apigenin from Extracts of Pigeon Pea Roots by Macroporous Resins. Bioresour Technol. 2010; 101(12): 4667-75.

Lv GP, Huang WH, Yang FQ, Li J, Li SP. Pressurized Liquid Extraction and GC–MS Analysis for Simultaneous Determination of Seven Components in Cinnamomum cassia and the Effect of Sample Preparation. J Sep Sci. 2010; 33(15): 2341-8.

Mander LN, Williams CM. Chromatography with Silver Nitrate: Part 2. Tetrahedron. 2016; 72(9): 1133-50.

Meng FC, Wu QS, Wang R, Li SP, Lin LG, Zhang QW, Chen P. A Novel Strategy for Quantitative Analysis of Major Ginsenosides in Panacis Japonici Rhizoma with a Standardized Reference Fraction. Molecules. 2017; 22(12): 2067.

Newman DJ, Cragg GM. Natural Products as Sources of New Drugs from 1981 to 2014. J Nat Prod. 2016;79(3): 629-61.

Newman DJ, Cragg GM. Natural Products as Sources of New Drugs over the 30 Years from 1981 to 2010. J Nat Prod. 2012; 75(3): 311-35.

Skalicka-Wozniak K, Walasek M, Ludwiczuk A, Glowniak K. Isolation of Terpenoids from *Pimpinellaanisum* Essential Oil by High-performance Counter-current Chromatography. J Sep Sci. 2013; 36(16): 2611-4.

Strati IF, Gogou E, Oreopoulou V. Enzyme and High Pressure Assisted Extraction of Carotenoids from Tomato Waste. Food Bioprod Process. 2015; 94: 668-74.

Tang Q, Wang Y, Chen M, Zhang Q, Fan C, Huang X, Li Y, Ye W. Application of High-speed Counter-current Chromatography Preparative Separation of Flavone C-glycosides from *Lophatherum gracile*. Sep Sci Technol. 2013; 48(12): 1906-12.

Vergara-Salinas JR, Bulnes P, Zuniga MC, Perez-Jimenez J, Torres JL, Mateos-Martin ML, Agosin E, Perez-Correa JR. Effect of Pressurized Hot Water Extraction on Antioxidants from Grape Pomace before and after Enological Fermentation. J Agric Food Chem. 2013; 61(28): 6929-36.

Verma SK, Goswami P, Verma RS, Padalia RC, Chauhan A, Singh VR, Darokar MP. Chemical Composition and Antimicrobial Activity of Bergamot-mint (*Menthacitrata* Ehrh.) Essential Oils Isolated from the Herbage and Aqueous Distillate using Different methods. Ind Crops Prod. 2016; 91: 152-60.

Vinatoru M, Mason TJ, Calinescu I. Ultrasonically Assisted Extraction (UAE) and Microwave assisted Extraction (MAE) of Functional Compounds from Plant Materials. TrAC Trends Anal Chem. 2017; 97: 159-78.

Wan JB, Li P, Yang RL, Zhang QW, Wang YT. Separation and Purification of 5 Saponins from *Panaxnotoginseng* by Preparative High-performance Liquid Chromatography. J Liq Chromatogr Relat Technol. 2013; 36(3): 406-17.

Wan JB, Zhang QW, Ye WC, Wang YT. Quantification and Separation of Protopanaxatriol and Protopanaxadiol type Saponins from *Panaxnotoginseng* with Macroporous Resins. Sep Purif Technol. 2008; 60(2): 198-205.

Wang X, Zhao C, Peng X, Tang K. Adsorption Mechanism of Methoxy Modified macro porous cross linked resin for phenol. Huaxue Xuebao. 2010; 68(5): 453-6.

Wei Q, Yang GW, Wang XJ, Hu XX, Chen L. The Study on Optimization of Soxhlet Extraction Process for Ursolic Acid from Cynomorium. ShipinYanjiu Yu Kaifa. 2013; 34(7): 85-8.

Wang Y, Du Al, Du Aq. Isolation of Zingiberene from Ginger Oleoresin by Silver Ion Coordination Column Chromatography. Jingxi Huagong. 2012; 29(7): 672-7.

WHO traditional medicine strategy: 2014-2023; 2013. http://www.who.int/medicines/publications/traditional/trm_strategy14_23/en/. Accessed 29 Dec 2017.

Wu QS, Wang CM, Lu JJ, Lin LG, Chen P, Zhang QW. Simultaneous Determination of Six Saponins in Panacis Japonici Rhizoma using Quantitative Analysis of Multi-components with Single-marker method. Curr Pharm Anal. 2017; 13(3): 289-95.

Xiong W, Chen X, Lv G, Hu D, Zhao J, Li S. Optimization of Microwave-assisted Extraction of Bioactive Alkaloids from Lotus Plumule using Response Surface Methodology. J Pharm Anal. 2016; 6(6): 382-8.

Xs Li, Bq Jiang, Jl Mao. Study on Extraction Separation and Pharmacodynamics of Effective Components in Kuqingcha. Guangxi Yixue. 2013; 35(5): 637-8.

Xu FX, Yuan C, Wan JB, Yan R, Hu H, Li SP, Zhang QW. A Novel Strategy for Rapid Quantification of 20(S)-protopanaxatriol and 20(S)-protopanaxadiolsaponins in *Panaxnotoginseng, P. ginseng* and *P. quinquefolium* Nat Prod Res. 2015; 29(1): 46-52.

Xu J, Zhao WM, Qian ZM, Guan J, Li SP. Fast Determination of Five Components of Coumarin, Alkaloids and Bibenzyls in Dendrobium spp. using Pressurized Liquid Extraction and Ultra-performance Liquid Chromatography. J Sep Sci. 2010; 33(11): 1580-6.

Yahya A, Yunus RM. Influence of Sample Preparation and Extraction Time on Chemical Composition of Steam Distillation Derived Patchouli Oil. Proc Eng. 2013; 53: 1-6.

Yan Y, Wang X, Liu Y, Xiang J, Wang X, Zhang H, Yao Y, Liu R, Zou X, Huang J, *et al.* Combined Urea-thin Layer Chromatography and Silver Nitrate-thin Layer Chromatography for Micro Separation and Determination of Hard-to-detect Branched Chain Fatty Acids in Natural Lipids. J Chromatogr A. 2015; 1425: 293-301.

Yang X, Wang J, Luo J, Kong L. One-step Large-scale Preparative Isolation of Isoquinoline Alkaloids from Rhizoma coptidis chinensis by Polyamide Column Chromatography and their Quantitative Structure-retention Relationship Analysis. J Liq Chromatogr Relat Technol. 2012; 35(13): 1842-52.

Yi Y, Zhang QW, Li SL, Wang Y, Ye WC, Zhao J, Wang YT. Simultaneous Quantification of Major Flavonoids in "Bawanghua", the Edible Flower of Hylocereusundatus using Pressurised Liquid Extraction and High Performance Liquid Chromatography. Food Chem. 2012; 135(2): 528-33.

Zhang H, Wang W, Fu ZM, Han CC, Song Y. Study on Comparison of Extracting Fucoxanthin from *Undariapinnatifida* with Percolation Extraction and Refluxing methods. Zhongguo Shipin Tianjiaji. 2014; 9: 91-5.

Zhang Q, Wang CH, Ma YM, Zhu EY, Wang ZT. UPLC-ESI/MS Determination of 17 Active Constituents in 2 Categorized Formulas of Traditional Chinese Medicine, Sanhuang XiexinTang and Fuzi Xiexin Tang: Application in Comparing the Differences in Decoctions and Macerations. Biomed Chromatogr. 2013; 27(8): 1079-88.

Zhang L. Comparison of Extraction Effect of Active Ingredients in Traditional Chinese Medicine Compound Preparation with Two Different method. Heilongjiang XumuShouyi. 2013; 9: 132-3.

Zhang Wm, ZhaiYc, Yang Hj, Zhang Rg, Hao J, Han Jq, Zhang Yl. Silver Nitrate-silica gel Column Chromatography Purification Linolenic Acid in Walnut Oil. Shipin Gongye Keji. 2015; 36(10): 229-32.

Zhou YQ, Wang CM, Wang RB, Lin LG, Yin ZQ, Hu H, Yang Q, Zhang QW. Preparative Separation of Four Sesquiterpenoids from *Curcuma longa* by High-speed Counter-current Chromatography. Sep Sci Technol. 2017; 52(3): 497-503.

Zhang Z, Su Z. Catalysis Mechanism to Increase Taxol from the Extract of *Taxus cuspidate* Callus Cultures with Alumina Chromatography. Sep Sci Technol. 2002; 37(3): 733-43.

Zhang Z, Su Z. Recovery of Taxol from the Extract of *Taxuscuspidata* callus Cultures with Al2O3 Chromatography. J Liq Chromatogr Relat Technol. 2000; 23(17): 2683-93.

Zhou YQ, Zhang QW, Li SL, Yin ZQ, Zhang XQ, Ye WC. Quality Evaluation of Semen Oroxyli through Simultaneous Quantification of 13 Components by High Performance Liquid Chromatography. Curr Pharm Anal. 2012; 8(2): 206-13.

ZtGuo, Xq Luo, Jp Liang, Yang Z, Ai X. Comparative Study on Extraction of Febrifugine from Traditional Chinese Medicine Dichroafebrifuga by Reflux method and Ultrasonic method. Shizhen Guoyi Guoyao. 2015; 26(6): 1532-3.

Pages: 111-117

Current Research in Biochemistry and Molecular Biology
Edited by: Dr. Prasann Kumar and Dr. Pawan Kumar 'Bharti'
ISBN: 978-93-88854-33-7
Edition: **2020**
Published by: **Discovery Publishing House Pvt. Ltd., New Delhi (India)**

CHAPTER
8

Silage and Hay

Prasann Kumar[1,2*], Johnson Yumnam[1]

GRAPHICAL ABSTRACT

Keywords: Agriculture, Crop, Hay, Silage

INTRODUCTION

- Grass conservation involves the restricting of bacterial growth and other organisms, which would otherwise cause spoilage.

[1] Department of Agronomy, School of Agriculture, Lovely Professional University, Jalandhar - 144 411 (Punjab) (India)
[2] Divison of Research and Development, Lovely Professional University, Jalandhar - 144 411 (Punjab) (India)

- This can be achieved by two contrasting methods:
  1. Controlled Fermentation – reducing the pH (acidity) of the grass to a level where growth of bacteria is inhibited.
  2. Dehydration– removing the level of water to inhibit microbial activity.
  3. Silage is produced by controlled fermentation above while hay involves dehydration.
  4. Silage is much more independent of the weather, so this makes it a better system for Indian farmers.
  5. Grass can be cut for silage in May, when the grass is at its most digestible (highest DMD).
  6. Hay cannot, however, as long periods of good weather cannot be expected.
- Hay is allowed to grow to a more mature stage and is generally cut in June where the weather is warmer.
- Therefore hay has less food value than silage.
- Silage making is more expensive though but the product is of a higher quality.
- Silage accounts for nearly 70% of conserved grassland now (45% in the 1970's).

Silage Making

Biochemical Processes

- When grass is cut and placed in a heap, respiration continues to occur.
- Respiration is the burning of Carbohydrates in Oxygen to CO_2 and Water.
- This means that food value is being removed.
- Therefore if grass is to be conserved after cutting, all air should be removed as to conserve the food value.
- When oxygen is removed the environment is said to be anaerobic.
- In anaerobic conditions, bacteria present cause fermentation to occur.
- Fermentation is the natural conversion of Carbohydrates to Organic Acids by bacteria.
- The presence of acids lower the pH of the environment, to a level where the bacterial growth and actions cease.
- At this stage the environment is said to be "pickled" or preserved.
- The bacteria that is involved depends on the amount of Carbohydrates present.

- The bacteria that is involved depends on the amount of Carbohydrates present.
- High levels of Carbohydrates allow *Lactobacillus* and *Streptococcus* to produce Lactic Acid in the silage.
- Low levels of carbohydrates allow *Clostridium* to produce Butyric Acid.
- Lactic acid silage is palatable, highly nutritious and can be stored safely for years.
- Butyric acid silage is unpalatable to stock, less nutritious and may only last a couple of months.
- Therefore to encourage good quality silage i.e. High Levels of Carbohydrates and the production of Lactic Acid the farmer should:
  1. Do not cut the crop immediately after rain – *wet grass reduces carbohydrate concentration.*
  2. Allow the crop wilt for a period of time after cutting (1 – 2 days) –*increases Carbohydrate concentration.*
  3. Using precision chop harvesting equipment – *makes the crop more accessible to bacterial activity.*
  4. Using a Carbohydrate rich additive (e.g. Molasses) -*to increase the chance of lactic acid production.*
  5. Most silage is cut from fields of permanent grassland.
  6. Two cuts are normal, the first in Mid – May, and the second around July 1st.
  7. The grass should be cut when the plant is at its height of digestibility.
  8. This is at the "heading out" stage, where the DMD is 75 – 80%.
  9. The Heading Out stage is the stage where half of the crop are showing their seed-heads
- Silage may be stored in Round bales or in Silage Pits. The procedures for cutting and storage of silage for pits are shown below:
  1. The Grass is cut, macerated and blow into a silage trailer using a forage harvester.
  2. The silage is transported to the pit and heaped out.
  3. An additive is used either at the pit or at harvesting (If necessary)
  4. Matted lumps of grass are removed and the surface levelled to remove air pockets.
  5. The grass is rolled repeatedly with the tractor to remove trapped air.
  6. When sufficiently rolled the pit is covered with at least two layers of heavy-duty polythene.

7. This should be further covered with tyres, manure or ground limestone, to further seal the pit.
8. The edges of the plastic sheets are pulled tightly and further sealed.
9. This should be repeated 2-3 times as the silage subsides over the coming weeks.

Round Bale Silage

- For round bale silage, the steps are similar but the following is required.
  1. The grass is cut and allowed to wilt for 1-2 days.
  2. An additive is added if required.
  3. A specialised machine is used to collect the grass and make it into round bales by covering it with plastic to remove any air.
  4. The plastic may be a wrap or a large bag.

Silage Additives

- Additives are used when the level of carbohydrates is expected to be low.
- There are two types of additive for silage:
  - Stimulants – are sources of sugars, which ensure lactic acid production. Molasses is a stimulant.
  - Inhibitors – These are acids which are used to lower the pH more quickly than is natural. E.g. Sulphuric Acid.
- Molasses is used commonly by farmers on a small scale, while acids are used by contractors and large farmers.

Silage Storage

- Silage is more commonly stored in pits or clamps.
- These may be wedge clamps or run over clamps.
- These should be located on concrete as to aid in the collection of effluent.
- Clamps/pits are most effective with sidewalls.
- Without walls there is a risk of tractor accidents and of the escape of effluent

Advantages of Round Bales

- The use of round bales in Ireland has advantages but is generally more expensive than clamp silage.
- Round bale silage is used in the following situations:

1. Silage can be made on soft, wet land where conventional equipment would be unsuitable.
2. Round bales can be made on rented land or land far away from the farm.
3. It can be used where the silage is to be sold.

Silage Effluent

- Silage effluent is a by-product of the fermentation process.
- It is acidic, rich in nutrients and appears about 2-3 weeks after the silage is sealed.
- Effluent has a high BOD (Biological Oxygen Demand), which means it can be a serious pollutant.
- Effluent should be collected and stored in underground pits, before being diluted and disposed of safely.
- The amount of effluent depends on the moisture content of the silage.
- After rain, huge amounts of effluent are produced.
- After wilting, very little effluent is produced.
- Therefore, wilting not only ensures high carbohydrate levels but also reduces the level of effluent.

Table 8.1: % moisture at ensiling

% Moisture at ensiling	Amount of Effluent Produced per tonne of Silage, L
85-90	400
80-84	150
75-79	60
< 75	0

Source: based on review of literature

Hay Making

- Baled hay is a clean, conveniently handled winter feed with very little waste.
- It is very useful for farmers who wish to feed out-wintered animals, which are far away from the farmyard.
- It does however have very little feeding value and can prove difficult to harvest correctly.
- The following are the principles for "Good hay making":
- Cut as close to June 1 as possible to ensure suitable drying conditions – the field should be closed to grazing from mid – April.
- Cut when dry weather is expected – a hot dry (and windy) spell is required to bring the moisture content to 20%.

- Use the correct machinery – Unrestricted access to these 3 pieces of machinery are essential:
- Rotary Mower – can cut 1.2-1.5 Ha/hour.
- Power Driven Rotary Tedder – Can work at high speeds to separate and shake out the grass – leaves a "fluffed up" swath of grass which dries quickly.
- Baler – essential as the dried hay must be baled and stored as quickly as possible (from 10 Ha/Day)

Good Silage Quality

Parameter	Correct Value	Factors Affecting
pH	4	Procedures at ensiling (e.g. additive etc)
DM (%)	20	Stage of growth at cutting, wetness
DMD (%)	70 – 75	Stage of growth, wetness and procedures at ensiling.
Protein	14 - 16	Stage of growth at cutting.

Fig. 8.1: Good silage quality
Source: based on review of literature

Fig. 8.2: Hay Making
Source: based on review of literature

- Cut the crop in manageable amounts – only cut enough that can (a) be tedded twice in a day and (b) baled in a day.
- Ted frequently to ensure fast drying – This reduces risk of weather damage and also maintains high Carbo levels – reduce roughness of tedding, as the grass gets drier.
- Bale and remove to storage without delay – Tedder is used to align into rows before baling – bales should be removed as soon as possible.

CONCLUSION

Silage underneath plastic sheeting is held down by scrap tires. Silage is fermented, high-moisture stored fodder which can be fed to cattle, sheep and other such ruminants (cud-chewing animals) or used as a biofuel feedstock for anaerobic digesters. It is fermented and stored in a process called *ensilage, ensiling* or *silaging,* and is usually made from grass crops, including maize, sorghum or other cereals, using the entire green plant (not just the grain). Concrete beneath the silage prevents fermented juice from leaching out. Silage is made by one or more of the following methods: placing cut green vegetation in a silo or pit; piling the vegetation in a large heap and compressing it down so as to purge as much oxygen as possible, then covering it with a plastic sheet; or by wrapping large round bales tightly in plastic film.Silage can be made from many field crops, and special terms may be used depending on type: *oatlage* for oats, *haylage* for alfalfa; but see below for the different British use of the term *haylage.*

REFERENCES

https://en.wikipedia.org/wiki/Silage

https://www.dpi.nsw.gov.au/agriculture/pastures-and-rangelands/silage

https://www.horsejournals.com/horse-care/.../hay-haylage-and-silage-whats-difference

krishisewa.com/articles/livestock/163-hay-silage.html

https://pediaa.com › Science › Biology

https://hayandforage.com/article-permalink-355.html

https://grdc.com.au/resources-and-publications/all-publications/.../hay-and-silage

Pages: 118-133

Current Research in Biochemistry and Molecular Biology
Edited by: Dr. Prasann Kumar and Dr. Pawan Kumar 'Bharti'
ISBN: 978-93-88854-33-7
Edition: 2020
Published by: Discovery Publishing House Pvt. Ltd., New Delhi (India)

CHAPTER 9

Polyamine and Plant Stress Response *Potential Mechanism of Action*

Prasann Kumar[1,2*], Shipa Rani Dey[1]

GRAPHICAL ABSTRACT

Keywords: Abiotic, Botany, Crop, Plant, Stress

INTRODUCTION

A compatible solute in higher plants Metabolic acclimation via the accumulation of compatible solutes is regarded as a basic strategy for the

[1] Department of Agronomy, School of Agriculture, Lovely Professional University, Jalandhar - 144 411 (Punjab) (India)
[2] Divison of Research and Development, Lovely Professional University, Jalandhar - 144 411 (Punjab) (India)

protection and survival of plants under abiotic stresses (Bartels and Hussain, 2008). Compatible solutes are non-toxic molecules, serve in turgor maintenance and stabilize macromolecular structures under unfavorable conditions (Bohnert and Shen, 1999; McNeil *et al.*, 1999). The notion of PA as a compatible solute is controversial in plants and needs further investigation. However, stress-induced PAs are often considered better stabilizers than others for protecting biomolecules and preventing the membrane system from denaturing under stress conditions (Liu *et al.*, 2007). PAs share many properties, for example, hydropholicity, protection of macromolecules, active oxygen scavengers, maintenance of cellular pH etc., which are close to those of proline and other compatible solutes (Liu *et al.*, 2007; Wi *et al.*, 2006). However, the concentration of stress-induced PAs is lower than proline and other solutes, which suggests that PAs are not compatible solutes. On the other hand, Duhazé *et al.* (2002) showed that products of PA catabolism, like β-alanine, can convert into β-alanine betaine which is required for osmoregulation in some halophytes. Proline is one of the most common osmolytes in stressed plants(Bartels and Hussain, 2008; Delauney and Verma, 1993; Sharma and Dietz, 2006; Urano *et al.*, 2009). Polyamine catabolism is closely related to proline accumulation in response to stress conditions (Aziz *et al.*, 1998; Bouchereau *et al.*, 1999). Öztürk and Demir (2003) showed that exogenous PA increases activity of peroxidase (POD) and catalase (Cat), along with proline production. PA metabolism is unique in that Put, proline and GABA share a common substrate, glutamate, and these metabolites often respond similarly to abiotic stresses (Seki *et al.*, 2007; Sharma and Dietz, 2006; Simon-Sarkadi *et al.*, 2005, 2006). There is no evidence yet about the mechanism of their coordinated accumulation (Radukina *et al.*, 2007). However, it is possible that a common signal triggers all three sub-pathways in a coordinated manner. Ornithine is a key intermediate in the biosynthesis of both Put and proline (Coruzzi and Last, 2000; Roosens *et al.*, 2002; Slocum, 2005) and is a possible candidate for a regulatory role in coordinating biosynthesis of these metabolites (Mohapatra *et al.*, 2010). Similarly, a hierarchical accumulation of PAs in differenttransgenic tissues/organs has been observed (Lepri *et al.*, 2001) which suggest that PAs might act as compatible solute in specific organs, cells or organelles.

POLYAMINE AND ANTIOXIDANT RESPONSE

Reactive oxygen species (ROS) production is a common plant response under both abiotic and biotic stresses (Miller *et al.*, 2008). ROS is characterized by the accumulation of toxic molecules $\bar{O}_2$, H_2O_2, and OH– in tissues which are capable of causing damage to plant cell membranes and macromolecules (Apel and Kirt, 2004). Plants have several antioxidant strategies (Rea *et al.*, 2004) like ROS-scavenging enzymes such as superoxide dismutase (SOD) (Aronova *et al.*, 2005), different peroxidases (POD; Hiraga *et al.*, 2000), catalase (Cat), and glutation reductase (GR; Bartels and Hussain, 2008). PAs may be related to their multi-faceted nature, which includes working as an antioxidant, a free radical scavenger and a membrane stabilizer (Larher *et al.*, 2003; Velikova *et al.*, 2000). The generation of ROS is tightly linked to catabolic processes of PAs, by PAO (Cona *et al.*, 2006) which is associated with plant defense and abiotic stress responses (Liu *et al.*, 2005). Verma and Mishra (2005) demonstrated that positive effects of Put on Brassica juncea seedlings under NaCl stress are evident from reduced H2O2 and lipid peroxidation. Similarly, Put increased activity of antioxidant enzymes and carotenoids in leaf tissues of salt stressed Brassica. Based on these results, they concluded that PAs may exhibit antioxidant properties under some conditions. Conclusive evidence regarding antioxidant roles of PAs were provided Nayyar and Chander (2004), who observed that exogenous application of PAs reduced H2O2 levels and molandialdehyde (MDA) content, and raised the antioxidant level in 15-day-old chickpea plants subjected to drought and cold stress for 4 days. PAs are also involved in inhibition of DNA oxidative degradation by OH– as shown by an in vitro experiment. Total DNA from M. Crystallinum is degraded, when incubated with an OH– generating system and addition of Spm suppressed DNA damage (Kuznetsov and Shevyakova, 2007). At the same time, some reports have demonstrated that PA conjugates are more efficient compared to parent compounds with stronger protective antioxidant activities (Edreva *et al.*, 2007). Nevertheless, it can be concluded that plants not only accumulate free PAs to function as scavengers of free radicals but also produce their conjugates which are more efficient antioxidants (Edreva *et al.*, 2007).

POLYAMINE: A SIGNAL MOLECULE DURING STRESS RESPONSE

In contrast to the trustworthy establishment of the role of PA in plant defense against abiotic (Bartels and Hussain, 2008) and biotic (Walters, 2003 and references therein) stresses, few reports recently indicated that PAs may act as cellular signals in intrinsic talk with hormonal pathways including ABA (Alcázar *et al.*, 2010a,b; Gill and Tuteja, 2010). It is well-known that ABA concentrations increase under water and salt stress as well as other abiotic stresses (Christmann *et al.*, 2005). It is also well-documented that ABA induces the expression of multiple genes involved in abiotic stress tolerance (Bartels and Hussain, 2008; Bartels and Souer, 2003), e.g. PA biosynthesis genes in Arabidopsis (Kasinathan and Wingler, 2004; Urano *et al.*, 2004). Exogenously applied ABA helped further to identify the possible roles of ABA in modulation of PA metabolism at the transcriptional level by up-regulating ADC2, SPDS and SPMS under stress conditions in plants (Alcázar *et al.*, 2006; Hanfrey *et al.*, 2001; Hanzawa *et al.*, 2002; Peréz- Amador *et al.*, 2002; Urano *et al.*, 2003). Similarly, a plethora of data on the analysis of mutant plants and transcript profiling suggest a positive feedback mechanism between Put and ABA, which permits a fresh insight that both Put and ABA reciprocally promote each other's biosynthesis under stress to increase plant adaptive potential (Cuevas *et al.*, 2008, 2009; Urano *et al.*, 2003, 2009; Yamaguchi *et al.*, 2006). PA catabolism produces H2O2 which was often considered mostly as a toxic metabolite. Only recently, our notions about H2O2 changed dramatically to a signalmolecule, capable of diffusion fromthe site of its production to neighbouring cells and tissues, resulting in activation of a defensive response (Neill *et al.*, 2002). Similarly, PAs like Spm and Spd are regarded as potent inducers of nitric oxide (NO) in plants (Tun *et al.*, 2006). Reports showing NO as a signaling molecule in plants appeared as late as 1998 (Delledonne *et al.*, 1998). These reports provoked an intensification of research on the role of NO in plants. In plant cells, several pathways coexist for NO-mediated signals including cyclic nucleotides, Ca2+ ions, protein kinases and others. Moreover, wheat plants subjected to drought had much higher ABA synthesis in roots in the presence of NO and ROS, which suggests synergistic action of ROS and NO (Zhao *et al.*, 2001). Also, the accumulation of NO proved necessary for ABA-induced closure of stomata in Viciafaba (Garia-Mata and Lamattina, 2002). Important clues about the functional cooperation between ABA, H2O2 and NO are also confirmed by a recent reportwhich found that ABA-induced stomatal closure in Arabidopsis is dependent not only on NO but also on H2O2 (Bright *et al.*, 2006). Recently, An *et al.* (2008) reported that PAs are involved in ABA-induced stomatal regulation under abiotic stresses. ABA, H2O2, NO and PAs are multifunctional molecules implicated in numerous physiological and biological responses during stress responses (Grün *et al.*, 2006; Neill *et al.*, 2003). Evidence obtained so far is being compiled, showing the involvement and interaction of ABA, H2O2, NO and PAs during stress responses by a complex network. Recently, Alcázar *et al.* (2010a,b) suggested a synergistic interplay between aforesaid molecules for abiotic stress tolerance in plants. However, whether or not the unique roles of these molecules in plants are attributable is still a matter of debate. 4.4. Polyamine: Regulation of ion channel and Ca2+ homeostasis Recently, it was found that PAs could substantially affect ion channel conductivity in plants (Kusano *et al.*, 2007a). At physiological pH, PAs are positively charged molecules, which interact with negatively charged proteins including ion channels. PAs are also potent blockers of fast and slow vacuolar channels, including calcium channels (Brüggemann *et al.*, 1999; Dobrovinskaya *et al.*, 1999a; 1999b). The effect of PAs on ion channels is proportional to its charge (Spm+4NSpd+3NPut+2) at both whole cell and single channel level, thus indicating a direct blockage of the channel by PAs (Brüggemann *et al.*, 1998).

These findings are in agreement with reports from animal literature, suggesting that PAs can block or modulate several types of cation channels (Bowie *et al.*, 1998; Gomez and Hellstrand, 1999; Huang and Moczydlowski, 2001; Lu and Ding, 1999; Oliver *et al.*, 2000; Williams, 1997a,b). As in the animal system, ion channels have been identified as PA targets in plants blocking inward rectifying K+ and Na+ channel and mediating additional aspects of ion fluxhomeostasis in cell type specific manner (Liu *et al.*, 2000; Zhao *et al.*, 2007). Furthermore, Garufi *et al.* (2007) suggested that PA may regulate the activity of numerous ion channels indirectly by affecting plasma membrane potential via activation of H+-ATPase through enhancement of interactions with 14-3-3 proteins. Consistent with the above data, it has been reported that Pas including spermine inhibit stomatal opening and induce closure by regulating KAT-1 like voltage-dependent inward K+ channel of Viciafaba guard cells. Similarly, exogenously applied PAs ameliorate the detrimental effects of salinity by reducing NaCl-induced K+ efflux through non-selective cation channels, a major route of Na+ uptake into plant cells (Demidchik and Tester, 2002; Shabala *et al.*, 2007). Yamaguchi *et al.* (2006) showed that acl5/spms mutant plant is hypersensitive to KCl and also Ca2+ deficient. The overall phenotype of mutant plants resembles transgenic plants over-expressing AtGluR2 and CAX1, which encode a Ca2+ influx channel at the plasma membrane and a vacuolar Ca2+/H+ exchanger, respectively (Hirschi, 1999; Kim *et al.*, 2001). Similarly, mutant plants lose more water than wild type plants due to failed stomatal closure upon onset of drought (Yamaguchi *et al.*, 2007). This phenomenon may again be explained by the impairment in Ca2+ homeostasis. It is documented that changes of free Ca2+ in the cytoplasm of guard cells are responsible for stomatal movement (Allen and Sanders, 1996; Peiter *et al.*, 2005; Rob *et al.*, 2005). On the other hand, spermine produced as a result of drought stress may modulate Ca2+ permeable channels, resulting in increased cytoplasmic Ca2+ concentration to trigger stomatal closure. Collectively, these results indicate that the absence of spermine may cause deregulation of Ca2+ trafficking, resulting in a lack of proper adaptation to high NaCl and drought stresses (Kusano *et al.*, 2007a,b). Taken together, this data points to a possible link between PAs, Ca2+ homeostasis and stress responses which should be further explored.

POLYAMINE AND PROGRAMMED CELL DEATH (PCD)

In plants, programmed cell death (PCD) can occur following both pathogen attack and environmental fluctuations (Reape and McCabe, 2008). For example, UV-C activate PCD in Arabidopsis (Danon *et al.*, 2004) and PCD can also be activated in tobacco by infection with Pseudomonas syringaepv. phsaeolicola (del Pozo and Lam, 1998). Polyamines are considered essential for cell growth and survival (Hanfrey *et al.*, 2001;

Thomas and Thomas, 2001) and homeostasis (Mittler and Shulaev, 2003). PAs have also been involved in regulation of PCD, apoptosis (Schipper *et al.*, 2000). There is substantial literature available indicating the involvement of PAs in apoptotic cell death in plants (Desicerio *et al.*, 1995; Ha *et al.*, 1997; Lindsay and Wallace, 1998). Furthermore, PA degradation seems to be important, leading to apoptosis in plants. In fact, Crowley and Walters (2002) observed an increase in PA catabolism by DAO and PAO in cells undergoing apoptosis which resulted in hypersensitive response in tobacco (Yoda *et al.*, 2003). Similarly, Yoda *et al.* (2003; 2006) demonstrated that cell death caused by TMV infection is partially mediated by H2O2 production through PA catabolism. Hydrogen peroxide has long been considered to be a causative element for apoptotic cell death in Plants. Apoptosis in plants follow similar interactions between PAs and components of PCD as described for animals. In numerous plant diseases, hypersensitive response (HR) is triggered when the host recognizes a pathogen affecter destined to suppress immunity (Jones and Dangl, 2006). It has been suggested that HR represents a form of PCD in plants (Greenberg *et al.*, 1994; Walters, 2003) and PAs have been implicated in a prominent role in this process. HR involves inducing localized cell death at the point of infection, thus limiting the progression of the pathogen. Similarly, PAs also affect conformation and function of specific proteins by forming covalent linkages mediated by the activity of transglutamines (TGase) enzymes (Griffin *et al.*, 2002). TGase activity has also been demonstrated in plants (Della Mea *et al.*, 2004). TGase activity is elevated, when apoptosis is induced in animals, and similar enhanced activity has also been shown during HR in tobacco/TMV interactions (Del Duca *et al.*, 2007). However, further investigations are required for conclusive evidence of PAs involvement in PCD in plants.

POLYAMINE AND PLANT RESPONSES TO BIOTIC STRESSES

Despite continued interest in polyamine metabolism in plants subjected to abiotic stresses (Bartels and Hussain, 2008), work on polyamine metabolism in plant-pathogen interactions relatively lags behind (Walters, 2000). Mostly, plant defense mechanisms against pathogen attack are triggered by a stimulus preceding the pathogen attack that reduces disease. The stimulus can boost the concentration of accessible defense compounds that include the assembly of new defensive structures and chemicals (Baileya *et al.*, 2005). PA metabolism has long been known to distort in plant cells responding to insightful changes in plants interacting with fungal (Asthir *et al.*, 2004; Greenland and Lewis, 1984), viral pathogens (Torrigiani *et al.*, 1997; Walters, 2003) and mycorrhizae (Walters, 2000). Nevertheless, much progress has been achieved regarding PA and plant diseases (Walters, 2000, 2003). For example, spermine (Spm) not only plays a role as a mediator in defense signaling against pathogen (Takahashi *et al.*, 2003, 2004) but is also important for resistance to virus infection (Yamakawa *et al.*, 1998).

POLYAMINE: ELICITOR OF THE PLANT DEFENSE RESPONSE

The coordination of internal processes in plants and their balance with the environment are connected with the excitability of plants cells. Yamakawa *et al.* (1998) reported that Spm accumulated in the apoplast of cells after lesion formation is an endogenous inducer of the expression of both pathogen-related (PR) proteins and resistance against TMV via salicylic acid (SA)-independent signaling pathway in tobacco plants. Later, it was known that Spm stimulates activity of (i) two important mitogen-activated protein kinases (MAPKs) involved in plant defense; wound-induced protein kinase (WIPK) and SAinduced protein kinase (SIPK) and (ii) defense gene expression (Takahashi *et al.*, 2003, 2004). Later, using a similar experimental system, it was discovered that exogenously applied spermine to tobacco leaves provokes a pathway involving mitochondrial dysfunction, activation of MAPKs, increased expression of hypersensitive response (HR) marker genes, induced defense responses and HR-like cell death (Mitsuya *et al.*, 2007, 2009; Uehara *et al.*, 2005). However, the mechanismof PAs as an elicitor of plant defense response requires further research.In soil, root development and acquisition of root architecture as well as root functions greatly rely on interactions of root tissues with the surrounding biotic environment, especially microorganisms. However, little is known about the interactions between plants and mycorrhizae, and the role of PAs in symbiotic relationships is less studied (Kytoviita and Sarjala, 1997). It has been shown that externally applied Put in arbuscular mycorrhizae increases the colonization frequency in pea roots (El-Ghachtouli *et al.*, 1995, 1996). A possible role of PAs in arbuscularmycorrhizal infection was, therefore, postulated. Later, Kytoviita and Sarjala (1997) showed that ectomycorrhizal symbiosis result in increased free Put levels in mycorrhizal roots of Scots pine. However, they found differences in PA levels between symbiotic and non-symbiotic roots and suggested that PA could create a carbon sink for symbionts, resulting in attraction ofphotoassimilates (Niemi *et al.*, 2002). Further, a high content of total free PAs in association with arbuscular mycorrhiza and Lotus glaber plants was detected compared to non-mycorrhizal plants (Sannazzaro *et al.*, 2007). This relationship also increased PA levels in both plants and mycorrhizae. The modulation of PA pools in symbionts could help to resist host defense responses induced at the start of the association. However, the roles of PAs in the plant–mycorrhizal associations remain elusive and await further research. Although long known for their pharmacology effects, there has been little investigation of defense responses of polyamine during pathogenic infection. We are now beginning to understand their role in plant biotic stresses through molecular biology and modern biochemical approaches (Mehta *et al.*, 2002; Walters, 2003). Early efforts found that in compatible interactions between barley and Pucciniahordei (brown rust fungus), polyamines particularly spermidine accumulate in infected leaves (Greenland and Lewis, 1984). Polyamine accumulation has also been reported in leaves of barley following infection by powdery mildew fungus (Blumeriagraminis f. sp. hordei) (Walters and Wylie, 1986; Walters *et al.*, 1985). The presence of PA in both plants and pathogenic fungi makes it difficult to identify their respective contribution to PA accumulation in infected organs. However, themost exciting and farreachingdevelopment in this area is the possibility of control of fungal plant diseases through specific inhibition of polyamine biosynthesis (Galston and Weinstein, 1988; Walters, 1989). Similarly,A inhibitors like DFMO, MGBG and CHA resulted in complete inhibition of microcycleconidiation at 5 mM levels (Khurana *et al.*, 1996). In relation to biotic stress responses and in order to identify regulatory components of the pathway involved in the hypersensitive response (HR) induced by tobacco mosaic virus (TMV) in tobacco plants, new developments are in the pipeline. Tobacco ZFT1 is a spermine-responsive gene encoding a zinc finger type transcriptional repressor, and is involved in spermine-signaling pathway (Uehara *et al.*, 2005). Interestingly, tobacco plants over-expressing ZFT1 are more resistant to TMV compared with control plants (Mitsuya *et al.*, 2007; Uehara *et al.*, 2005). Another important observation regarding PA implication in the signaling pathway involved in biotic stress response has been postulated. Accumulation of H2O2 as a result of PA catabolism and nitric oxide due to induction by spermine/spermidine plays an important signaling role in plant–pathogen interactions (Romero-Puertas *et al.*, 2004; Tun *et al.*, 2006; Walters, 2003; Yamasaki and Cohen, 2006). These studies suggest that manipulation of key factors present upstream of polyamine biosynthesis or in the polyamine-induced signaling pathway could render the host plant resistant to biotic stresses. Some recent studies explored another layer of complex polyamineinduced signaling pathway. Rhee *et al.* (2007) described that the polyamine adaptive response appears to be shared between pathogen (prokaryote) stringent responses and host (eukaryote) unfolded protein responses (UPR). AtbZIP60 belongs to the basic leucine zipper protein family and is a key transcription factor involved in Arabidopsis UPR. An orthologue of AtbZIP60 has been identified in tobacco (NtbZIP60) via screening of spermine-responsive genes (Tateda *et al.* 2008). It is further confirmed that AtbZIP60 is responsive to spermine and is also involved in modulation of UPR-responsive genes in Arabidopsis (Iwata and Koizumi, 2005). However, further research may highlight the cross-talk between spermine function and UPR/stringent response.

CONCLUDING REMARKS AND FUTURE PERSPECTIVES

We are as it were fair starting to comprehend the impact of PAs, and later inquire about on polyamine digestion system has built a solid case for assist thinks about towards cautious examination of PA qualities included in natural stresses. Tall throughput investigation counting advanced natural disciplines like electrophysiology, microarray, transcriptomics, proteomics, metabolomics approaches will too be accommodating to get it the association of the PA biosynthetic pathway in abiotic and biotic stretch resistance. Besides, biotechnological enhancement of trim abiotic and biotic stretch resistance at the atomic level is in advance. Hereditary control of polyamine digestion system has as of now given important data with respect to their part in stretch reaction.The exploitation of information revealed using plant models and the transfer of knowledge to a wide range of crop species for breeding purposes are current challenges for improvement of plant tolerance using the PA pathway. However, intelligent engineering of regulatory circuits involved in stress response requires detailed knowledge of signaling hierarchies and the impact of metabolic changes involved in this response. However, it is reasonable to assume that a thorough comparative analysis of the expression and function of PA genes and other genes involved in stress tolerance will be useful. Alternative approaches also include the use of PA as an external application which can also be administered for increasing tolerance to various stresses. In the long run, PA can be exploited in the same way as farm chemicals to mitigate stress-induced injury for crop protection. However, evidence from field level studies is still lacking. Some striking evidences of exogenous application of PA to counteract environment stresses are expected to promote its extended application to other crops. Nevertheless there are two main areas that need further investigation. Firstly, although there is a strong correlation between the presence of PAs and better tolerance to environmental stresses, intensive research at the molecular level is needed on signaling function. Secondly, current understanding of plant resistance to pathogens is that PA synthesis is stimulated by a plant–pathogen interaction. However, the role of PA in resistance to pathogens requires further research. Hence, research on PA and stress tolerance is at an interesting stage and has set the stage for intensive research to understand an array of functions of these relatively simple molecules.

REFERENCES

Afzal I, Munir F, Ayub CM, Basra SMA, Hameed A, Nawaz A. Changes in Antioxidant Enzymes, Germination Capacity and Vigour of Tomato Seeds in Response of Priming with Polyamines. Seed SciTechnol 2009; 37: 765-70.

Alcázar R, García-Martínez JL, Cuevas JC, Tiburcio AF, Altabella T. Over Expression of ADC2 in Arabidopsis induces Dwarfism and Late-flowering through GA Deficiency. Plant J 2005; 43: 425-36.

Alcázar R, Marco F, Cuevas JC, Patron M, Ferrando A, Carrasco P, Tiburcio AF, Altabella T. Involvement of Polyamines in Plant Response to Abiotic Stress. Biotechnol Lett 2006; 28: 1867-76.

Alcázar R, Altabella T, Marco F, Bortolotti C, Reymond M, Knocz C, Carrasco P, Tiburcio AF. Polyamines: Molecules with Regulatory Functions in Plant Abiotic Stress Tolerance. Planta 2010a; 231: 1237-49.

Alcázar R, Planas J, Saxena T, Zarza X, Bortolotti C, Cuevas J, Bitrian M, Tiburcio AF, Altabella T. Putrescine Accumulation Confers Drought Tolerance in Transgenic Arabidopsis Plants over-expressing the Homologous Arginine decarboxylase2 gene. Plant PhysiolBiochem 2010b; 48: 547-52.

Ali RM. Role of Putrescine in Salt Tolerance of Atropa belladonna Plant. Plant Sci 2000; 152: 173-9.

Allen KD. Assaying Gene Content in Arabidopsis. Proc Nat AcadSci USA 2002; 99: 9568-72.

Allen GJ, Sanders D. Control of Ionic Currents Guard Cell Vacuoles by Cytosolic and Luminal Calcium. Plant J 1996; 10: 1055-69.

Altabella T, Tiburcio AF, Ferrando A. Plant with Resistance to Low Temperature and method of Production thereof. 2009; Spanish Patent Application WO2010/004070.

An Z, Jing W, Liu Y, Zhang W. Hydrogen Peroxide Generated by Copper Amine Oxidase is Involved in Abscisic Acid-induced Stomatal Closure in Viciafaba. J Exp Bot 2008; 59: 815-25.

Apel H, Kirt H. Reactive Oxygen Species: Metabolism, Oxidative Stress and Signal Transduction. Annu Rev Plant Biol 2004; 55: 373-9.

Armengaud P, Breitling R, Amtmann A. The Potassium-dependent Transcriptome of Arabidopsis Reveals a Prominent Role of Jasmonic Acid in Nutrient Signaling. Plant Physiol 2004; 136: 2556-76.

Aronova EE, Shevyakova NI, Sretsenko LA, Kuznetsov VIV. Cadaverine-induced Induction of Superoxide Dismutase Gene Expression in Mesembryanthemum crystallinum L. Dokl Biol Sci 2005; 403: 25-9.

Asthir B, Spoor W, Duffus CM. Involvement of Polyamines, Diamine Oxidase and Polyamine Oxidase in Resistance of Barley to Blumeriagraminis f. sp. Hordei. Euphytica 2004; 136: 307-12.

Aziz A, Martin-Tanguy J, Larher F. Stress-induced Changes in Polyamine and Tyramine Levels can Regulate Proline Accumulation in Tomato Leaf discs Treated with Sodium Chloride. Plant Physiol 1998; 104: 195-202.

Bagni N, Tassoni A. Biosynthesis, Oxidation and Conjugation of Aliphatic Polyamines in Higher Plants. Amino Acids 2001; 20: 301-17.

Baileya A, Strema D, Baea H, Myolob G, Guiltinan J. Gene Expression in Leaves of Theobroma Cacao in Response to Mechanical Wounding, Ethylene, and/or Methyl Jasmonate. Plant Sci 2005; 168: 1247-58.

Bais HP, Ravishankar GA. Role of Polyamines in the Ontogeny of Plants and their Biotechnological Applications. Plant Cell Tissue Organ Cult 2002; 69: 1-34.

Bartels D, Hussain SS. Current Status and Implications of Engineering Drought Tolerance in Plants using Transgenic Approaches. CAB Reviews: Perspectives in Agri, Vet Sci, Nutri Natur Sci, 3. ; 2008. p. 020.

Bartels D, Souer E. Molecular Responses of Plants to Dehydration. In: Madhava KV, Editor. Plant Responses to Abiotic Stress. Berlin: Springer; 2003. p. 8-38.

Bartels D, Sunkar R. Drought and Salt Tolerance in Plants. Crit Rev Plant Sci 2005; 24: Bhatnagar P, Minocha R, Minocha S. Genetic Manipulation of the Metabolism of Polyamines in Poplar Cells: The Regulation of Putrescine Catabolism. Plant Physiol 2002; 128: 1455-69.

Bohnert HJ, Shen B. Transformation and Compatible Solutes. SciHortic 1999; 78: 237-60.

Bortolotti C, Cordeiro A, Alcázar R, Borrell A, Culiañez-Macià FA, Tiburcio AF, Altabella T. Localization of Arginine Decarboxylase in Tobacco Plants. Plant Physiol 2004; 120: 84-92.

Bouchereau A, Aziz A, Larher F, Martin-Tanguy J. Polyamines and Environmental Challenges: Recent Development. Plant Sci 1999; 140: 103-25.

Bowie D, Lange GD, Mayer ML. Activity-dependent Modulation of Glutamate Receptors by Polyamines. J Neurosci 1998; 18: 8175-85.

Bright J, Desikan R, Hancock JT, Weir IS, Neill ST. ABA-induced NO Generation and Stomatal Closure in Arabidopsis are Dependent on H2O2 Synthesis. Plant J 2006; 45: 113-22.

Brüggemann L, Pottosin I, Schönknecht G. Cytoplasmic Polyamines Block the Fast Activating Vacuolar cation Channel. Plant J 1998; 16: 101-5.

Brüggemann L, Pottosin I, Schönknecht G. Selectivity of the Fast Activating Vacuolar cation Channel. J Exp Bot 1999; 50: 873-6.

Camacho-Cristóbal JJ, Lunar L, Lafont F, Baumert A, González-Fontes A. Boron Deficiency Causes Accumulation of Chlorogenic Acid and Caffeoyl Polyamine Conjugates in Tobacco Leaves. J Plant Physiol 2004; 161: 879-81.

Capell T, Escobar C, Liu H, Burtin D, Lepri O, Christou P. Over-expression of Oat Arginine Decarboxylase cDNA in Transgenic Rice (Oryza sativa L.) Affects Normal Development Pattern in vitro and Results in Putrescine Accumulation in Transgenic Plants. TheorAppl Genet 1998; 97: 246-54.

Capell T, Bassie L, Christou P.Modulation of the Polyamine Biosynthetic Pathway Intransgenic Rice Confers Tolerance to Drought Stress. Proc Nat AcadSci USA 2004; 101: 9909-14.

Cheng L, Zou Y, Ding S, Zhang Y, Yu X, Cao J, Lu G. Polyamine Accumulation in Transgenic Tomato Enhances the Tolerance to High Temperature Stress. J Integr Plant Biol 2009; 51: 489-99.

Christmann A, Hoffmann T, Teplova I, Grill E, Müller A. Generation of Active Pools of Abscisic Acid Revealed by in vivo Imaging of Water Stresses Arabidopsis. Plant Physiol 2005; 137: 209-19.

Cona A, Cenci F, Cervelli M, Federico R, Mariottini P, Moreno S, Angelini R. Polyamine Oxidase, a Hydrogen Peroxide-producing Enzyme, is up-regulated by Light and Down-regulated by Auxin in the outer Tissues of the Maize Mesocotyle. Plant Physiol 2003; 131: 803-13.

Cona A, Rea G, Angelini R, Federico R, Tavladoraki P. Functions of Amine Oxidases in Plant Development and Defence. Trends Plant Sci 2006; 11: 80-8.

Coruzzi G, Last R. Amino Acids. In: Buchanan B, Gruissem W, Jones R, Editors. Biochemistry and Molecular Biology of Plants. American Society of Plant Physiologists MD; 2000. p. 358-410.

Crowley T, Walters DR. Polyamine Metabolism in an Incompatible Interaction between Barley and the Powdery Mildew Fungus, Blumeriagraminis f. sp. Hordei. J Phytopathol 2002; 150(11-12): 1-7.

Cuevas JC, Lopez-Cobollo R, Alcázar R, Zarza X, Koncz C, Altabella T, Salinas J, Tiburcio AF, Ferrando A. Putrescine is involved in Arabidopsis Freezing Tolerance and Cold Acclimation by Regulating Abscisic Acid Levels in Response to Low Temperature. Plant Physiol 2008; 148: 1094-105.

Cuevas JC, Lopez-Cobollo R, Alcázar R, Zarza X, Koncz C, Altabella T, Salinas J, Tiburcio AF, Ferrando A. Putrescine as a Signal to Modulate the Indispensable ABA Increase under Cold Stress. Plant Signal Behav 2009; 4: 219-20.

Danon A, Botari VI, Gordon A, Mailhac N, Gallois P. Ultraviolet-C overexposure Induces Programmed Cell Death in Arabidopsis, which is Mediated by Caspase-like Activities and which can be Suppressed by Caspase Inhibitors, p35, and Defender against Apoptotic Death. J BiolChem 2004; 279: 779-87.

Del Duca S, Betti L, Trebbi G, SeraWni-Fracassini D, Torrigiani P. Transglutaminase Activity Changes during the Hypersensitive Reaction, a Typical Defense Response of Tobacco NN Plants to TMV. Plant Physiol 2007; 131: 241-50

delPozo O, Lam E. Caspases and Programmed Cell Death in the Hypersensitive Response of Plants to Pathogens. CurrBiol 1998; 8: 1129-32.

Delauney AJ, Verma DPS. Proline Biosynthesis and Osmoregulation in Plants. Plant J 1993; 4: 215-23.

Della Mea M, Caparros-Ruiz D, Claparols I, SeraWni-Fracassini D, Rigau J. AtPng1p: The First Plant Transglutaminase. Plant Physiol 2004; 135: 2046-54.

Delledonne M, Xia Y, Dixon RA, Lamb C. Nitric Oxide Functions as a Signal in Plant Disease Resistance. Nature 1998; 394: 585-8.

Demidchik V, Tester M. Sodium Fluxes through Non-selective cation Channels in the Membrane of Protoplasts from Arabidopsis Thaliana Roots. Plant Pgysiol 2002; 128: 379-87.

Desiderio MA, Grassilli E, Bellesia EE, Salomoni P, Franceschi C. Involvement of ornithine Decarboxylase and Polyamines in Glucocorticoid-induced Apoptosis of Rat Thymocytes. Cell Growth Differ 1995; 6: 505-13.

Dobrovinskaya OR, Muñiz J, Pottosin II. Asymmetric Block of the Plant Vacuolar Ca2+ Permeable Channel by Organic cations. EurBiophys J 1999a; 28: 552-63.

Dobrovinskaya OR, Muñiz J, Pottosin II. Inhibition of Vacuolar ion Channels by Polyamines. J MembrBiol 1999b; 167: 127-40.

Duan JJ, Li J, Guo SR, Kang YY. Exogenous Spermidine Affects Polyamine Metabolism in Salinity-stressed Cucumissativus Roots and Enhances Short-term Salinity Tolerance. J Plant Physiol 2008; 165: 1620-35.

Duhazé C, Gouzerh G, Gagneul D, Larher F, Bouchereau A. The Conversion of Spermidine to Putrescine and 1,3-deaminopropane in the Roots of Limoniumtataricum. Plant Sci 2002; 163: 639-46.

Edreva AM, Velikova VB, Tsonov TD. Phenylamides in Plants. Russ J Plant Physiol 2007; 54: 289-302.

El-Ghachtouli N, Paynot M, matin-Tanguy J, Dorandi D, Gianinazzi S. The Effect of Polyamines on Endomycorrhizal Infection of Wild-type Pisumsativum, cv Frisson (nod +myc+) and Rwo Mutants (nod+myc- and nod-myc+). Mycorrhiza 1995; 5: 189-92.

El-Ghachtouli N, Paynot M, matin-Tanguy J, Dorandi D, Gianinazzi S. Effect of Polyamines and Polyamine Biosynthesis Inhibitors on Spore Germination and Hyphal Growth of Glomus Mosseae. Mycol Res 1996; 100: 597-600.

Evans PT, Malmberg RL. Do Polyamines have Roles in Plant Development? Ann Rev Plant Physiol Plant MolBiol 1989; 40: 235-69.

Franceschetti M, Hanfrey C, Scaramagli S, Torrigiani P, Bagni N, Burtin D, Michael AJ. Characterization of Monocot and dicot Plant S-adenosyl-L-methionine Decarboxylase Gene Families including Identification in the mRNA of a Highly Conserved Pair of Upstream Overlapping open Reading Frames. Biochem J 2001; 53: 403-9.

Franceschetti M, Fornale S, Tassoni A, Zuccherelli K, Mayer MJ, Bagni N. Effects of Spermidine Synthase Overexpression on Polyamine Biosynthetic Pathway in Tobacco Plants. J Plant Physiol 2004; 161: 989-1001.

Galston AW, Weinstein LH. Control of Phytopathogen by Inhibitors of Polyamine Biosynthesis. AdvExp Med Biol 1988; 250: 589-99.

Galston AW, Kaur-Sawhney R, Altabella T, Tiburcio AF. Plant Polyamines in Reproductive Activity and Response to Abiotic Stress. Bot Acta 1997; 110: 197-207.

Garia-Mata C, Lamattina L. Nitric Oxide and Abscisic Acid Cross Talk in Guard Cells. Plant Physiol 2002; 128: 790-2.

Garufi A, Visconti S, Camoni L, Aducci P. Polyamines as Physiological Regulators of 14-3-3 Interaction with the Plant Plasma membrane H+ -ATPase. Plant Cell Physiol 2007; 48: 434-40.

Ge C, Cui X, Wang Y, Hu Y, Fu Z, Zhang D, Cheng Z, Li J. BUD2, Encoding an Sadenosylmethionine decarboxylase, is required for Arabidopsis Growth and Development. Cell Res 2006; 16: 446-56.

Gill SS, Tuteja N. Polyamines and Abiotic Stress Tolerance in Plants. Plant Signal Behav 2010; 51: 26-33.

Gomez M, Hellstrand P. Endogenous Polyamines Modulate Ca2+ Channel Activity in Guinea-pig Intestinal Smooth Muscle. Pflugers Arch 1999; 436: 445-51.

Greenberg JT, Guo A, Klessig DF, Ausubel FM. Programmed Cell Death in Plants: A Pathogen-triggered Response Activated Coordinately with Multiple Defense Functions. Cell 1994; 77: 551-63.

Greenland AJ, Lewis DH. Amines in Barley Leaves Infected with Brown Rust and their Possible Relevance to Formation of 'Green Islands'. New Phytol 1984; 96: 283-91.

Griffin M, Casadio R, Bergamini CM. Transglutaminases: Nature's Biological Glues. Biochem J 2002; 368: 377-96.

Groppa MD, Benavides MP. Polyamines and Abiotic Stress: Recent Advances. Amino Acids 2008; 34: 35-45.

Groppa MD, Benavides MP, Tomaro ML. Polyamine Metabolism in Sunflower and Wheat Leaf discs under Cadmium or Copper Stress. Plant Sci 2003; 16: 481-8.

Grün S, Lindermayr C, Sell S, Durner J. Nitric Oxide and Gene Regulation in Plants. J Exp Bot 2006; 57: 507-16.

Ha HC, Woster PM, Jager JD, Casero RAJ. The Role of Polyamine Catabolism in Polyamine analogue-induced Programmed Cell Death. Proc Natl AcadSci USA 1997; 94: 11557-62.

Hanfrey C, Sommer S, Mayer MJ, Burtin D, Michael AJ. Arabidopsis Polyamine Biosynthesis: Absence of Ornithine Decarboxylase and the Mechanism of Arginine Decarboxylase Activity. Plant J 2001; 27: 551-60.

Hanzawa Y, Takahashi T, Komeda Y. ACL5: An Arabidopsis Gene Required for Internodal Elongation after Flowering. Plant J 1997; 12: 863-74.

Hanzawa Y, Takahashi T, Michael AJ, Burtin D, Long D, Pineiro M, Coupland G, Komeda Y. ACAULIS5, an Arabidopsis Gene required for Stem Elongation, Encodes a Spermine Synthase. EMBO J 2000; 19: 4248-56.

Hanzawa Y, Imai A, Michael AJ, Komeda Y, Takahashi T. Characterization of the Spermidine Synthase-related Gene Family in Arabidopsis Thaliana. FEBS Lett Hashimoto T, Tamaki K, Suzuki K, Yamada Y. Molecular Cloning of Plant Spermidine Synthases. Plant Cell Physiol 1998; 39: 73-9.

He L, Nada K, Kasukabe Y, Tchibana S. Enhanced Susceptibility of Photosynthesis to Low Temperature Photohibition due to Interruption of Chill-induced Increase of Sadenosyl methionine Decarboxylase Activity in Leaves of Spinach (Spinaciaoleracea L.). Plant Cell Physiol 2002; 43: 196-206.

He L, Ban Y, Inoue H, Matsuda N, Liu J, Moriguchi T. Enhancement of Spermidine Content and Antioxidant Capacity in Transgenic Pear Shoots overexpressing Apple Spermidine Synthase in Response to Salinity and Hyperosmosis. Phytochem 2008; 69: 2133-41.

Hiraga S, Ito H, Yamakawa H, Ohtsubo N, Seo S, Mitsuhara I, Matsui H, Honma M, Ohashi Y. An HR-induced Tobacco Peroxidase Gene is Responsive to Spermine, but not to Salicylate, Methyl Jasmonate, and Ethephon. Mol Plant-Microbe Interact 2000; 13: 210-6.

Hirschi KD. Expression of Arabidopsis CAX1 in Tobacco: Altered Calcium Homeostasis and Increased Stress Sensitivity. Plant Cell 1999; 11: 2113-22.

Hu WW, Gong H, Pua EC. Molecular Cloning and Characterization of S-adenosylmethionine Decarboxylase Genes from Mustard (Brassica juncea). Plant Physiol 2005; 124: 25-40.

Huang CJ, Moczydlowski E. Cytoplasmic Polyamines as Permeant Blockers and Modulators of the Voltage-gated Sodium Channel. Biophys J 2001; 80: 1262-79.

Hummel I, Gouesbet G, El Amrani A, Ainouche A, Couee I. Characterization of the Two Arginine Decarboxylase (Polyamine Biosynthesis) Paralogues of the Endemic Subantarctic Cruciferous species Pringleaantiscorbutica and Analysis of their Differential Expression during Development and Response to Environmental Stress. Gene 2004; 342: 199-209.

Igarashi K, Kashiwagi K. Polyamines: Mysterious Modulators of Cellular Functions. Biochem Biophys Res Commun 2000; 271: 559-64.

Illingworth C, Mayer MJ, Elliott K, Hanfrey C, Walton NJ, Michael AJ. The Diverse Bacterial Origins of the Arabidopsis Polyamine Biosynthetic Pathway. FEBS Lett 2003; 549: 26-30.

Imai R, Ali A, Pramanik HR, Nakaminami K, Sentoku N, Kato H. A Distinctive Class of Spermidine Synthase is involved in Chilling Response in Rice. J Plant Physiol 2004; 161: 883-6.

Iqbal M, Ashraf M. Changes in growth, Photosynthetic Capacity, and Ionic Relations in Spring Wheat (Triticumaestivum L.) due to Pre-sowing Seed Treatment with Polyamines. Plant Growth Regul 2005; 46: 19-30.

Iwata Y, Koizumi N. An Arabidopsis Transcription Factor, AtbZIP60, Regulates the Endoplasmic Reticulum Stress Response in a Manner Unique to Plants. Proc Natl AcadSci USA 2005; 102: 5280-5.

Janowitz T, Kneifel H, Piotrowski M. Identification and Characterization of Plant Agmatineiminohydrolase, the Last Missing Link in Polyamine Biosynthesis of Plants. FEBS Lett 2003; 544: 258-61.

Jones JDG, Dangl JL. The Plant Immune System. Nature 2006: 444: 323-9. Kakehi J, Kuwashiro Y, Niitsu M, Takahashi T. Thermospermine is Required for Stem Elongation in Arabidopsis Thaliana. Plant Cell Physiol 2008; 49: 1342-9.

Kakkar RK, Sawhney VK. Polyamine Research in Plants. A Changing Perspective. Physiol Plant 2002; 116: 281-92.

Kasinathan V, Wingler A. Effect of Reduced Arginine Decarboxylase Activity on Salt Tolerance and on Polyamine Formation during Salt Stress in Arabidopsis Thaliana. Plant Physiol 2004; 121: 101-7.

Kasukabe Y, He L, Nada K, Misawa S, Ihara I, Tachibana S. Overexpression of Spermidine Synthase Enhances Tolerance to Multiple Environmental Stresses and up-regulates the Expression of Various Stress-regulated Genes in Transgenic Arabidopsis Thaliana. Plant Cell Physiol 2004; 45: 712-22.

Kasukabe Y, He L, Watakabe Y, Otani M, Shimada T, Tachibana S. Improvement of Environmental Stress Tolerance of Sweet Potato by Introduction of Genes for Spermidine Synthase. Plant Biotechnol 2006; 23: 75-83.

Kaur-Sawhney R, Tiburcio AF, Altabella T, Galston A. Polyamines in Plants: An Overview. J. Cell MolBiol 2003; 2: 1-12.

Khurana N, Saxena RK, Gupta R, Rajam MV. Polyamines as Modulators of Microcycleconidiation in Aspergillus Flavus. Microbiology 1996; 142: 517-23.

Kim SA, Kwak JM, Jae SK, Wang MH, Nam HG. Overexpression of the AtGluR2 gene Encoding an Arabidopsis Homolog of Mammalian Glutamate Receptors Impairs Calcium Nutilization and Sensitivity to Ionic Stress in Transgenic Plants. Plant Cell Physiol 2001; 42: 74-84.

Knott JM, Römer P, Sumper M. Putative spermine Synthases from Thalassiosira pseudonana and Arabidopsis thaliana Synthesize Thermospermine rather than Spermine. FEBS Lett 2007; 581: 3081-6.

Kumar A, Altabella T, Taylor M, Tiburcio AF. Recent Advances in Polyamine Research. Trends Plant Sci 1997; 2: 124-30.

Kumria R, Rajam MV. Ornithine decarboxylase Transgene in Tobacco Affects Polyaminemetabolism, *in vitro* Morphogenesis and Response to Salt Stress. J Plant Physiol 2002; 159: 983-90.

Kusano T, Yamaguchi K, Berberich T, Takahashi Y. Advances in Polyamine Research in 2007. J Plant Res 2007a; 120: 345-50.

Kusano T, Yamaguchi K, Berberich T, Takahashi Y. The Polyamine Spermine Rescues Arabidopsis from Salinity and Drought Stresses. Plant Signal Behav 2007b; 2: 250-1.

Kusano T, Berberich T, Tateda C, Takahashi Y. Polyamines: Essential Factors for Growth and Survival. Planta 2008; 228: 367-81.

Kuthanová A, Gemperlová L, Zelenková S, Eder J, Macháèková I, Opatrñy Z, Cvikrová M. Cytological Changes and Alterations in Polyamine contents induced by Cadmium in Tobacco BY-2 Cells. Plant PhysiolBiochem 2004; 42: 149-56.

KuznetsovVl, Shevyakova NI. Proline under Stress: Biological Role, Metabolism and Regulation. Russ J Plant Physiol 1999; 46: 274-87.

KuznetsovVl, Shevyakova NI. Polyamines and Stress Tolerance of Plants. Plant Stress 2007; 1: 50-71.

KuznetsovVl, Shevyakova NI. Polyamines and Plant Adaptation to Saline Environments. In: Remawat KG, Editor. Desert Plants. Springer-Verlag Berlin-Heidelberg; 2010. p. 261-98.

Kytoviita MM, Sarjala T. Effects of Defoliation and Symbiosis on Polyamine Levels in Pine and Birch. Mycorrhiza 1997; 7: 107-11.

Larher FR, Aziz A, Gibon Y, Trotel-Aziz P, Sulpice R, Bouchereau A. An Assessment of the Physiological Properties of the so-called Compatible Solutes using *in vitro* Experiments with Leaf discs. Plant PhysiolBiochem 2003; 41: 657-66.

Lepri O, Bassie L, Safwat G, Thu-Hang P, Trung-Nghia P, Hölttä E, Christou P, Capell T.Over-expression of Human Ornithine Decarboxylase cDNA in Transgenic Rice Plants alters the Polyamine Pool in a Tissue-specific manner. Mol Genet Genomics 2001; 266: 303-12.

Levine A, Pennell RI, Alvarez ME, Palmer R, Lamb C. Calcium-mediated Apoptosis in a Plant Hypersensitive Disease Resistance Response. CurrBiol 1996; 6: 427-37.

Lindsay GS, Wallace HM. Changes in Polyamine Catabolism in HL-60 Human Promyelogenous leukaemic Cells in Response to Etoposide Induced Apoptosis. Biochem J 1998; 337: 83-7.

Liu K, Fu H, Bei Q, Luan S. Inward Potassium Channel in Guard Cells as a Target for Polyamine Regulation of Stomatal Movements. Plant Physiol 2000; 124: 1315-26.

Pages: 134-146

Current Research in Biochemistry and Molecular Biology
Edited by: Dr. Prasann Kumar and Dr. Pawan Kumar 'Bharti'
ISBN: 978-93-88854-33-7
Edition: 2020
Published by: Discovery Publishing House Pvt. Ltd., New Delhi (India)

CHAPTER 10

Photosynthesis
It's Significance in Plant Growth, Development and Bio Productivity Gaseous Fluxes in Atmosphere

Prasann Kumar[1,2*], Shipa Rani Dey[1]

GRAPHICAL ABSTRACT

Photosynthesis: The movie

Keywords: Atmosphere, Bio-productivity,Crop, Development, Gases

INTRODUCTION

The earth is very dynamic and has undergone dramatic changes in its history. All of the elements, including those common in living things, were

[1] Department of Agronomy, School of Agriculture, Lovely Professional University, Jalandhar - 144 411 (Punjab) (India)
[2] Divison of Research and Development, Lovely Professional University, Jalandhar - 144 411 (Punjab) (India)

synthesized from primordial hydrogen in the interior of stars. Supernovas and other stellar instabilities dispersed many elements into space. Because hydrogen and the noble gases are greatly depleted on earth as compared with their cosmic abundances, it is likely that the chunks of matter giving rise to the protoplanet did not carry with them gaseous shells of their own.The biological conversion of light quanta energy into chemical energy is known as photosynthesis. Photosynthesis supports all life on earth and in eukaryotes occurs exclusively in chloroplasts. All green tissues contain chloroplasts, but most photosynthesis, by far, occurs in leaves. Rough estimate give a value of 3×10^{21} J for the overall biomass produced by autotrophic organism and 13×10^{18} J for the energy uptake by mankind. In any case and without overestimating the correctness of the given value, it is clear that less than 1% of the available radiation energy is converted into biomass. Of this value, less than 1% is actually taken up as nutrition (of any type) by mankind. Thus the significance and the importance of photosynthesis (and the organism involved) can hardly be overvalued. In evolutionary terms, blue- green algae (Cyanobacteria) must be mentioned in the first place because they were the organisms that "invented" an "improved" and most important form of photosynthesis, namely oxygenic photosynthesis, about 3-4 billion years ago. It must be emphasized that this process took place in a reducing atmosphere that consisted of nitrogen and carbon dioxide (possibly some hydrogen) with virtually no oxygen present. This generally accepted view, however, does not completely hold, as small but substantial amounts of oxygen must have been present at the time. In Photosynthesis, molecular water is oxidized and oxygen is produced as a waste product of the reaction. However, physiological processes in photosynthesis organism include (various) reaction that require or include the oxidation or oxygenation of compounds so that technically an oxygen uptake from the surrounding atmosphere takes place. On the basis of the overall oxygen gas exchange, the immanent problem for scientific investigation is obvious. Normally, oxygen gas analyses are carried out using oxygen electrodes, which, however, cannot discriminate between evolution and concomitant uptake processes. Consequently, such systems quantify the overall balance or difference following an "event" (e.g., illumination) by simple adding up positive and negative changes. Thus, an important goal of plant physiological investigation has been to develop techniques allowing the simultaneous recording of gas evolution and uptake reactions, e.g., in a liquid reaction assay and from an artificial gas atmosphere over the aqueous phase without interference.

PHOTOSYNTHESIS

The terminus photosynthesis defines and summarizes the complex process(es) by which radiation energy of light is used to form carbohydrates according to the simple formula

$$CO_2 + D^{2-} / 2H^+ \rightarrow CH_2O + DO$$

Where D (onor) means any reduced photo-oxidizable compounds. Thus, in the case of anoxygenic photosynthesis D might be a sulfide or a ferric salt, whereas $D^{2-}/2H = H_2O$ for oxygenic photosynthesis. In the course of the Light – induced electron transport from an ultimate donor through two consecutively operating photosystems, energy is conserved in the form of ATP and reducing equivalents ($NADPH_2$) are built.

PHOTOSYNTHETIC RATE

Photosynthetic rate in strong light is important parameters characterizing the photosynthesis capacity of the photosynthesis apparatus. Apparently, it is not a notion of efficiency because the efficiency is the ratio of the output to input energy. In fact, it is also a notion of the efficiency because it is a determinant of crop yield and light use efficiency. Under same light intensity, especially saturating light for photosynthesis, leaves with a higher photosynthesis rate necessarily have a higher photosynthesis capacity and higher light use efficiency compared with leaves with a lower one.

RELATION BETWEEN LEAF PHOTOSYNTHESIS RATE AND CROP YIELD

Except for the mineral nutrient elements, accounting for about 5% of the total, all of the dry matter of crop plants is derived from photosynthesis CO2 assimilation. From this fact it naturally expected that a higher photosynthetic rate will lead to a higher yield or that there is a positive correlation between leaf photosynthesis and crop yield. However, a positive relation is not often observed, and it has been stated that in most cases there no association between them and in some cases even a negative correlation between leaf photosynthesis rate and yield. This paradox puzzled many plant physiologist and agronomists for quite a long time. In fact, the apparent lack of a positive correlation is not surprising because this is a very complex problem and leaf photosynthetic rate is an important but not the sole factor determining crop yield.

1. Reflection of the Essence- Positive Correlation

It is well known that about 95% of the dry matter of plants comes from photosynthesis. This fundamental fact determines that the essence of the relationship between leaf photosynthetic rate and crop yield is positive but not or no correlation.

The economic yield(Y) of crops is a function of photosynthetic production, respiratory consumption(R), and harvest index (HI). The amount of photosynthetic production depends on photosynthetic rate(P), leaf area(A), and photosynthetic duration (T). Their relationship can be very roughly expressed in the following equation:

Y=HI (P X A X T-R)

From this equation, it is very clear that Y must increase when P increase and Y must decrease when P decrease provided that HI, A, T, and R remains constant.

2. Factor masking the intrinsic relation

Yield formation of a crop plant is a complex process involving many factors. In other words, crop yield is influenced and determined by several factors, external and internal. Among internal factors, leaf photosynthetic rate is the basic but not the sole factor. Thus, the intrinsic relation between leaf photosynthetic rates is the basic but not the sole factor. Thus, the intrinsic relation between leaf photosynthetic rate and crop yield may be masked by other factors changed in the opposite direction.

Leaf Functional Duration: Leaf functional duration is also an important factor affecting yield, and a lower yield is often related to a shorter leaf functional duration.

Harvest Index: A change in the harvest index opposite to that in leaf photosynthesis may mask the intrinsic relation between leaf photosynthetic rate and yield. It was reported that there was a significant positive correlation between leaf photosynthetic rate and biomass and seed yield.

RESPIRATORY LOSS

Developmental Stage

C3 and C4 Photosynthesis Models: An Overview from the Perspective of Crop Modelling

Photosynthesis is the primary physiological process that drives plant growth and crop productivity and influences many other plant processes. It is also strongly affected by environmental stresses. Its study becomes increasingly important in the context of assessing the impact of climate change on agro-ecosystem function and of exploring opportunities for bio-based energy production. Therefore, mechanistic quantification of photosynthesis deserves further attention in dynamic simulation models of crop growth (Figure 10.1).

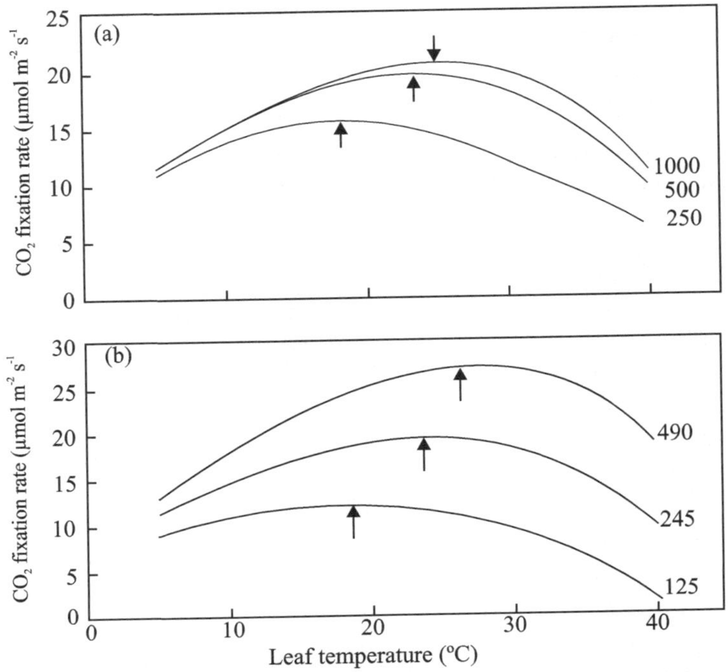

Fig. 10.1: An example of response curves of net CO2 assimilation rate in a C3 plant to leaf temperature, modelled using the FvCB model, (a) at three levels of irradiance (µmolm^{-2} s^{-1}) when Cc was fixed at 245µbar, and (b) at three levels of Cc (µbar) when irradiance was fixed at 500molm^{-2} s^{-1}. Arrows indicate the position of the optimum temperature

Source: based on review of literature

SIMULATION OF DIURNAL VARIATIONS OF CO_2, WATER AND HEAT FLUXES OVER WINTER WHEAT WITH A MODEL COUPLED PHOTOSYNTHESIS AND TRANSPIRATION

A model was developed that couples canopy photosynthesis and transpiration of winter wheat. The model combined a two-layer evapotranspiration model with a coupled photosynthesis–stomatal conductance model to study the diurnal variations of CO_2, water and heat fluxes of winter wheat. Photosynthesis and transpiration are two basic processes in forming crop productivity. Accurate estimation of photosynthesis and water consumption is important not only in directing irrigation and improving water use efficiency of cropland, but also in studying the interactions between plant and atmosphere. The simulation of photosynthesis and evapotranspiration has been intensively studied in the past decades at all levels, from individual leaf, canopy and region scale to the global scale. An analysis of measured flux data showed that there was an evident midday depression of photosynthesis, caused by stomatal closure due to high vapor water deficit and canopy temperature though the soil was well irrigated. There was a close agreement between simulated and measured net radiation, CO_2 flux, sensible and latent heat fluxes, which proved the predictive power of the coupled photosynthesis and transpiration model. Photosynthesis and transpiration are interdependent and inseparable since they take place in the leaf. Many models combine photosynthesis and transpiration through a model for stomatal resistance (Figure 10.2).

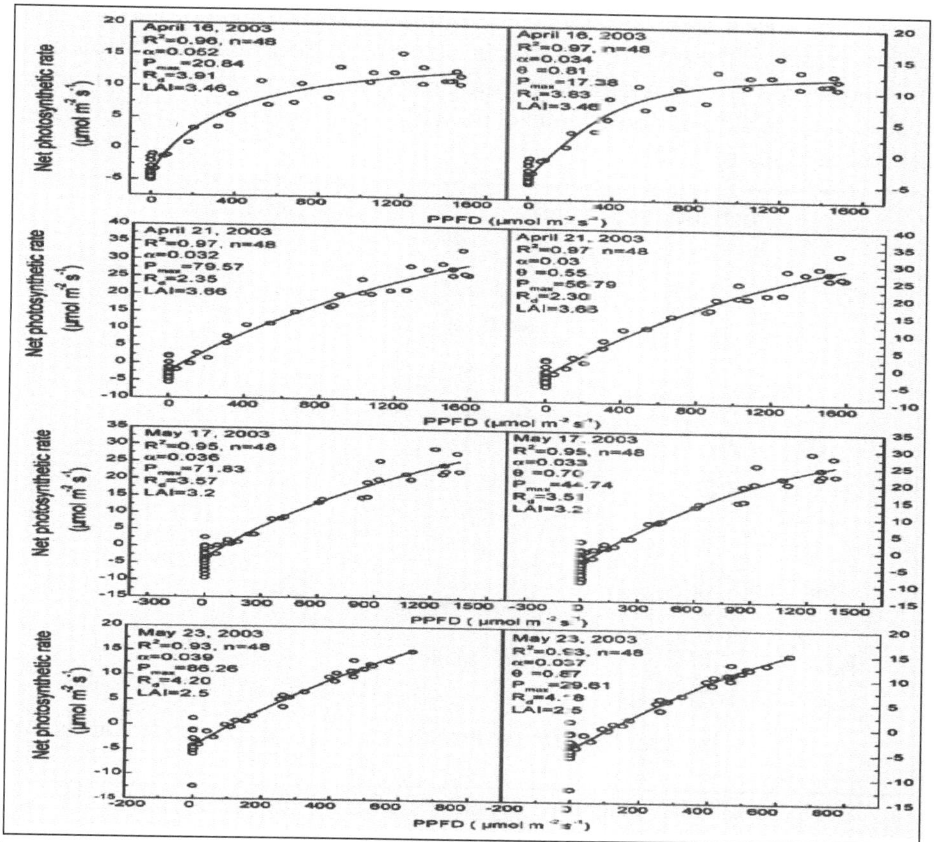

Fig. 10.2: The response curve of canopy net photosynthetic rate to photosynthetic photo flux density (PPFD) (left is a rectangular hyperbola and right is a non-rectangular hyperbola)

Source: based on review of literature

PHOTOSYSTEMS AND GLOBAL EFFECTS OF OXYGENIC PHOTOSYNTHESIS

Because life on earth is governed by the second law of thermodynamics, it is subject to increasing entropy. Oxygenic photosynthesis, the earth's major producer of both oxygen and organic matter, is a principal player in the development and maintenance of life, and thus results in increased order. The primary steps of oxygenic photosynthesis are driven by four multi-subunit membrane protein complexes: photosystem I, photosystem II, cytochrome b6f complex, and F-ATPase. Photosystem II generates the most positive redox potential found in nature and thus capable of extracting electrons from water. Photosystem I generates the most negative redoxPotential found in nature; thus, it largely determines the global amount of enthalpy in living systems. The recent structural determination of PSII and PSI complexes from Cyanobacteria and plants sheds light on the evolutionary forces that shaped oxygenic photosynthesis. This newly available structural information complements knowledge gained from genomic and proteomic data, allowing for a more precise description of the scenario in which the evolution of life systems took place (Figure 10.3).

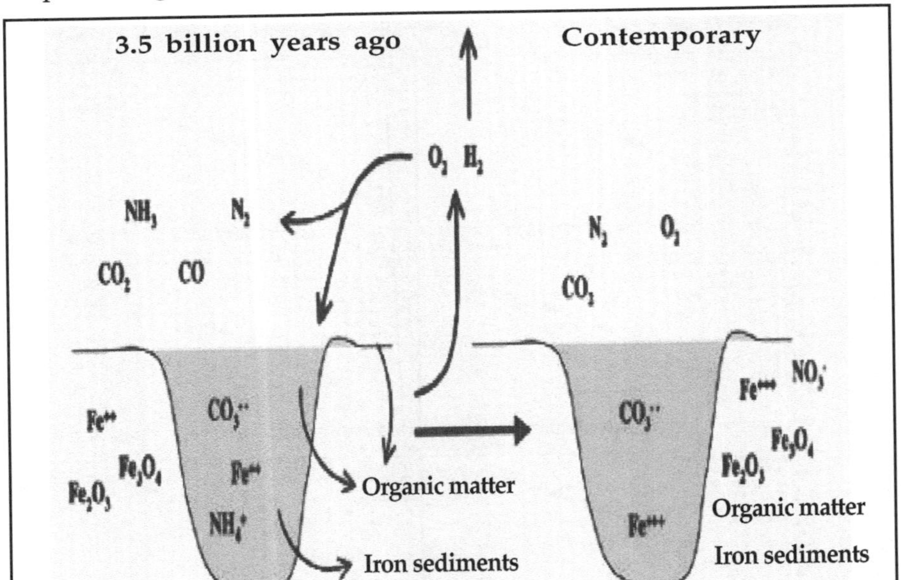

Fig. 10.3: Global major events resulted from oxygenic photosynthesis

Source: based on review of literature

A DYNAMIC MODEL OF CROP GROWTH AND PARTITIONING OF BIOMASS

A model is presented of growth and partitioning to leaves, stems and roots in herbaceous, vegetative crops in response to atmospheric conditions and water supply. It comprises 12 state variables and 33 parameters (including four functional relationships), all of direct physiological significance. The important characteristic of the model is the simultaneous consideration of crop assimilate and water balances achieved by calculations made at short time steps (1 h or less) in order to capture the physiological responses of crop growth and water use as they respond to diurnal environmental patterns. In the model, root-zone water content decreases with transpiration and soil evaporation, and increases with rainfall, irrigation and deepening of the root zone as the crop develops. Photosynthesis depends upon intercepted radiation and temperature and also on canopy conductance determined from crop water status. Respiration of organs is calculated as separate requirements for maintenance and growth. Transpiration proceeds with photosynthesis but in response to evaporative demand, reducing crop water content, which is in turn replenished from the root zone based on its water content and the rootlength that explores it. Partitioning of assimilate to leaves, stems, and roots depends upon diurnal oscillations in assimilate supply, temperature, and crop water content within limits set by phenological development. Phenological development, here the initiation and expansion of leaves and the maturity and senescence of canopy and root systems, is determined by temperature. Examples, and trends, of model performance are compared with measured physiological and agronomic responses of sunflower to strategies of irrigation (Figure 10.4).

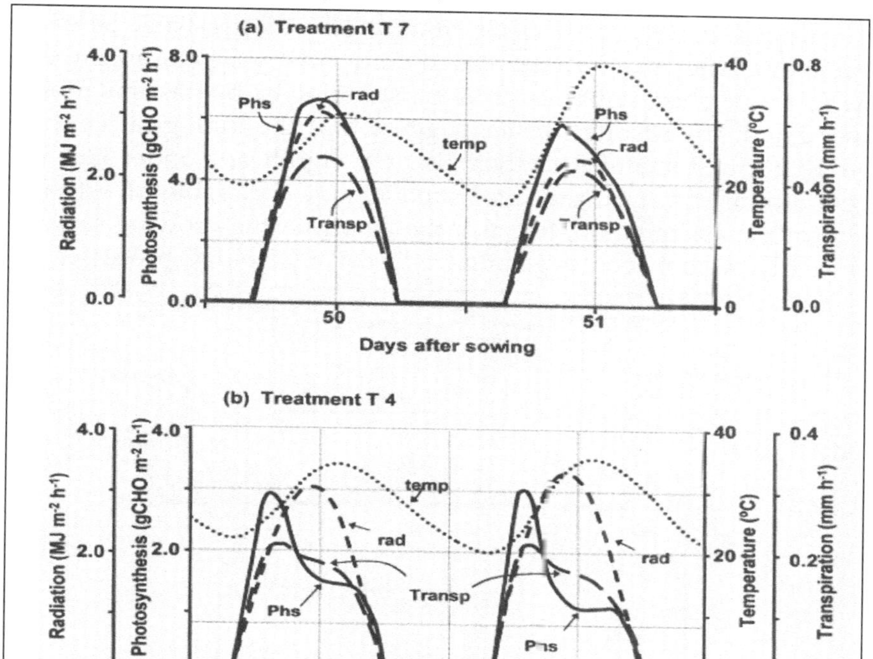

Fig. 10.4: Simulation of diurnal gross photosynthesis (Phs) and transpiration (Transp) of sunflower crops

Source: based on review of literature

INCORPORATING CANOPY PHYSIOLOGY INTO A HYDROLOGICAL MODEL: PHOTOSYNTHESIS, DYNAMIC RESPIRATION, AND STOMATAL SENSITIVITY

Vegetation modulates the effects of climate variability through soil–vegetation–atmosphere (SVAT) interactions. A quantitative understanding of such interactions requires the proper integration of the water cycle and photosynthesis. While biochemical models have widely been used to estimate primary production, the effects of water stress on transpiration and carbon assimilation rates, and its feedbacks into the water cycle are not generally represented. The objective of this study is to investigate the limiting effects of soil moisture and evaporative demand on photosynthesis, and to understand its interactions with other hydrological processes. Our approach consists of integrating a physically based land surface hydrological model (LSHM) with a biochemical model for leaf photosynthesis and a substrate-structure separation model for respiration, including parameterizations of the diurnal cycle of Rubisco concentration and species-specific stomatal conductance (resistance). Exploratory simulations to evaluate the model against results from previous studies indicated that the model captures basic processes of canopy physiology well. Sensitivity analysis shows that water stress at sub-daily time-scales is an important limiting factor of photosynthesis, thus constraining carbon assimilation. On the other hand, the results further suggest that the biological control of transpiration via stomatal sensitivity is only significant under soil water stress conditions. Overall, the integrated model is capable of estimating not only carbon assimilation, but also the length of the growing season, as well as feedbacks between vegetation and soil hydrology processes.

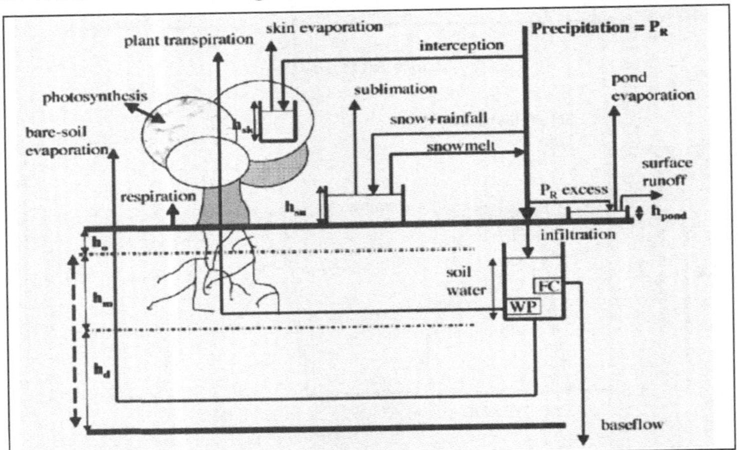

Fig. 10.5: Conceptual depictions of essential water fluxes and reservoirs in the land surface hydrology model (LSHM)

Source: based on review of literature

E-photosynthesis: Web-based platform for modeling of complex photosynthetic processesE-photosynthesis framework is a web-based platform for modeling and analysis of photosynthetic processes. Compared to its earlier version, the present platform employs advanced software methods and technologies to support an effective implementation of vastly diverse kinetic models of photosynthesis. We report on the first phase implementation of the tool new version and demonstrate the functionalities of model visualization, presentation of model components, rate constants, and initial conditions and of model annotation. The demonstration also includes export of a model to the Systems Biology Markup Language format and remote numerical simulation of the model.

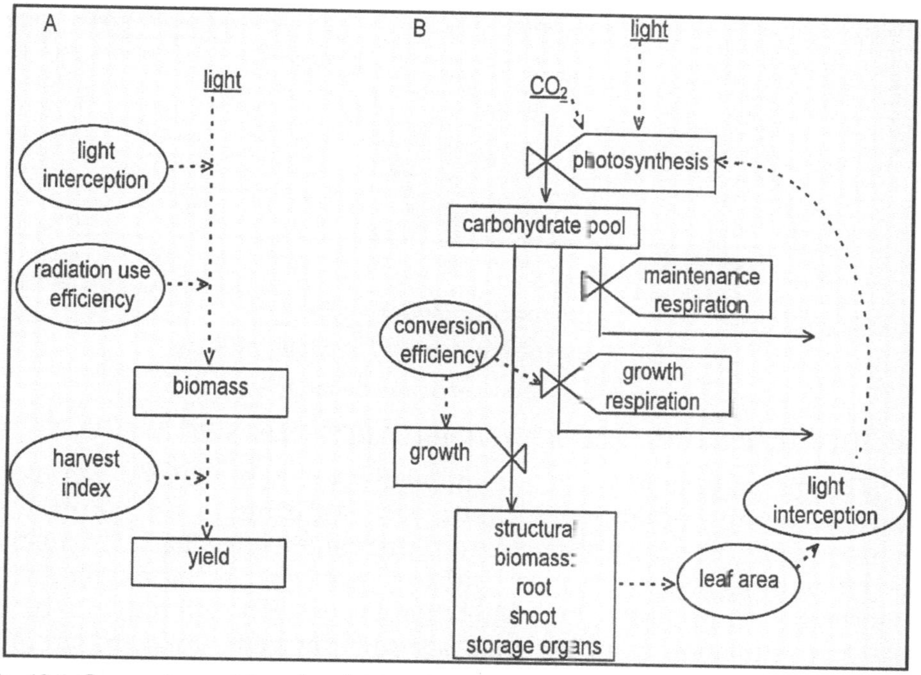

Fig. 10.6: Comparison of functional (a) and mechanistic (b) approaches of yield prediction

Source: based on review of literature

PLANTS, CO_2 AND PHOTOSYNTHESIS IN 21st CENTURY

Inorganic carbon is the basis for organic life on earth. Plants are the central link in this transformation, converting inorganic carbon dioxide (CO_2) in the atmosphere to organic carbon in the biosphere by photosynthesis. As the primary biological process within the global carbon cycle, photosynthesis also directly links changes in the earth's atmosphere caused by humans to the biological functioning of both natural and agricultural ecosystems. In this review we will examine the effects of rising atmospheric CO, partial pressure (pCO) on the process of photosynthesis.

We describe the critical components of photosynthesis that ultimately control atmosphere-biosphere interactions, explain how these processes may be altered by the rise in pCO,), due to human activity, and speculate on how these changes may affect the global carbon cycle of the 21st century and beyond (Figure 10.7).

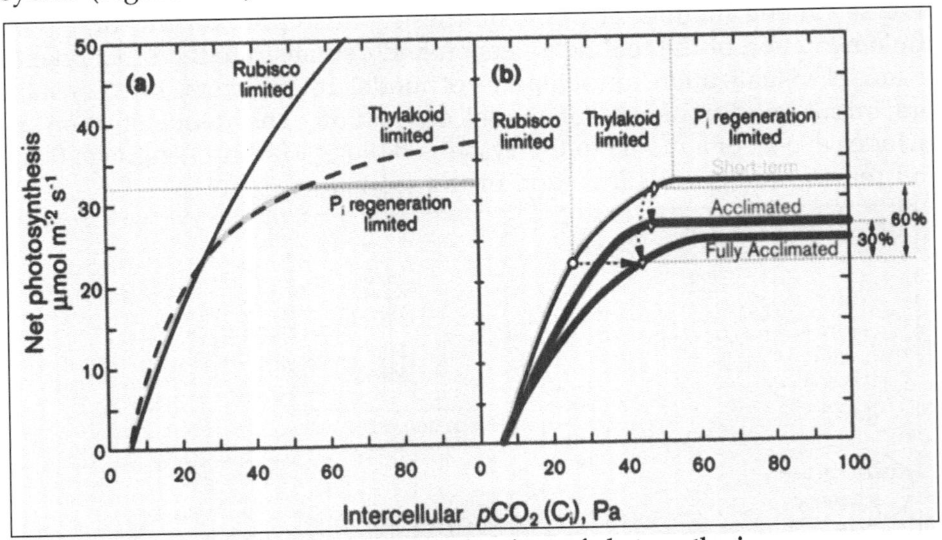

Fig. 10.7: CO_2 and the biochemistry of photosynthesis

Source: based on review of literature

A MODEL TO PREDICT PHOTOSYNTHETIC RESPONSES TO ELEVATED CO_2

The model assumes that the initial response to elevated CO_2 is an increase in the net photosynthetic rate; leading to an increase in photosynthetic products (carbohydrates) that can then feedback to influence the net photosynthetic rate. A pathway for short-term regulation of photosynthesis resulting from a limitation in Pi regeneration is in red and long-term regulation resulting from a change in gene transcription is in blue. Circled symbols (h = leaf mass per unit area and nm = nitrogen per unit area) are model inputs, whereas the boxed symbols (Amax = photosynthetic capacity) are model outputs. Steps colored green relate to whole-plant morphological and physiological traits.

Model of cellular short- and long-term feedback regulation of photosynthesis resulting from elevated CO,. Key regulatory enzymes (boxes) of the photosynthetic carbon reduction cycle (Calvin cycle) are shown in the scheme of the chloroplast; light energy (hv) supplies the ATP to reduce the C, products generated by Rubisco (see Fig. 10.3) into sugar phosphates (triose phosphates). An intermediate step catalyzed by glyceraldehydes 3-phosphate dehydrogenase (GAPDH) requires the consumption of NADPH (not shown), which is also produced in the light reactions. Fructose 1, 6-bisphosphatase (FBPase) is a key regulatory enzyme; it catalyzes the conversion of fructose bisphosphate to fructose 6-phosphate + inorganic phosphate (P,) as the Calvin cycle continues. The regeneration of RuBP is completed by phosphoribulokinase (PRK), which also consumes ATP. For the cycle to continue, the Pi consumed during the reduction processes (from ATP) must be replaced. Triose phosphates can be exported from the chloroplast envelope (Pi transporter) in exchange for Pi. When starch and sucrose synthesis is limited, however, Pi regeneration will slow and may limit ATP production and eventually the functioning of the Calvin cycle. This is known as short-term feedback regulation (red). Long-term feedback (blue) is probably realized through reduced gene transcription. Excess sucrose produced in the cytosol can enter the vacuole, where invertase can act upon it to produce hexoses. Glucose seems to be the primary active sugar for feedback regulation; it exits the vacuole, and is phosphorylated by hexokinase, initiating the feedback signal. Effecters may interact with hexokinase at this point to propagate a signal that enters the nucleus and acts as a repressor (R) of transcription of photosynthetic genes (e.g., by decreased translation Rubisco, rbcS). Rubisco levels may also be decreased by increased mRNA turnover.

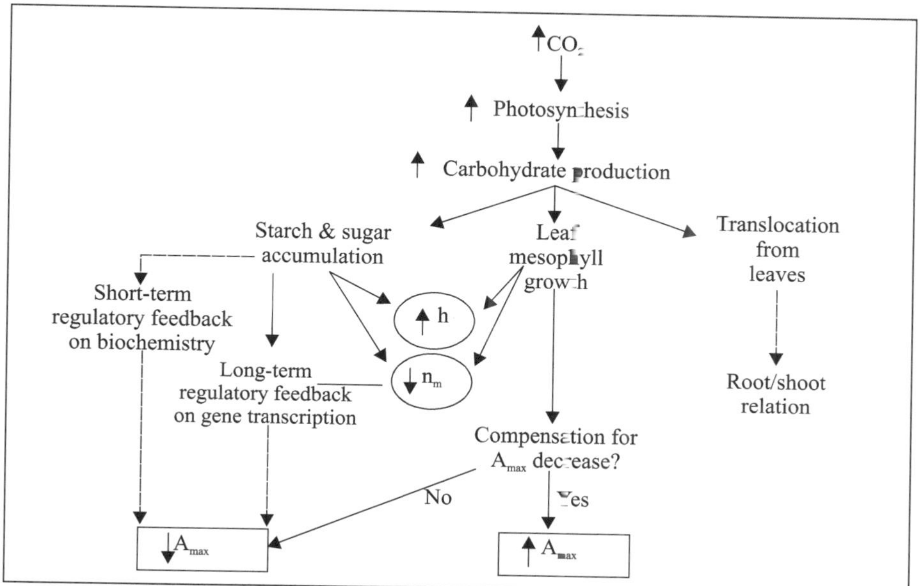

Fig. 10.8: A model to predict photosynthesis and its responses

CONCLUSION

There is a new interest in plant morphogenesis and architecture because molecular genetics is providing new information on their genetic and physiological control. From a crop modeller's point of view, this requires particular attention paid to the regulation of sinks associated with organ development, as well as their interactions with assimilate sources. Existing agronomic and architectural crop models are not capable of simulating such interactions. A conceptual framework is presented for the analysis and simulation of crop growth driven by either assimilate source or sink dynamics, building on the assumption that meristems are the main sites in the plant architecture where sinks are initiated and adjusted to resources. Among the numerous sink–source feedbacks to be considered are sensing of the plant's resource and stress status by meristems (enabling adjustment of morphogenesis), as well as transitory reserves, organ senescence and end-product inhibition of photosynthesis (necessary for the plant to cope with acute imbalances). These feedbacks are to a large extent related to sugar metabolism and can be explained with recent molecular findings on the prominent place in plant development of sugar sensing and the regulation of sucrose cleavage at sink sites. A model integrating these phenomena in a simplified manner, called EcoMeristem, was developed and is being applied in phenotyping for functional-genomics studies on rice. Theoretical evidence and model sensitivity analyses suggested that sink regulation during vegetative growth has a strong effect on plant vigour and growth rate, even at given levels of leaf photosynthetic capacity. However, the usefulness of complex, whole-plant models such as EcoMeristem for heuristic phenotyping approaches remains to be demonstrated. Specific problems are related to the stability of process-based crop parameters across environments, as well as the measurement of such crop parameters that are inaccessible to direct observation. But it is argued that integrated, structural-functional models may be the only means to quantify complex traits, such as those governing adaptive morphology (phenotypic plasticity). Furthermore, such models may be well suited to develop improved plant type concepts *in silico*.

REFERENCES

https://en.wikipedia.org/wiki/Photosynthesis

https://www.livescience.com › Planet Earth

https://www.rsc.org/Education/Teachers/Resources/cfb/Photosynthesis.htm

https://ssec.si.edu/stemvisions-blog/what-photosynthesis

https://www.britannica.com/science/photosynthesis

www.biology4kids.com/files/plants_photosynthesis.html

https://www.bbc.co.uk/bitesize/articles/zn4sv9q

https://www2.estrellamountain.edu/faculty/farabee/BIOBK/BioBookPS.html

https://www.toppr.com/guides/biology/photosynthesis.../introduction-to-photosynthesis/

Pages: 147-156

Current Research in Biochemistry and Molecular Biology
Edited by: Dr. Prasann Kumar and Dr. Pawan Kumar 'Bharti'
ISBN: 978-93-88854-33-7
Edition: **2020**
Published by: **Discovery Publishing House Pvt. Ltd., New Delhi (India)**

CHAPTER 11

Transpiration
An Unavoidable Evil

Prasann Kumar[1,2*], Shipa Rani Dey[1]

GRAPHICAL ABSTRACT

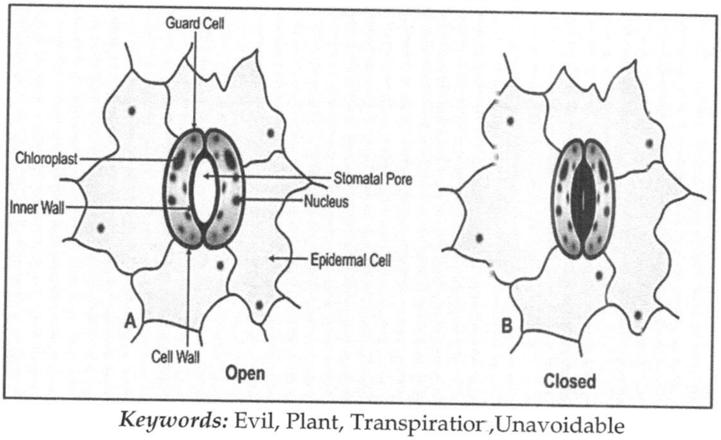

Keywords: Evil, Plant, Transpiration,Unavoidable

INTRODUCTION

- **Transpiration** is the evaporation of water from the aerial parts of plants.Of all the water plant absorbs, over 95-99% is transpired to the air as water vapor.From where water is transpired? Aerial parts of whole young plant

[1] Department of Agronomy, School of Agriculture, Lovely Professional University, Jalandhar - 144 411 (Punjab) (India)

[2] Divison of Research and Development, Lovely Professional University, Jalandhar - 144 411 (Punjab) (India)

- Lenticels (lenticular transpiration) 0.1%
- Cutin (cuticular transpiration) 3%~10% Stomatum (stomatal transpiration) ~ 90%

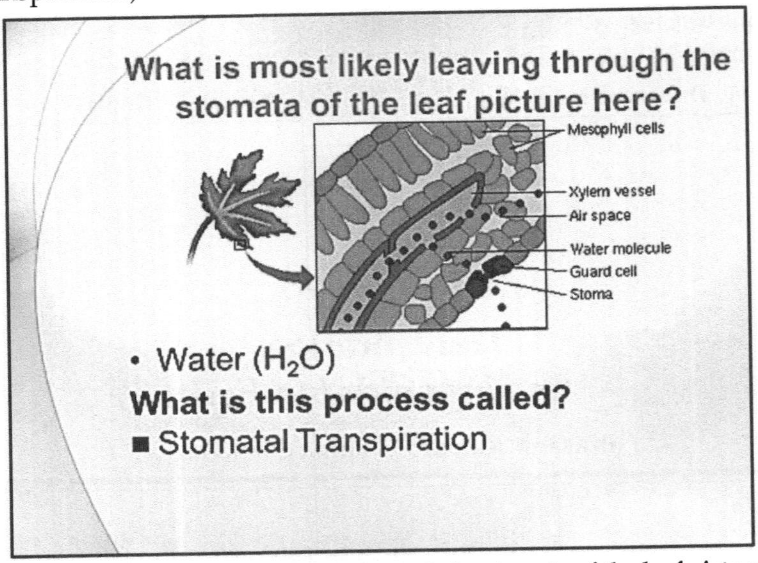

Fig. 11.1: What is most likely leaving through the stomata of the leaf picture here?

Source: based on review of literature

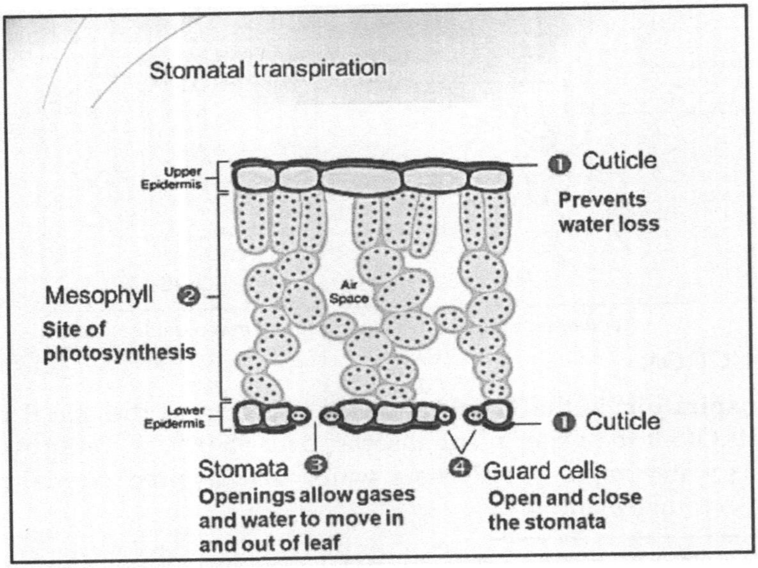

Fig. 11.2: Stomatal transpiration

Source: based on review of literature

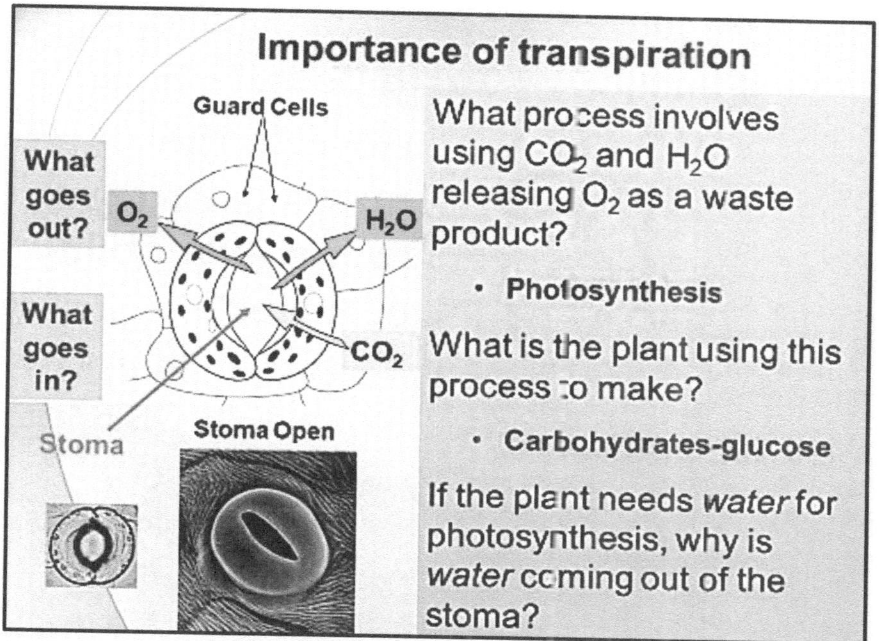

Fig. 11.3: Importance of transpiration

Source: based on review of literature

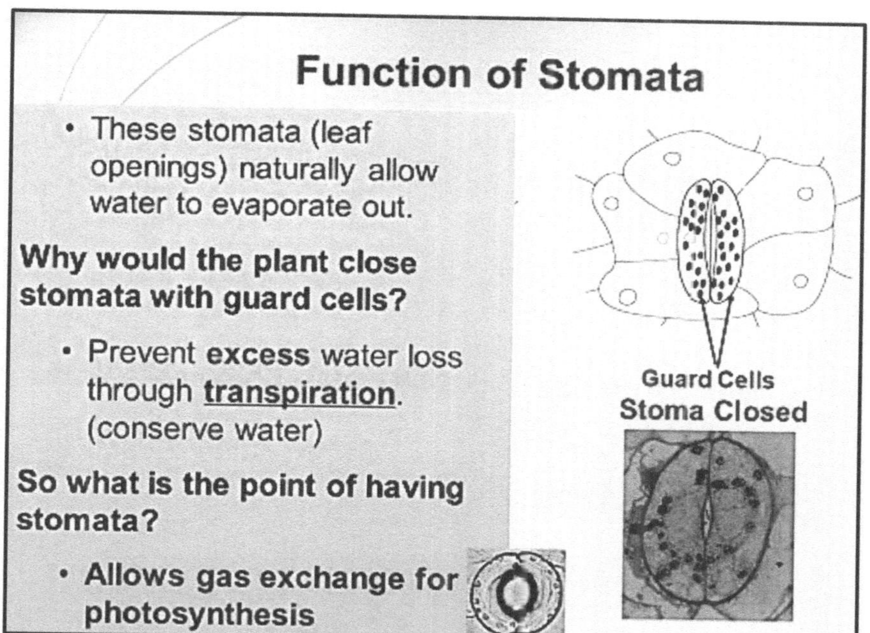

Fig. 11.4: Function of stomata

Source: based on review of literature

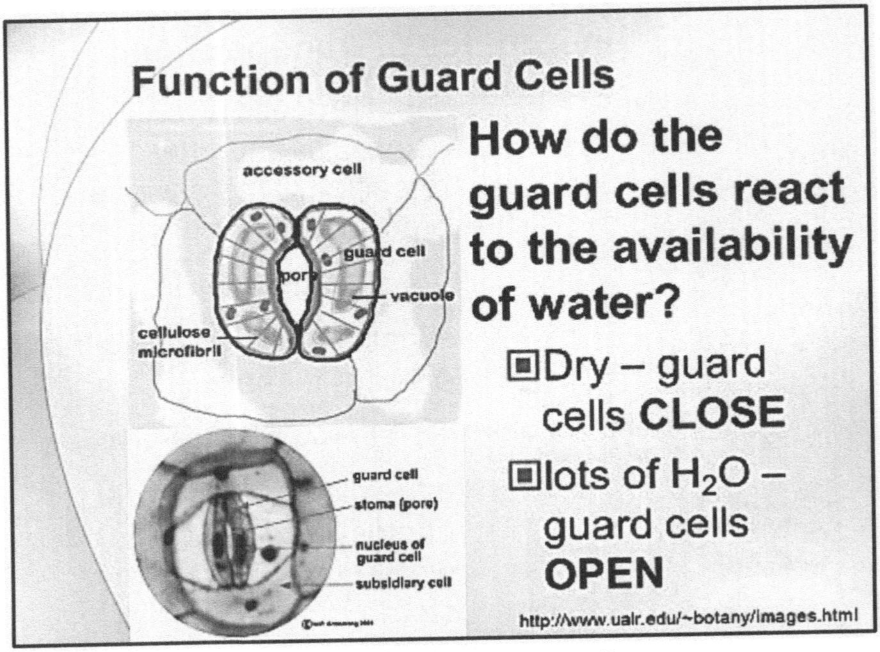

Fig. 11.5: Function of Guard cells
Source: based on review of literature

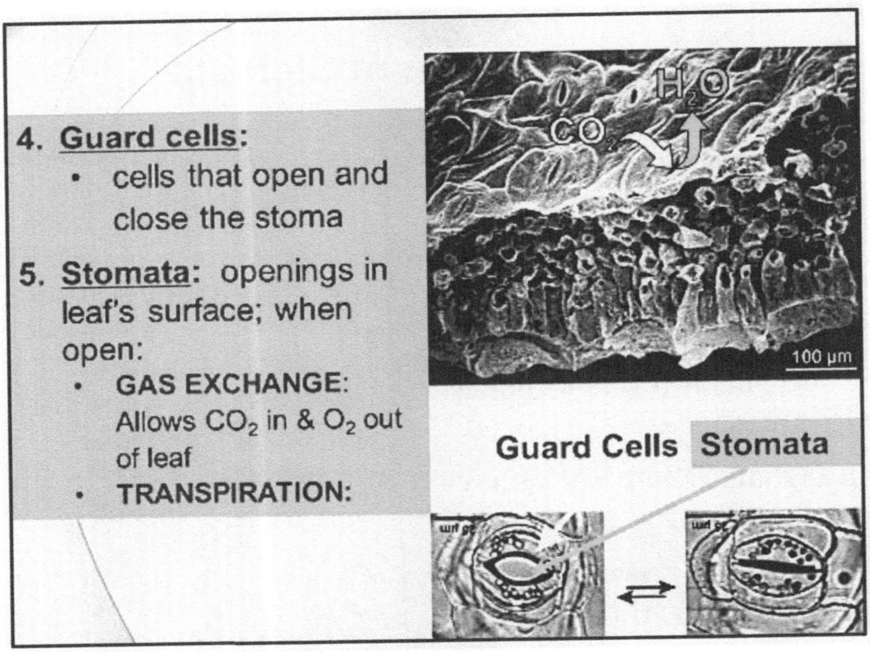

Fig. 11.6: Guard cells and stomata
Source: based on review of literature

Fig. 11.7: Stomata an in plants
Source: based on review of literature

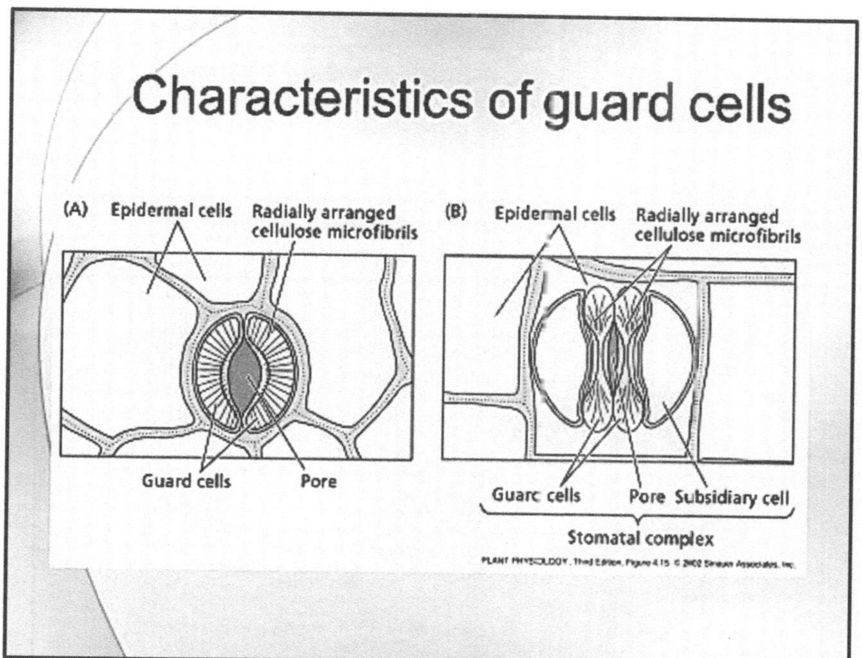

Fig. 11.8: Characters of guard cells
Source: based on review of literature

Guard cell properties and their relationship with stomatal control

- Thickness of CW varies in the ventral and dorsal part of the guard cells
- Contains chloroplast and can perform light reaction. (not dark reaction for the lack of key enzymes)
- Structurally isolated from epidermal cells for the lack of plasmodesmata (water and ions transmit only through cellular pathway, thus helps to build up water gradient)
- Little volume, little amount of water absorption or loss controls stomatal aperture.

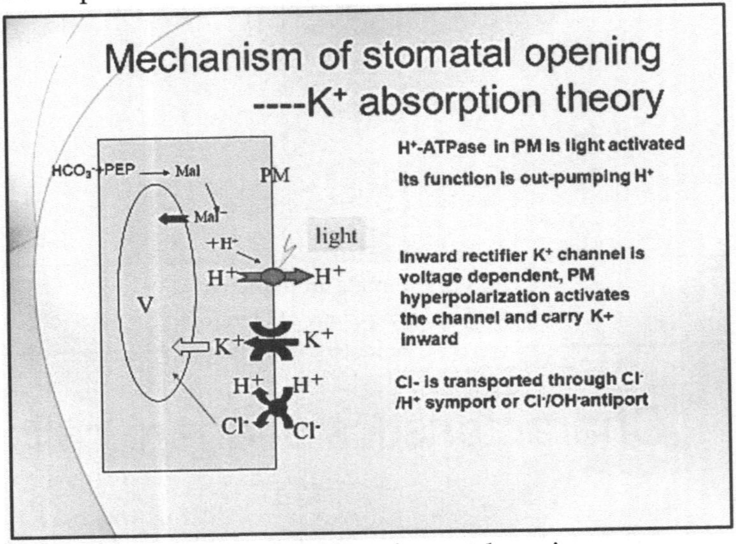

Fig. 11.9: Mechanism of stomatal opening

Source: based on review of literature

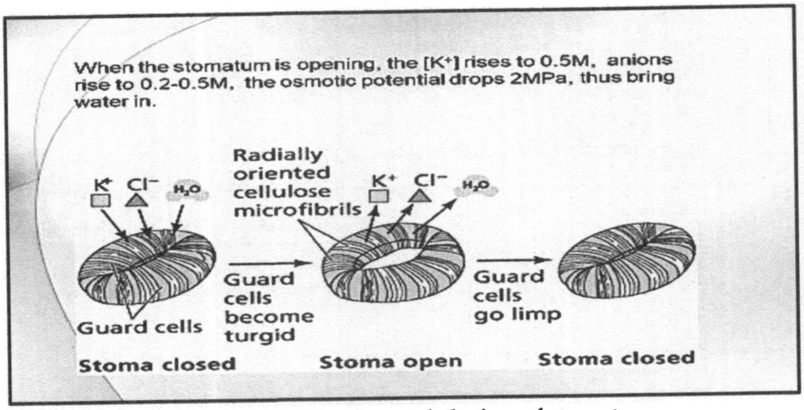

Fig. 11.10: Opening and closing of stomata

Source: based on review of literature

Factors influencing stomatal aperture

- Light
- Temp.
- CO_2
- Water content
- Plant hormone

1. **Light**

   - Stomata of most plant open in the day and close at night, while CAM plants are just the opposite.
   - Stomata opening are sensitive to red light and blue light, and blue light is more effective, it stimulates opening by a blue-light receptor: zeaxanthin.

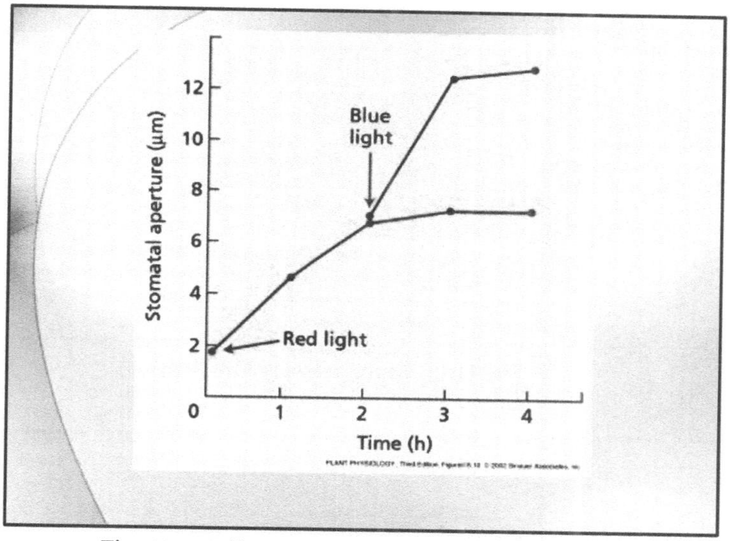

Fig. 11.11: Effect of light on stomatal aperture

Source: based on review of literature

2. **Temperature**

   - Stomatal aperture increase with Temp, within 20- 30! (the optimal).

3. **CO_2**

   - Low CO_2 conc. promotes stomatal opening, while high CO_2 conc. inhibits stomatal opening through its acidification of the guard cell thus inhibits PM hyperpolarization.

4. **Water content**
5. **Plant hormones**
    - CTK promotes opening
    - ABA inhibits

FACTORS THAT INFLUENCE TRANSPIRATION

Transpiration from the leaf depends on two major factors:

1. Difference in water vapor gradient
2. Diffusional resistance

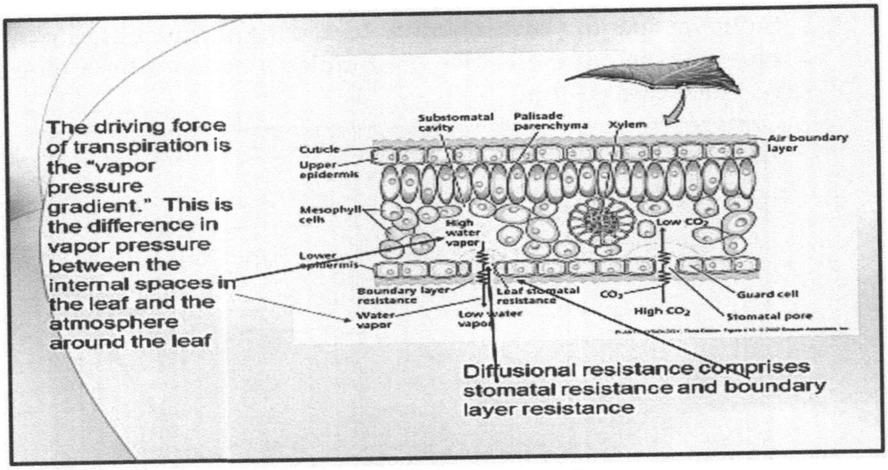

Fig. 11.12: Vapor pressure Gradient

Source: based on review of literature

$$\text{Transpiration rate} = \text{Driving force/resistance}$$

$$= \frac{\text{water vapor inside the leaf} - \text{water vapor of the air}}{\text{stomatal resistance} + \text{boundary layer resistance}}$$

Fig. 11.13: Transpiration force

Source: based on review of literature

Environmental factors that affect the rate of transpiration

1. Light

Plants transpire more rapidly in the light than in the dark. This is largely because light stimulates the opening of the stomata, Light also speeds up transpiration by warming the leaf.

2. Temperature

Plants transpire more rapidly at higher temperatures because water evaporates more rapidly as the temperature rises.

3. Humidity

When the surrounding air is dry, diffusion of water out of the leaf goes on more rapidly.

4. Wind

When a breeze is present, the humid air is carried away and replaced by drier air.

5. Soilwater

A plant cannot continue to transpire rapidly if its water loss is not made up by replacement from the soil. When absorption of water by the roots fails to keep up with the rate of transpiration, loss of turgor occurs, and the stomata close. This immediately reduces the rate of transpiration. If the loss of turgor extends to the rest of the leaf and stem, the plant wilts.

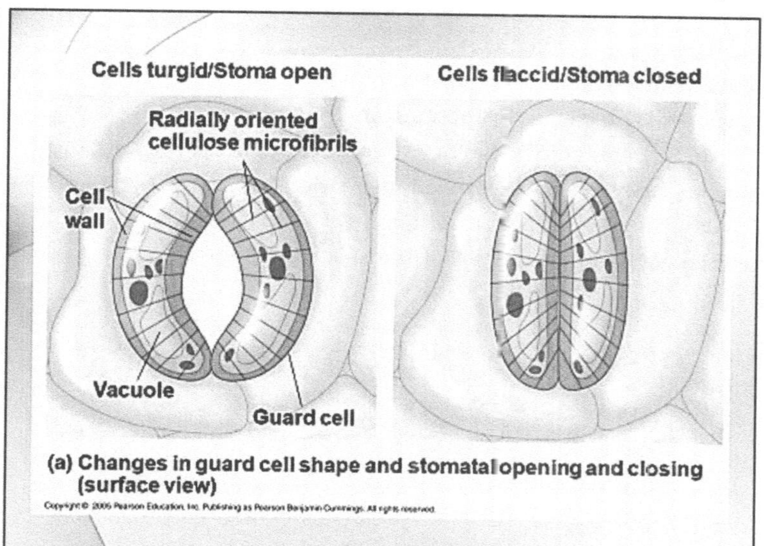

Fig. 11.14: Cells turgid/Stoma open

Source: based on review of literature

CONCLUSION

Transpiration is the process of water movement through a plant and its evaporation from aerial parts, such as leaves, stems and flowers. Two major factors influence the rate of water flow from the soil to the roots: the hydraulic conductivity of the soil and the magnitude of the pressure gradient through the soil.Water is necessary for plants but only a small amount of water taken up by the roots is used for growth and metabolism. The remaining 97–99.5% is lost by transpiration and guttation. Transpiration occurs through the stomatal apertures, and can be thought of as a necessary "cost" associated with the opening of the stomata to allow the diffusion of carbon dioxide gas from the air for photosynthesis. Transpiration also cools plants, changes osmotic pressure of cells, and enables mass flow of mineral nutrients and water from roots to shoots.Leaf surfaces are dotted with pores called stomata, and in most plants they are more numerous on the undersides of the foliage. The stomata are bordered by guard cells and their stomatal accessory cells (together known as stomatal complex) that open and close the pore. Both of these factors influence the rate of bulk flow of water moving from the roots to the stomatal pores in the leaves via the xylem.

REFERENCES

https://en.wikipedia.org/wiki/Transpiration

https://simple.wikipedia.org/wiki/Transpiration

https://en.wikipedia.org/wiki/Talk%3ATranspiration

https://en.wikipedia.org/wiki/Transpiration_stream

https://en.wikipedia.org/wiki/Potometer

https://en.wikipedia.org/wiki/Evapotranspiration

https://www.toppr.com/guides/biology/transport-in-plants/transpiration/

https://water.usgs.gov/edu/watercycletranspiration.html

https://en.wiktionary.org/wiki/transpiration

https://www.cropsreview.com/types-of-transpiration.html

Pages: 157-165

Current Research in Biochemistry and Molecular Biology
Edited by: **Dr. Prasann Kumar and Dr. Pawan Kumar 'Bharti'**
ISBN: 978-93-88854-33-7
Edition: **2020**
Published by: **Discovery Publishing House Pvt. Ltd., New Delhi (India)**

CHAPTER
12

Plant Hormones, Senescence and Abscission in Crops

Prasann Kumar[1,2*], Shipa Rani Dey[1]

GRAPHICAL ABSTRACT

Keywords: Abscission, Crops, Senescence, Water

INTRODUCTION

Abscission the separation of leaves, flowers, and fruitsfrom plants after the formation of an abscission zoneat the base of their petioles,

[1] Department of Agronomy, School of Agriculture, Lovely Professional University, Jalandhar - 144 411 (Punjab) (India)

[2] Divison of Research and Development, Lovely Professional University, Jalandhar - 144 411 (Punjab) (India)

peduncles, and pedicels. Abscission, a physiologically determined program of cell separation, provides a mechanism whereby every discrete, multicellular plant organ, such as leaves,flowers, or fruits, becomes detached from the plantbody in a controlled manner. It can be a programmed shedding of organs that no plant, exemplified by the flower after aiding in pollination. The process requires the formation of an anatomically distinct structure, the abscission zone (AZ), which constitutes the region where organs are detached fromthe plant body. Very littleis known about which developmental signals and how cell–cell interactions inform primordial AZ cells to differentiate.

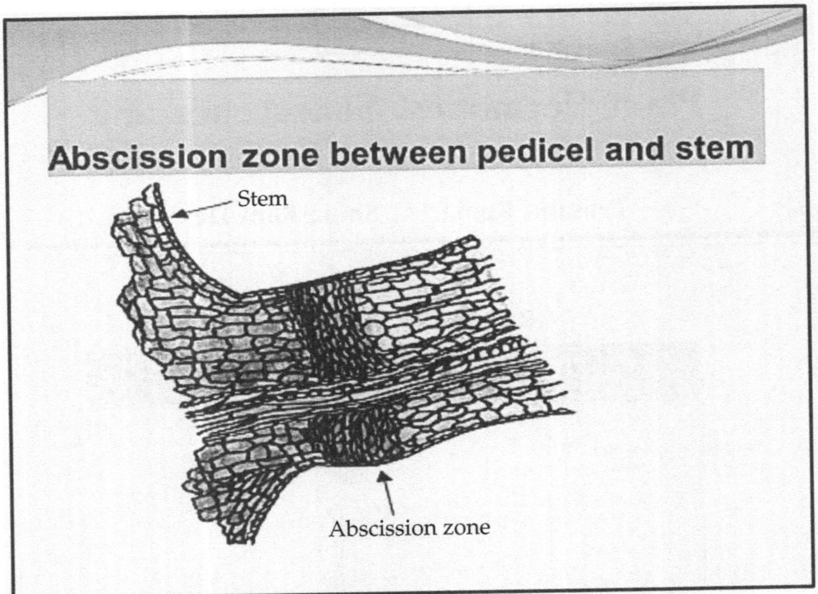

Fig. 12.1: Abscission zone between pedicle and stem

Source: based on review of literature

STRUCTURAL MECHANISM

In deciduous trees, an abscission zone, also called a separation zone, is formed at the base of the petiole. It is composed of a top layer which has cells with weak walls, and a bottom layer which expands in the autumn, breaking the weak walls of the cells in the top layer. This allows the leaf to be shed.

LACK OF CHLOROPHYLL AS A TRIGGER

The reduction of chlorophylls production inleaves due to decreased sunlight in the fall explains why some leaves turn yellow. However, the yellow color can attract aphids, so some trees turn the leaves red instead by injecting a bright pigment. The loss of chlorophyll may also contribute to the abscission process.

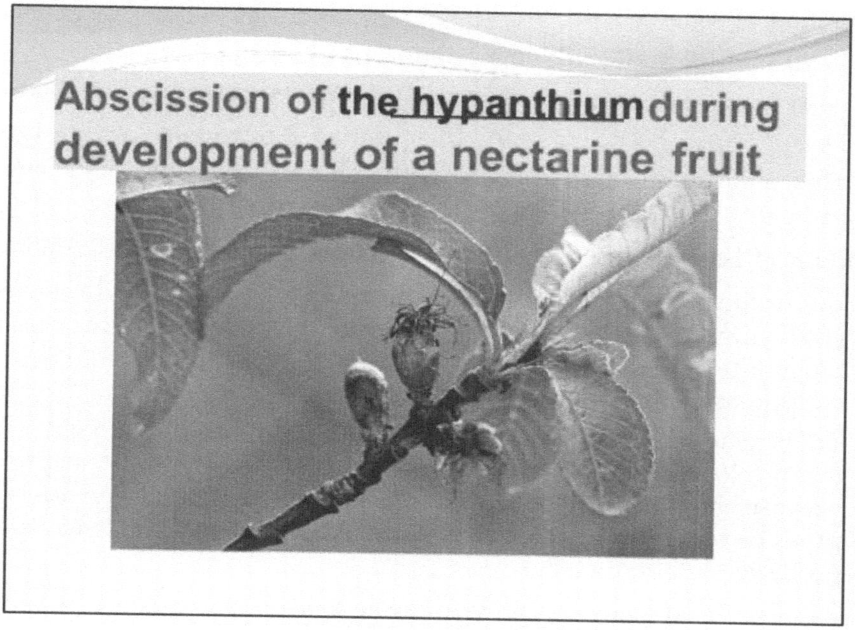

Fig. 12.2:Abscission of the hypanthium
Source: based on review of literature

Senescence

- Life comprises of following sequential events germination/birth, juvenile state, maturation, old age and death.
- Old age called senescence in plants.
- Senescence biological process of deterioration with age.
- This stage leads to complete loss of organization and function and finally complete inhibition of life activity i.e. death, thus senescence is penultimate phase of life. But death is not part of senescence.
- Meristem don't undergo senescence and are considred as potetially immortal.

Types of senescence

- Top senescence:- occurs in aerial parts of plant. Common in perennials.
- Deciduous senescence:- Occursin deciduous plants. Only occurs in leaves.
- Overall senescence:- seen inannual plants. Senescence occurs orderly in flower, fruits, leaves androot.
- Progressive senescences:- It is common in annual plants. First seen on old leaves and then newleaves.

Retardation of senescence

- It means that delay the degradation of plant.
- Also increase the life of plant and getting more and more yield.
- Delay the senescence of many plant parts i.e. flowers, leaves and fruits.
- This retardation of senescence with the help of many factor studied by many people these are as follows:

Inhibition of Leaf Senescence by Auto regulated Production of Cytokinin

- Controlling expression of *IPT*, a gene encoding isopentenyl transferase (the enzyme that catalyzes the rate-limiting step incytokinin biosynthesis), with a senescence- specific promoter results in the suppression of leaf senescence.
- Transgenic tobacco plants expressing this chimeric gene do not exhibit the developmental abnormalities usually associated with *IPT* expression because the system is auto regulatory. Because sufficient cytokinin is produced to retard senescence, the activity of the senescence-specific promoter is attenuated.

Retardation of Leaf Senescence by Ascorbic acid

- Leaf discs of *Solatiummelongena* were floatedon various concentrations of ascorbic acid (AA), gibberellic acid (GA_3), and kinetin in order to study their effect on senescence.
- AA was highly effective in retarding senescence as shown by the arrest of the fall in levels of chlorophyll, DNA, RNA, and proteins.
- AA was effective at a lower concentration than that of GA_3 orkinetin.

Plant Hormones

How do we know they exist?

Why do the shoots grow up, but the roots grow down?

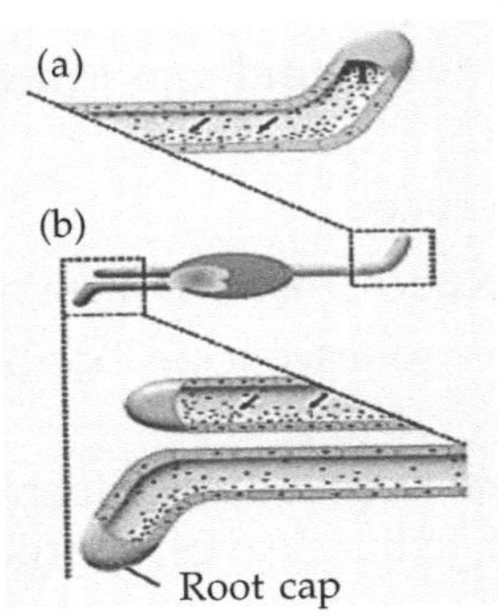

Fig. 12.3: Plant hormones and its role in tropic moment

Source: based on review of literature

Plant Hormones

Phototropism experiments by Charles and Francis Darwin

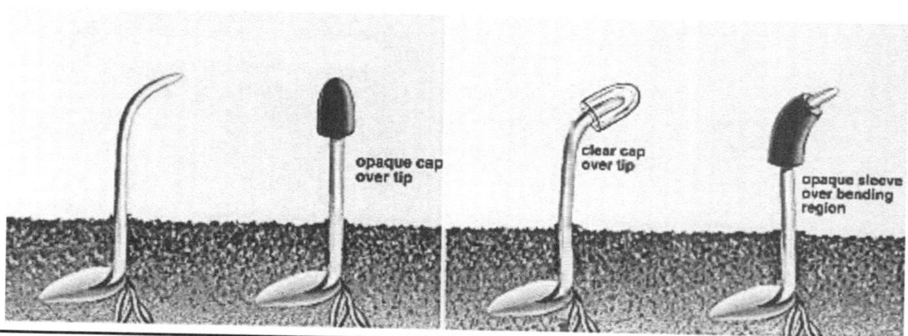

Fig. 12.4: Experiment with hormones
Source: based on review of literature

Plant Hormones

Boysen-Jensen's experiments

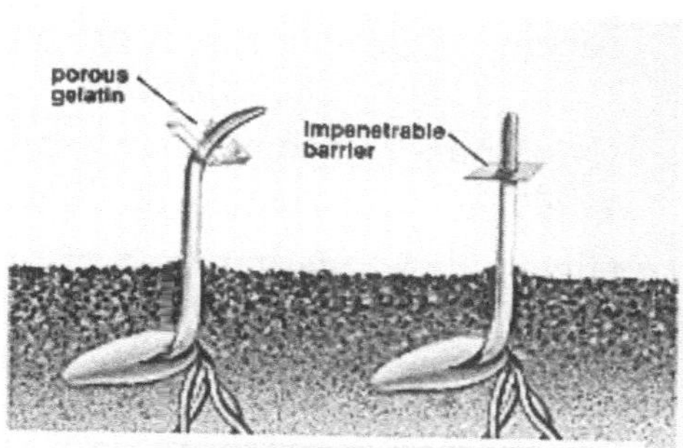

Mechanisms of bending:

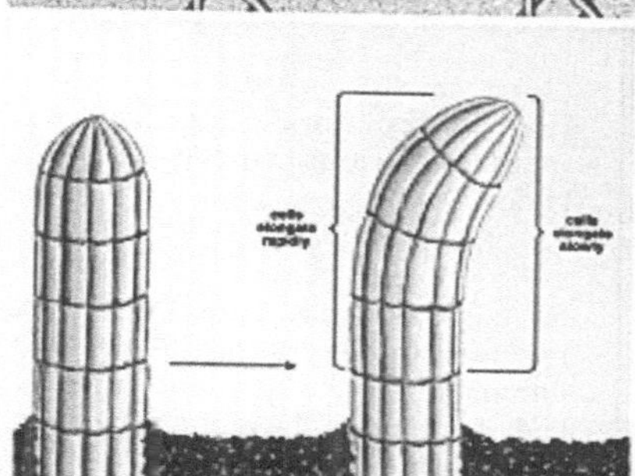

Fig. 12.5: Boysen –Jensen's experiments
Source: based on review of literature

Plant Hormones

Frits went discovered the hormone Auxin. Concentration of auxins in different parts of roots and shoots determine growth rates of the cells ... Since distribution of auxins is affected by both light and gravity, auxins are involved in plants' phototropic and gravotropic growth patterns.

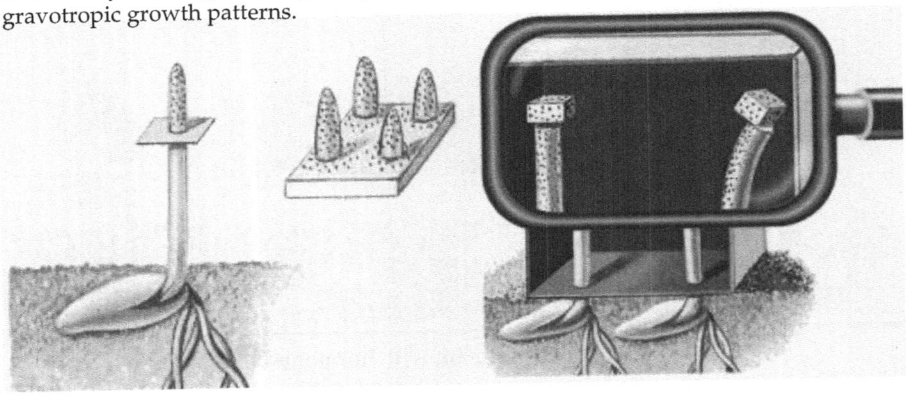

Fig. 12.6: Auxin and its distribution in different parts

Source: based on review of literature

Major plant hormones and their action:

Abscisic acid	closing of stomata; seed dormancy
Auxins	elongation of shoots and roots, gravotropism, phototropism
Cytokinins	promotion of sprouting of lateral buds
Ethylene	ripening of fruit
Gibberellins	germination of seeds and sprouting of buds; elongation of stems; stimulation of flowering; development of fruit

Plant Hormones

Hormones can work with each other to regulate various aspects of plant biology.

Here, auxin and cytokinin work together in regulating lateral bud information ... the sprouting of lateral buds depends on the ratio of cytokinin to auxin...

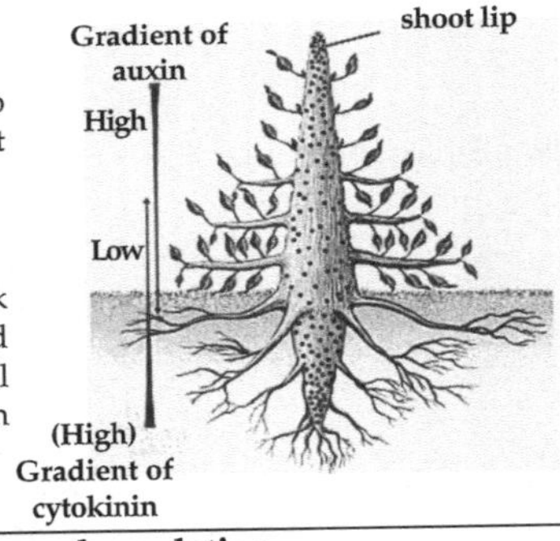

Fig. 12.7: Hormonal regulation

Source: based on review of literature

Plant Hormones

Plants use starch-filled organelles called statoliths to detect gravity ... this is very similar to how jellyfish detect gravity, and in some ways, it is even similar to how humans keep themselves balanced ...

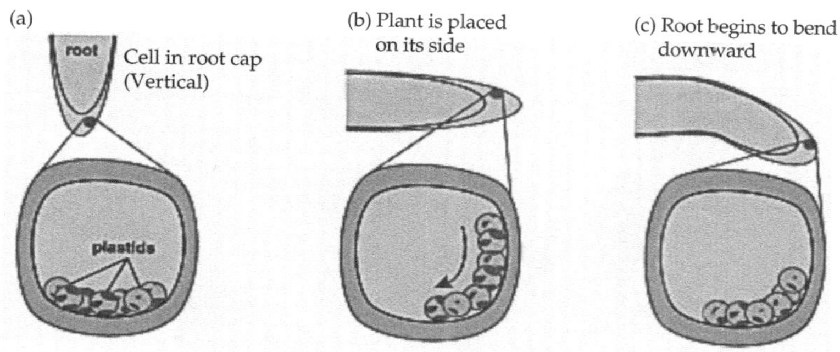

Fig. 12.8: Statoliths and its role in gravity detection

Source: based on review of literature

Plant Hormones

A hormone called florigen both stimulates and inhibits flowering. Since flowering is sometimes a function of day length, pigments called phytochromes are involved in "measuring" day length. The ratio of different forms of this pigments change as a function sunlight exposure and can thus be used by the plants to set their "internal biological clocks".

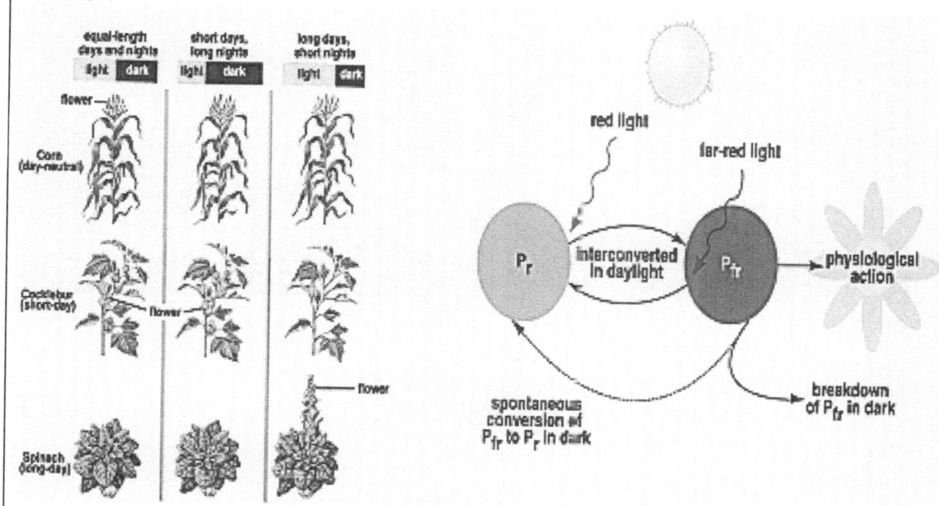

Fig. 12.9: Role of florigen

Source: based on review of literature

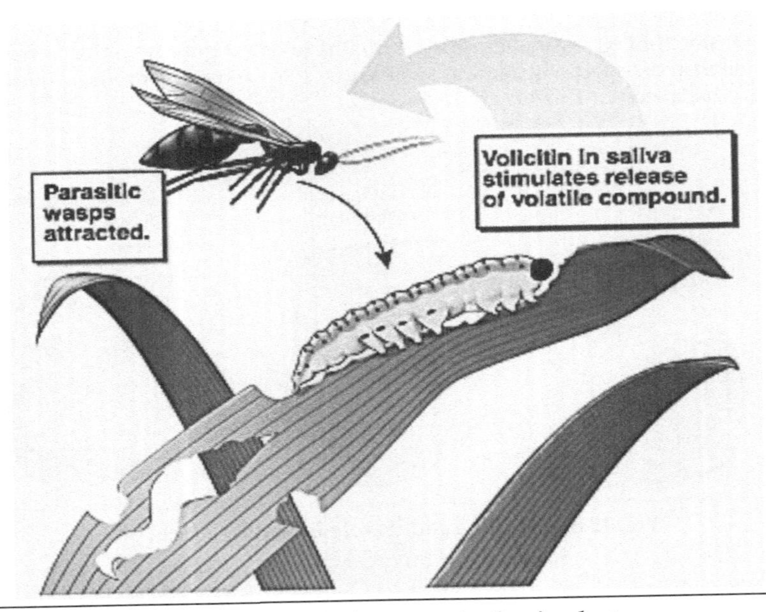

Fig. 12.10: Chemical communication in plants

Source: based on review of literature

Plant Communication

(a) (b)

The Venus flytrap catches files as a source of nitrogen.

Insects are attracted to the nectar in the trap, but when they trigger sensory "haris" within the trap, they are captured ...

What is the mechanism ?

Fig. 12.11: Plant communications

Source: based on review of literature

CONCLUSION

Abscission (from Latin *ab*, "away", and *scindere*, "to cut'") is the shedding of various parts of an organism, such as a plantdropping a leaf, fruit, flower, or seed. In zoology, abscission is the intentional shedding of a body part, such as the shedding of a claw, husk, or the autotomy of a tail to evade a predator. In mycology, it is the liberation of a fungal spore. In cell biology, abscission refers to the separation of two daughter cells at the completion of cytokinesis.

REFERENCES

https://en.wikipedia.org/wiki/Abscission

https://www.dictionary.com/browse/abscission

https://study.com/academy/lesson/leaf-abscission-definition-lesson.html

www.biologydiscussion.com/plants/growth-hormones/abscission-of...in.../23473

https://www.cell.com/current-biology/comments/S0960-9822(18)30289-6

https://www.javatpoint.com/senescence-vs-abscission

https://www.britannica.com/science/abscission-layer

https://www.britannica.com/science/abscission

https://www.sciencedirect.com/topics/agricultural-and-biological-sciences/abscission

https://www.sciencedirect.com/topics/agricultural-and-biological.../leaf-abscission

Index

❑ ❑ ❑ ❑ ❑ ❑